Substance Abuse Disorders in Clinical Practice

Edward C. Senay

Substance Abuse Disorders
in Clinical Practice

Second Edition

W. W. Norton & Company
New York • London

For information about permission to reproduce selections from this book, write to
Permissions, W. W. Norton & Company, Inc., 500 Fifth Avenue, New York, NY 10110

Composition and design by Kenet Books
Manufacturing by Royal Book

Library of Congress Cataloging-in-Publication Data

Senay, Edward C.
Substance abuse disorders in clinical practice /
Edward C. Senay. —2nd ed.
p. cm.
"A Norton professional book"—Cover p. 4.
Includes bibliographical references and index.
ISBN 0-393-70291-X
1. Substance abuse. 2. Family medicine. I. Title.
[DNLM: 1. Substance-Related Disorders. 2. Family Practice. WM
270 S474s 1998]
RC564.S459 1998
616.86—dc21
DNLM/DLC
for Library of Congress   98-21154   CIP

W. W. Norton & Company, Inc., 500 Fifth Avenue, New York, NY 10110
http://www.wwnorton.com

W. W. Norton & Company Ltd., 10 Coptic Street, London WC1A 1PU

1 2 3 4 5 6 7 8 9 0

Table of Contents

Introduction

This book attempts to respond to the need for a single-author book in the field of addiction medicine that is comprehensive in its coverage of all common intoxicants and that is comprehensive in its coverage of treatment. It will introduce the reader to the spectrum of current treatment methods. The focus of the book is clinical rather than academic; it attempts to provide an understanding of a therapeutic community, a detoxification ward, and a methadone clinic, as well as other common treatment programs. It presents common clinical problems encountered in these environments together with generally practiced responses. Physicians are the central but by no means the only population for whom this book is written. Nurses, psychologists, social workers, counselors, and a variety of other health care workers may find a clinically oriented primer on substance abuse useful.

The conditions in which clinicians operate have changed considerably, and this edition describes clinical problems in the managed care environment. The concept of a continuum of care and the placement of a patient on it, according to the patient placement criteria of the American Society of Addiction Medicine (ASAM), are reviewed. In this new environment, diagnosis must be explicit and based on the criteria given in the *Diagnostic and Statistical Manual on Mental Disorders* (DSM-4) of the American Psychiatric Association (e.g., "This 23-year-old white married musician meets criteria 1, 2, 3 and 7 for Cocaine Dependence 304.20"). In addition, where Joint Commission on Accreditation of Health Care Organizations (JCAHO) criteria require clinical action, as in the instance of mental status examination and literacy probes, they are also described.

If in my judgment, recent research findings appear likely to be introduced broadly into real-world drug and alcohol treatment units, they are described and appropriate references given. If not, they do not appear in this book. This might be one of a number of books one could study for Addiction Medicine Boards, but it would be a mistake to base a board attempt solely on this book, with its strictly clinical orientation. There is not enough space to describe important information from other fields, such as pharmacology and epidemiology, which are of interest and should be known by the educated addiction medicine specialist but are of no immediate clinical relevance.

The fact that benzodiazepines act at the GABA receptor as do alcohol and barbiturates, thus accounting for cross-tolerance, is discussed in this book. But from a pharmacological perspective, the phrase "act at the GABA receptor" is very imprecise. There are fourteen different subunits of the receptor, and various benzodiazepines act at some of them, while other benzodiazepines act at others. This level of information is not presented, as the clinical significance of these facts is not yet clear; but for someone taking boards, it would be good to know the pharmacology of the benzodiazepines thoroughly.

Similar remarks could be made about epidemiology and many other sciences with important bearing on addiction medicine. A knowledge base has been developed in the neuroscience of addiction medicine that holds promise of ultimate control over substance abuse, pain, and mood disorders, but this book provides only a glimpse of this knowledge base, because its readers are going to be busy in the emergency room, outpatient clinic, therapeutic community, or some other clinical venue.

If managed care is not itself managed better, it will increase, not decrease, the historic division of care that splits primary care from mental health and these two from substance abuse. This division is as enormously costly and inefficient as it is unnecessary. The most recent national studies disclose a 26.6 percent lifetime occurrence of substance abuse disorders in the United States. Coupled with the fact that medical, psychiatric, social, legal, familial, community, and financial problems tend to cluster—that is, 14 percent of the population have over 40 percent of all the problems—in all these domains, the need for comprehensive biopsychosocial assessment of each patient should be clear.

There is heightened recognition now that a host of problems seen in medical practice are intoxicant related (e.g., cancers, cardiovascular disease, trauma, burns, vehicular and industrial accidents, infections like HIV, hepatitis, and others), and a parallel recognition in psychiatric practice that suicide, homicide, sleep disorders, and the like are often complicated by substance related disorders. Hopefully, policy will unite the divisions of the past, and we will have a medical care system in which all three efforts can be combined.

I do not attempt to be encyclopedic, as I want to have a book of manageable size. I do not attempt to provide more than important reference materials in areas in which I have little clinical experience, such as family therapy, geriatric addiction, psychometric assessment, cognitive and behavioral treatments, and many others.

In referring to people in treatment, I use *patient* or *client* or *resident*, according to what service is being delivered. Effective treatment for substance abuse requires teamwork that is sometimes primarily medical or psychiatric, sometimes psychological and social, sometimes educational, and so forth, so there is no conflict among the terms.

In closing I want to cite the ethic that informs our work. It has three parts. The first is absolute respect for the humanity of every patient; in a sense, we should not need the term *special population,* because every patient, from every population, should be special. The second part is a sustained commitment to the development and maintenance of a professional level of skill in listening and in organizing data to serve patients. The last part is to maintain a knowledge of the neuroscience of addiction so that care of patients is based on current science. Respect, commitment, and knowledge are the three bases for the best in clinical care.

1. Substance Abuse/Dependence and Treatment Defined, General Background, and Introductory Treatment Guidelines

The definition that follows is the author's. While it attempts to incorporate the views of the American Psychiatric Association (as implicit in the *Diagnostic and Statistical Manual of Mental Disorders 4*) the American Society of Addiction Medicine (ASAM), and the Joint Commission on Accreditation of Health Care Organizations (JCAHO), it does not represent any official view that they have endorsed either singly or collectively. My definition is based on 30 years of clinical experience and a long exposure to the neuroscience of addiction; it attempts to provide the reader with a unifying, explanatory theory for the assessment of clinical problems and their management.

NATURE OF SUBSTANCE ABUSE/DEPENDENCE

Substance abuse/dependence, as defined by DSM-4 criteria, is a complex biopsychosocial disorder. It is expressed in biologic, psychologic, familial, social, and cultural spheres in varying degrees for each individual afflicted. There are many factors important in initiating a behavioral pattern that leads to substance abuse/dependence. These include novelty seeking, genetic predisposition, alienation, rejection of family and social values, childhood physical and/or sexual abuse, self-medication for dysphoric mood, and participation in antisocial groups. These predisposing factors are different from the factors that are important in maintaining the pattern once it is established, such as withdrawal dysphoria, craving, and conditioning. When the behavioral pattern acquires an inherent automaticity, it meets criteria for a disease in that it has an offending agent, it has specific criteria for its diagnosis, it has a defined course, and it is reproducible in animals.

The central tendency of this disease is characterized by chronic relapse and remission. It frequently has severe consequences in multiple spheres, including death. Although forces in the individual combine with forces outside the individual—sometimes very remote from the individual—to produce this disease, the individual must take full responsibility for managing it and its consequences. A few with this disease are able to control it and to achieve recovery without treatment, but, empirically, a great many individuals meeting DSM-4 criteria for drug related disorders require treatment if they are to achieve full or even partial recovery. A large and growing body of experiential, epidemiologic, biologic, social, and behavioral evidence indicates that the development of this disease, in many domains, has differing origins, courses, and consequences for males versus females.

As discussed in further detail in the next chapter, the more recent classification systems incorporate the consensus that one cannot separate these biopsychosocial disorders from the contexts in which they occur. This is the basis for multiaxial assessment.

PHILOSOPHY OF TREATMENT

Treatment for substance abuse/dependence is biopsychosocial; it is largely, but no longer solely, empirical in nature and consists of self-help groups and pharmacologic, psychiatric, psychological, social, familial, cognitive, educational, vocational, and social-learning components in varying mixes according to the unique needs, resources, and coping skills of individuals. Because the problem is both episodic and recurring, it is best responded to by a continuum of care that provides for both active treatment of episodes and prevention of recurrences. The continuum of care used in this text is that developed by ASAM and JCAHO. Recovery must be active for long periods. For most, recovery must be a lifetime commitment. Because the disease is frequently influenced by or has primary interactions with psychological and social domains, it requires multiaxial description, including the psychological, medical, and social/cultural/environmental domains that are captured in DSM-4's five axes. These axes and the ASAM/JCAHO criteria for the continuum of care are reviewed in this text in detail.

GENERAL BACKGROUND

The second national study of the epidemiology of mental disorders in the United States was conducted from 1990 to 1992 and was published in 1994.[1] The lifetime prevalence for substance abuse disorders was an astounding 26.6 percent. The Surgeon General's Office has determined that intoxicants are related to morbidity and mortality from (and this is only a partial list) cancers, immune system diseases, emphysema, cardiovascular disease, liver disease, vehicular and industrial accidents, homicides, suicides, and overdoses. The most lethal of all the intoxicants is nicotine, with approximately 419,000 deaths per year; in second place is alcohol, with approximately 110,000 deaths; 10,000 deaths from direct effects of drugs such as cocaine and heroin are a distant third.[2] One in five hospital admissions is related to use of intoxicants.

For the clinician, such figures mean that drug disorders are very frequent and that a high index of suspicion is warranted. One might not think of a drug problem in a comatose 3-month-old infant, but death and serious neurological syndromes have been reported in infants from passive inhalation of phencyclidine (PCP) and cocaine base vapors.

Treatment for drug problems, like treatment for major psychiatric syndromes such as depression, anxiety, bipolar affective disorder, or schizophrenia, is symptom specific, not syndrome specific; and it is ameliorative, not curative. For occasional individuals and in occasional syndromes, treatment is curative, but for most of the 26.6 percent of the population who meet criteria for a drug disorder, the central tendency is to develop a decades-long career of episodes of abuse/dependence interspersed with periods of abstinence. One should expect, from an episode of treatment, improvement in the quality of life and prevention of some or all of the debilitating and/or lethal consequences of untreated episodes. The most striking illustration of the preventive power of treatment is evident in the fact that rates of HIV infection in methadone treated opiate dependent people are much closer to the rate in the general population than they are to the rate in untreated opiate dependent populations.[3]

Treatment is effective in proportion to the load of problems that can accompany substance abuse/dependence, the resources of the individual affected, and the strength of family and community support systems. Drug dependent physicians, for example, with no other accompanying psychiatric disorders and a stable relationship with a nondrug using spouse, have positive treatment outcomes 80 to 90 percent of the time and have longer remissions and fewer secondary problems than a multiproblem minority group member with poor education, no marketable job skills, a second major DSM-4 disorder, and many family members who are current drug abusers and who are all embedded in a dysfunctional community. For the latter cases, only 20 percent have positive treatment outcomes, with shorter remissions and more secondary problems. When the whole population of substance abusers is considered, one third get well, one third vacillate between dependent and abstinent, and one third are not helped by a given treatment episode. There is considerable evidence that the more treatment substance abusers get, the better the long-term outcomes.

There is a clinically important spectrum in the population meeting criteria for a substance abuse disorder. At one end of this spectrum are individuals who make a rational appraisal of their problem; decide, without assistance, to stop; and then do so with complete permanent success. Most of the 26.6 percent fall between this end of the spectrum and the other end, which is defined by repeated nonstop abuse of chemicals ending with an early death. Locating an individual on this spectrum is important from a number of perspectives—need for treatment, recognition that some can recover without treatment, and so forth. For most of the 26.6 percent there is a decades-long career of episodes of dependence interspersed with episodes of abstinence. Variability is the hallmark of the relationship between individuals and treatment need and responsiveness. Most nicotine dependent people who are able to stop smoking do so without help, but there are nicotine dependent people who smoke although it hastens death; these individuals are totally unresponsive to treatment even when it is intense and prolonged. Most 12-year-olds who use inhalants stop after a few months and then use alcohol and/or marijuana. Hallucinogens tend to be given up as an age cohort matures. Alcohol, nicotine, and marijuana are started in early adolescence and then are continued for decades, if not for life.

The psychology of substance abuse/dependence is not characterized by denial alone; it is characterized by ambivalence. Denial alternates with healthy striving. It is this tension that probably accounts for the fact that most drug dependent people have careers of episodes of abstinence interspersed with periods of dependence. The clinician must address the positive, striving pole of the ambivalence and build a relationship with that part of the patient's personality. Another important aspect of the psychology of drug dependence is that taking the drug, talking about the drug, and using the drug come to take on the characteristics of social relationship, which is expressed in such terms as "I've got a jones" or "I've got a monkey on my back" to describe a heroin habit, or "my friend the bottle" to refer to alcoholism. Clinically, this relationship must be mourned, and we know, empirically, that it is difficult for many people. It is also difficult for the people who were displaced by the heroin or alcohol habit to return. The clinician needs to be sensitive to these issues.

GENERAL CLINICAL GUIDELINES

The physician's role with respect to substance abuse disorders should stress the partnership rather than the directive aspect of the physician–patient relationship. A successful partnership with respect to substance abuse disorders requires a set of attitudes that permits a partnership to occur. Frequently, medical school and postgraduate training engender attitudes that prevent a physician from contributing to the treatment of people afflicted with drug and alcohol problems. During training, a physician may be exposed solely to patients with end-stage disease (e.g., cirrhosis with oesophageal varices or heroin addicts with severe endocarditis) who are slowly and inexorably committing suicide while doctors and nurses are forced to look on helplessly. Given such experiences, negative attitudes toward alcoholism and drug abuse are understandable, but end-stage patients do not characterize the population of people with substance abuse disorders. This much larger population is responsive to intervention. Modern industries, for example, have developed employee assistance programs that successfully treat approximately 70 percent of substance abusers. A doctor needs only one exposure to a grateful patient and/or family to develop the motivation to engage with these pervasive and costly public health problems.

Substance abusers respond well to physicians who try to learn about the substance abuser's lifestyle and perspectives. If you can generate in the patient a recognition that "The doctor listens and tries to understand me," you will have created a force that is central to successful management.

Because training in basic psychiatric techniques and in substance abuse varies so much from medical school to medical school and is often fragmentary, I begin this chapter with a general review of how to get clinical information before proceeding to the specifics of substance abuse history-taking and treatment.

INTERVIEW TECHNIQUES

The goal of the interview is to examine the patient's history for the presence or absence of the DSM-4 criteria for the substance related disorders, as well as any other medical or psychiatric problems the patient might have. The product of this examination is a brief statement delivered nonjudgmentally, according to the paradigm "This is the problem" followed by "This is the solution." The problem should be expressed in language as close to that of the DSM-4 criteria as one can make it. "You have been using more cocaine than you intended; the cost of the cocaine is draining resources away from your family; you have continued to use despite the fact that you might lose your spouse; and you now have legal problems." This is the "Here's the problem" part of the paradigm. "I want you to get into treatment at X clinic with Dr. Y." is the solution. The interview should have this underlying paradigm.

Basic interview techniques are as follows:

1. *Structure the situation so you can give your undivided attention to the patient.* Cut off phones, request no intrusion by staff, and interview the patient, if at all possible, in a quiet and private place. If you are in a situation in which you cannot avoid intrusion, make it clear to the patient that this is the case and try to schedule time when you can focus exclusively on the patient. The first encounter with a patient is important in beginning to reverse the demoralization that frequently characterizes the substance abuser seeking treatment. If the first encounter with a physician produces feelings in the patient such as "The doctor is too busy for me," "There's no time for my problems here," "The doctor is really judgmental," a serious breach of professionalism has occurred.

2. *Get yourself and the patient comfortable.* If possible, seat yourself so you are at the same eye level as the patient. Some substance abusers, particularly younger ones imbued with counterculture beliefs, may be sensitive to an authoritarian structure such as may be conveyed by being seated lower than the doctor.

3. *Give the "set" of the interview:* "I want to know about your problem, but I also need to know about you and how your life is going." "All I know is that your husband said you have a problem taking pills." "Tell me what's happening and how you see things." "Let's try to understand the problem you mentioned on the phone."

   Maintain frequent eye contact and note whether or not the patient maintains frequent eye contact with you. Note also the relationship between what is being discussed and such behaviors as looking away, looking down, facial expressions, and body movements. If you fear that you might offend a patient by asking about lifestyle issues, you might begin the history-taking session by commenting that it is routine to ask questions about a patient's lifestyle because lifestyle can have very serious health consequences. Every case should have a complete drug and alcohol history in the modern context. Explain that you would be delinquent in your medical duty if you did not take a drug and alcohol history.

4. *Use few words, and use simple words and phrases:* "When did you start using heroin?" "Did you have shaking hands?" "What happened next?" "How badly did it hurt?"

   If you find yourself doubling up—that is, repeating a question in slightly different words or taking more time than you need to communicate a simple question—you should regard such phenomena as possible expressions of anxiety on your part. Attempt to understand the source of your anxiety. The pressure of time is frequently the culprit, but time pressure can be used by physicians defensively to cover up common sources of anxiety, such as feelings of clinical inadequacy with respect to these problems, anger generated by the provocative behavior of the substance abuser, sexual feelings, envy of the hedonism of the substance abuser, or fear of the violence inherent in the destructive behavior of the substance abuser toward self, family, and community.

5. *Be nonjudgmental.* Your acceptance of the humanity of the patient is the centerpiece of your therapeutic efforts. It can be an important stimulus to the growth of self-esteem in the patient. Substance abuse is associated with violence, either real or psychological, and violence generates negative feelings in everyone. The patient's behavior (e.g., neglect of a child, violent crime) may also generate anger that cannot be expressed in any constructive way in ordinary clinical contacts. Feelings like these are unavoidable and expectable. An effective clinician knows they are there but does not permit these feelings to interfere with empathetic interviewing. From one perspective, a substance abuser may be antisocial; but from another, he or she is our husband or wife or our son or daughter.

   If you find that you cannot surmount feelings that a particular substance abuser should be punished, seek out a colleague and discuss the role of a physician with respect to deviance. The physician's role is to give the best possible care to every patient regardless of age or socioeconomic, ethnic, sexual, criminal, or psychiatric status. To confuse medicine with punishment is a serious error.

6. *Get to the point:* "I understand your father and mother believe that you use marijuana and that it's harming you. How do you see it?" "My examination strongly suggests that you use alcohol excessively."

7. *Settle the question of confidentiality explicitly and early in the interview.* Discuss with the patient the constraints placed on you by federal and state laws concerning confidentiality. In general, drug abuse information is absolutely confidential and cannot be released to anyone without written authorization by the patient specifying the information that can be released, to whom it may be released, and for what period of time the authorization is valid. Medical emergency, federal audit when federal funds support part or all of treatment, and an order from a court constitute the only conditions under which a physician is obliged to release information concerning drug abuse without written consent of the patient.

   Confidentiality laws vary much more for alcohol related problems than for drug abuse. The physician needs to learn about state laws not only because legal realities need to be clear but also because of the clinical impact they have. For example, laws governing confidentiality for minors vary widely; in many states minors have a right to treatment without parental knowledge. In such states a physician may have to respect this right, although parental involvement may be indicated clinically; conversely, in other states a physician may have to notify parents even though this may not be indicated or is contraindicated clinically. In any event, make clear to the patient who may and who may not have access to the information the patient may divulge. Many young people need to discuss their feelings about their parents without having to face the parental anger or depression the disclosure of such feelings might stimulate. If the law permits, make clear to such a patient that you will maintain absolute confidentiality unless you have specific written permission from the patient to do otherwise. On occasion the police may request information about a substance abuser. Frequently, police officers are not aware of the stringent federal and state laws concerning disclosure. Without a properly executed order, issued by a court of competent jurisdiction, a physician should not respond to such requests because improper disclosure may result in the physician receiving a fine and/or jail sentence. If questions concerning confidentiality arise, one should seek legal consultation.

8. *Managing the interview.* Break the interview into an initial phase in which you try to elicit from the patient, in the patient's words, what the problems are. In the second phase, you become much more active and ask whatever questions are necessary for diagnostic patient decisions.

In the first segment of the interview, do not interrupt the patient. Let the patient talk about whatever the patient wants to talk about. Doing so may be fostered by picking up on the last thing said by a patient when the patient ends a segment of communication: "You were arguing with your wife and she left your house," in response to a patient's description of his recent drinking habits and the arguments they led to with his wife. The technique of picking up on the last thing said by a patient is an element in the Rogerian counseling technique.

As noted, you should initially give the "set" of the interview—for example, "I want to know about your life and particularly how drugs/alcohol affect you and the people around you," but then, at least in the early stages of the interview, you should yield to the patient. As the interview progresses, because of time pressure, you may have to take charge in order to obtain a complete history, but, as much as possible, use silence as an interview technique. Technically, this means allowing the patient pauses and silences of 15 to 30 seconds or more. Pauses this long are sometimes necessary for patients to define what they are thinking and feeling. By permitting patients to reflect on what they are saying, a more emotionally meaningful interview results than is the case if you control by frequent interruptions.

Substance abuse may be just one of many problems a patient is seeking help for. If a patient does not get time to express an opinion of what her or his problems are, clinically important information will have been lost. If you have to, you can interrupt a patient and say, for example, "There are things I have to know about, and time is getting short. Have you ever had convulsions?"

If you encounter a patient who talks a lot but says little, you may have a patient whose verbal output seems to create a feeling of control in what is possibly a frightening situation. Less commonly, excessive verbalization may be part of the repertoire of "con." By talking in irrelevancies but controlling the airwaves, so to speak, the "conning" person creates a sense of control and, more importantly, studies how you respond to being controlled in this way and how you react to the different subjects advanced.

9. *Blend open-ended questions* (e.g., "What do you feel when you take Valium?") *with closed-ended questions* (questions that can be answered with yes or no) according

to the fluctuating needs of the interview. In general, open-ended questions are best when exploring new topic areas. Closed-ended questions are preferable when the details relating to the topic area come under discussion.

10. *Use whatever vocabulary you are comfortable with.* After some experience with substance abusers, it may be more effective to use their slang than to use more formal terms; "Are you shooting or snorting coke?" may be better than "Are you taking the cocaine intravenously or by insufflation?" But again, the style is not as important as your concern and your basic pharmacologic knowledge. If you express concern by taking time, listening attentively, and responding with care and honesty, lack of knowledge of street slang is irrelevant.

11. *Project confidence.* If you do not know much about drugs/alcohol, you must make the effort to acquire the relevant knowledge. Patients commonly believe they know more about "street" drugs than their doctors, and they are often correct. Such a situation is not conducive to effective clinical work. If you know the pharmacology of psychoactive substances, lack of familiarity with street names for drugs will not be troublesome. These names change from time to time and from area to area of the country. In addition, repeated studies demonstrate that street buys are for substances different from those thought to be sold by street dealers as much as 50 percent of the time. Many substance abusers are aware of the fact of false buys but are not aware of their extent, nor are they aware that this has been much studied.

12. *A little empathy is worth a lot of sympathy.* A clinician working with substance abusers frequently feels that what has happened to the patient could happen to anyone. From some points of view, the miracle is that more people are not drug dependent. Patients may attempt to manipulate clinicians around such feelings. A common sequence for a physician with strong initial negative attitudes toward substance abusers is for the feeling of rejection to turn into identification with the addicts' position. Addicts usually report many experiences in which they were, in fact, demeaned by families, by society, or by both. These experiences are genuinely moving, but a correct clinical posture is to remain empathic rather than identifying with the patient.

　　An empathic interviewer tries to evoke from the patient the patient's story, feelings, perception, and analyzes. Empathy requires work; sympathy does not. Sympathy is tangential to the real job of serving patients and more often than not inhibits communication.

13. *At some point near the end of the interview, summarize with the patient the major findings.* This practice often brings out important information that might not have otherwise come out, such as the patient commenting, "It was after my parents' divorce that I started getting high every day."

14. *The JCAHO guidelines suggest that formal assessment of mental status should be carried out "as appropriate" or "when indicated."* The problem for the clinician is to know when it is appropriate, because the results are occasionally surprising. Patients who appear to be articulate and oriented may reveal serious problems on testing. Mental status testing should therefore be routine. The test that follows is an ex-

ample, not a standard. It is important to make clear to all patients that this type of test is a part of the workup for every patient.

Mini–Mental Status Assessment
(Source: Adapted from R. Katzman, T. Brown, P. Fuld, et al. Validation of short orientation-memory-concentration test of cognitive impairment. *American Journal of Psychiatry* 1983;140:743–739.)

		Points	
1.	What year is it now?	4	*for any error*
2.	What month is it now?	3	*for any error*
3.	Please repeat this phrase after me: John Brown, 42 Market Street, Detroit.	0	*use for 7 below*
4.	About what time is it?	3	*for any error*
5.	Please count backwards from 20 to 1.	2	*per error; stop at four points*
6.	Please say the months of the year in reverse order.	2	*per error; stop at four points*
7.	Please repeat the phrase I asked you to repeat before. [John Brown/42 Market Street/Detroit]	2	*for any error*
	Total of the errors scored	—	

- Add up the number of errors and record the score.
- If the total is greater than 10, terminate the assessment and consult a supervisor or a consultant about whether to reattempt the test later.
- If the score is less than or equal to 10, continue.
- If a client appears to "become" impaired during the assessment, you can readminister this exam.

CONSTRUCTING A TREATMENT PROGRAM FOR THE SUBSTANCE ABUSER

There is a set of common elements that should be considered when creating a treatment program for a substance abuser. In some cases, one or another of these elements will be inappropriate or inapplicable, but a clinician should consider each of the following:

1. *Substance abuse disorders are independent problems.* They are not expressions of other problems; rather, they are disorders that must be regarded as primary and not secondary to whatever other psychological or social problems may exist in a given patient or group of patients. The treatment goal is complete and permanent cessation of use of the chemicals—alcohol, cannabis, and so forth—save in the instance of the opioids, where medically supervised subintoxicating intake of methadone may be necessary in lieu of abstinence.

9

2. *A program is necessary.* Substance abuse disorders cannot be treated by writing a prescription and/or by a doctor-patient relationship alone. Instruct the patient that a program is required and that this program has varied elements. Each element in the program is useful but serves a different purpose. Make it clear that the burden for carrying out the program is on the patient. Others can assist, but the patient must implement the program, and that requires independent effort.

3. *Management of substance abuse disorders requires a long-term program.* Work with the patient to create an understanding that the program has to be carried out over a long period, possibly a lifetime. A change in lifestyle is needed, and although instant "cures" occur in some people through religious conversion or herculean self-effort, for almost all substance abusers a long-term effort is required. The physical and psychological reasons why this is so are reviewed in this text.

4. *The key to the program is change.* Change of friends, change of family dynamics, change of attitude, perhaps even change of neighborhoods or cities may be required. The clinical challenge is to examine the fit of the drugs in the patient's life and then to map out a strategy to change the dynamics of the situation. Heroin addicts who live in heavy drug using neighborhoods close to drug abusing relatives, for example, may have to move to a new neighborhood if they are to have any chance of successful treatment. An alcoholic who lives with a spouse who is a heavy drinker may have to separate from or divorce the spouse if the spouse will not recognize and change his or her role as a co-alcoholic.

   A classic example of the necessity for change in family dynamics is illustrated in a case I saw a few years ago. The patient was a 45-year-old woman with a history of hospitalization for severe alcohol withdrawal 10 years previously. She had been sober for many years but had resumed drinking heavily in the year prior to consultation with me. I saw her and her husband together. During the history, they described their pleasure at dining out in restaurants four or five nights a week, a practice they had engaged in for years. Further history revealed that the woman sat with her husband, frequently together with his mother, for one to two hours before eating, while the husband and the patient's mother-in-law had three to five cocktails. Initially, both the patient and her husband denied that this constituted a difficult experience for the patient.

5. *A treatment program requires formal assessment of the psychiatric status of the patient.* A psychiatric consultation may be advisable. Substance abusers have rates of depression, anxiety disorders, and antisocial personality disorders higher than those observed in community samples; rates of other psychiatric disorders do not seem to be grossly different between substance abusers and the general population, but these relationships are just coming under systematic scrutiny.[4] The family history should be carefully reviewed for evidence of affective disorder or other major mental illness.

6. *A treatment program should involve the family.* If a heroin addict wants treatment and is living with a spouse who is an active heroin addict and who will not come in for treatment, the program will probably fail. There is evidence that some drug abusers are playing roles assigned to them by their pathologic families. In gener-

al, try to obtain the patient's permission to interview family members. An occasional patient may be quite suspicious of your motives and the motives of his or her relatives. In this case, have the patient present when you talk to family members.

While you should try to involve the family, common clinical experience indicates that it is frequently difficult to do so. Male heads of households most often will not cooperate. Your expectations with respect to therapeutic use of family dynamics have to be grounded in the reality that it is often not possible to engage the entire family. You may have to work with one or two concerned family members. Interest in the relationship between family dynamics and substance abuse is growing, and a number of centers are exploring ways of improving the therapeutic use of family dynamics.

7. *Putting a program together may involve confrontation.* That is, presenting your conclusion that the patient has a problem with alcohol abuse or drug dependence. Patients' responses to such presentations vary. Many react with denial and hostility, but frequently patients experience relief when a physician makes the diagnosis. As mentioned many times in this text, patients are ambivalent about alcohol and drugs, and many will be able to admit this.

The principles of confrontation are as follows:

- Make a succinct summary of the findings when confronting a patient: "Your liver enzymes are elevated. This finding, in combination with the history of drinking you gave me, suggests you are abusing alcohol." Note that this first principle is based on a thorough workup. Confrontation is effective in proportion to the completeness of the workup.
- Be nonjudgmental. Use precise diagnostic terms—alcohol abuse, nicotine dependence—and tell the patient what you think needs to be done: go into a hospital, join Alcoholics Anonymous (AA), and so forth.
- Attempt to assess the reaction of the patient before the confrontation. If you have worked up the patient thoroughly, you should have some assessment of his or her probable response. You might preface the confrontation by assuring the patient that what you are about to say is in complete confidence, or you may want to schedule the confrontation when you will have enough time to discuss why you reached your decision.
- A strategy that might avoid a confrontation is to ask the patient if the patient's family has considered that a drug/alcohol problem is present. Frequently, a patient will admit that the question has come up but that his or her case does not conform to a stereotype of substance abuse—"I'm not a skid row drinker," for example. The doctor can then correct the stereotype and describe the reasons why a substance abuse problem is present.

8. *The modern pattern of multiple drug use, including alcohol, requires constant clinical monitoring by random urinalysis and breathalyzer tests.* In general, the therapeutic value of monitoring urine and breath has not been utilized by the alcohol treatment community. Alcohol can be detected by breathalyzers for only a few hours in low levels of use, but for many hours when drinking has been heavy, simple-to-

use, pocket-size intoximeters are feasible for monitoring the breath. For maximum impact, monitoring has to be random and should include breath and urine. All urine specimens should be taken under direct observation or with temperature monitoring to avoid substitution.

Monitoring provides for early detection of relapse. It is difficult for a patient to develop a pattern of sustained covert alcohol and/or drug use when random once-a-week or twice-a-week monitoring is employed. Monitoring provides structure and control, and both elements are usually needed and appreciated by patients. Substance abusers lack control and feel safer when they know that they may be able to fool themselves, but they are not going to be able to fool their counselor or doctor for very long. Monitoring also is a potent legal tool. Possible suits brought against substance abusers are easier to defend against when there is a history of participation in urine and breath monitoring. It is especially potent if there is a record of negative random urine and breath tests. Monitoring costs somewhere between $5 and $15 per week, depending on the number and types of drugs tested for. A nurse or counselor can be instructed to call a patient on varying days of the week. Drug testing methods and results are discussed later in this book.

9. *Take advantage of community-based programs.* In the instance of alcoholism, consider referral to AA; for drug abusers, consider referral to Narcotics Anonymous, a therapeutic community, detoxification program, drug free program, or methadone maintenance program, as appropriate. In addition, in some communities, there are programs such as Tough Love and Families Anonymous, which can be important resources. Clinical aspects of referral to AA, therapeutic communities, methadone maintenance programs, and so forth are discussed in detail in later chapters.

10. *Consider enlisting the assistance of a recovering substance abuser.* A recovering substance abuser can provide a role model for the patient, who may gain hope and social support from such a person. Frequently, one of the substance abuser's biggest problems is changing from old to new friends. Friendship networks provide important continuing reinforcement for drug and alcohol abuse, and breaking these bonds may be the most difficult part of the program. The recovering person can be instrumental in the effort. After some years, most clinicians who work with substance abusers have "recovering" patients, patients who are doing well and who benefit substantially from their assistance to another human being.

11. *Specific pharmacologic measures are discussed in the relevant chapters* (e.g., narcotic substitution or narcotic blocking agents for opioid dependent patients, disulfiram for alcoholics).

12. *Explore counseling or psychotherapy.* There has been much debate about the effectiveness of psychotherapy for substance abusers, but in my experience there is no question that it can be an important element in the general management plan for a substance abuser. If a patient does not do well with a particular therapy or therapist, do not hesitate to try a new therapy or therapist. Psychotherapy assists the patient in coming to terms with feelings and problems that cannot be effec-

tively overcome by the social support of AA or a methadone maintenance program or in a relationship with a recovering substance abuser. Frequently, a substance abuser refuses psychological help, but pressure should be kept on the patient to engage with this element of the program if recovery is not robust. At one time, many prominent clinicians considered psychotherapy contraindicated in alcoholics until they achieved one to two years of sobriety and were active in AA or some other support system. With the appearance of physicians trained and experienced in addiction medicine, there is much more skillful use of psychotherapy, which avoids the splitting and other problems seen in the past. My experience is that psychotherapy is not available or acceptable to many substance abusers, but, as reviewed later, it can contribute to successful recovery.

13. *Review general health measures.* Medical or surgical problems should be identified and treated. In addition, you should review with the patient diet and exercise patterns. Most substance abusers do not practice sound nutrition and do not exercise. They are often surprised at how good simple exercise can make people feel. If you are functioning as a family physician, your continuing interest in the recovery can be helpful for both patient and family members.

14. *If the patient is physically dependent, educate the patient about withdrawal.* You should review with the patient the certain existence of an acute withdrawal syndrome and the probable existence of a chronic withdrawal syndrome. Most patients have irrational attitudes and emotions concerning withdrawal. For example, some believe that they can be withdrawn in a few days when they are severely dependent; others believe that they must suffer extreme discomfort. An occasional patient may be phobic concerning withdrawal. The job is to identify the patient's beliefs and feelings and to respond by reassurance and presentation of specific data about withdrawal. Time should be spent with the patient discussing the patient's experiences and judgments concerning withdrawal before withdrawal is attempted.

The key to successful management of withdrawal is the determination of a dose decrement that is tolerable to the patient. The usual regimen for withdrawal is too fast and induces severe dysphoria, which the patient cannot tolerate. Self-treatment with drugs is assured in such instances.

With respect to the chronic withdrawal syndrome, the patient should be instructed that psychological dependency manifests itself for many months, if not many years, after the acute phase of physical dependency is over. In other words, the essence of dependence is psychological, not physical, as in the instance of the "dry drunk." In addition, several investigators have identified persisting physiologic changes that constitute a chronic abstinence syndrome following alcohol or drug withdrawal. The occurrence of a similar chronic abstinence syndrome is probable but has not been explored for other classes of drugs. Psychological dependency and, at least in the instances of alcohol and the opioids, a chronic abstinence syndrome dictate that the treatment program be projected for years.

15. *Consider hospitalization.* A 2- to 6-week hospitalization can be important in accomplishing detoxification, determining in depth the dynamics of the substance

abuse pattern, and treating medical or psychiatric conditions. The patient may learn under controlled conditions what it feels like to be drug free. Hospitalization may be inappropriate because of cost or because a patient will not accept it or cannot afford to take time from work, but it should be considered seriously for complicated problems of substance abuse.

16. *Educate the patient concerning psychoactive drugs and their effects.* Patients treated at Hazelden, a prominent treatment center, reported that learning about alcohol was one of the most valuable elements in their treatment experience. Education can be accomplished in groups and/or with pamphlets and books.

17. *Once the program is constructed, review the elements with the patient.* As the patient begins to appreciate that others have been through the same experience and that support is available, there will be an improvement of morale. Since demoralization is extreme with most substance abusers, an important hurdle will have been overcome.

Discuss how the program will be supported financially and if fees are involved. Make clear to the patient your guidelines with respect to payment of fees and contingencies if fees are not paid. Frequently, these matters do not receive the attention they deserve in the initial phase of implementation. They can then sometimes inject themselves into the program at times and in ways that strongly suggest they are being used defensively by the patient. It may not be possible to discuss fees, resources, and so forth in the first or even in the first few sessions, but as early as possible in the relationship these matters should be clarified.

In the following sections of this chapter, common drug related problems are introduced. General principles are presented with the understanding that problems specific to drug classes are covered in the drug specific chapters to come.

GENERAL PRINCIPLES OF MANAGEMENT OF SUBSTANCE INDUCED WITHDRAWAL

1. *A program is necessary.* Management of withdrawal requires more than a physician writing orders. The patient must be oriented and the staff assigned roles. A centerpiece of good management of withdrawal is the establishment of a working relationship with the patient. A program is carried out with an informed and participating patient; it is not something done to a patient. Other elements of the program are as follows:

2. *Assess the level of dependence.* In general, I determine level of dependence by frequent observation of the patient. If there are no withdrawal symptoms, then continued observation is indicated. If a patient is becoming increasingly sedated, then medical measures such as hemodialysis may be indicated. If withdrawal symptoms appear, then their severity and course determine clinical action. Many addiction medicine centers determine level of dependence by challenge with drugs from the class involved to determine how much tolerance is present, as discussed in the chapter on sedative hypnotics. In general, the history predicts level of dependence, as discussed in later chapters.

3. *Use a long-acting member of the class of drugs involved, if one exists.* There is considerable cross-tolerance between alcohol and sedative hypnotics, which makes the use of phenobarbital or diazepam logical for control of withdrawal from any of the members of the class. We do not have well-established studies comparing phenobarbital with diazepam, so current practice is based on the experience of clinicians.

4. *Clarify roles with the patient, if the patient's mental status permits.* With a patient undergoing severe withdrawal delirium from alcohol or other sedatives, it is not possible to establish any meaningful relationship, but with most patients one can and should assign roles. I usually tell the patient that my role is to keep the patient safe and to withdraw him or her at rates that may be uncomfortable but should be tolerable. The patient's job is to report symptoms and focus on things other than the withdrawal. I have always been struck by the dramatic difference between opioid withdrawal in jails and in therapeutic communities. In jail settings, frequently there is no program, and the patient lies in bed or sits around all day with nothing to focus on but the suffering of withdrawal. The severity of withdrawal in this circumstance is much worse than in a therapeutic community, where the patient is busy with demanding tasks and relationships.

5. *The lower the level of dependence, the slower the withdrawal.* At high levels of dependence one can reduce dose during withdrawal by 5 to 10 percent and have tolerable withdrawal symptoms, but as one approaches zero dose, such decrements can produce symptoms severe enough to drive the patient back to drug use.

6. *A wide range of drugs is used in different settings for withdrawal.* Clonidine, carbamazepine, beta blockers, hydroxyzine, and valproic acid are all utilized by some centers. In these centers, there are usually highly experienced addiction medicine physicians. My advice is to use the drugs most commonly used (e.g., benzodiazepines for alcohol or benzodiazepine withdrawal, phenobarbital for other sedative hypnotic withdrawal, methadone for opioid withdrawal). The newer drugs are still experimental, and the general physician who uses them without informed consent and institutional review board approval is risking medicolegal consequences that could be severe. We will return to this issue in the coming chapters.

GENERAL PRINCIPLES OF MANAGEMENT OF ACUTE DRUG INDUCED MENTAL DISORDERS: DRUG INDUCED PSYCHOSES, HALLUCINATIONS, DELIRIUM[5]

Diagnostic Criteria for Substance Intoxication Delirium

A. Disturbance of consciousness (i.e., reduced clarity of awareness of the environment) with reduced ability to focus, sustain, or shift attention.

B. A change in cognition (such as memory deficit, disorientation, language disturbance) or the development of a perceptual disturbance that is not better accounted for by a preexisting, established, or evolving dementia.

C. The disturbance develops over a short period (usually hours to days) and tends to fluctuate during the course of the day.

D. There is evidence from the history, physical examination, or laboratory findings of either (1) the symptoms in criteria A and B developed during substance intoxication; or (2) medication use is etiologically related to the disturbance. The diagnosis should be recorded as substance induced delirium if related to medication use. Refer to Appendix G for E-codes indicating specific medications.

Note: This diagnosis should be made instead of a diagnosis of substance intoxication only when the cognitive symptoms are in excess of those usually associated with the intoxication syndrome and when the symptoms are sufficiently severe to warrant independent clinical attention.

Code (specific substance) intoxication delirium:

291.0 alcohol   292.81 amphetamine (or amphetamine-like substance)
                          cannabis
                          cocaine
                          hallucinogen
                          inhalant
                          opioid
                          phencyclidine (or phencyclidine-like substance)
                          sedative, hypnotic, or anxiolytic
                          other (or unknown) substance
                          (e.g., cimetidine, digitalis, benztropine)

Diagnostic Criteria for Substance Withdrawal Delirium

A. Disturbance of consciousness (i.e., reduced clarity of awareness of the environment) with reduced ability to focus, sustain, or shift attention.

B. A change in cognition (such as memory deficit, disorientation, language disturbance) or the development of a perceptual disturbance that is not better accounted for by a preexisting, established, or evolving dementia.

C. The disturbance develops over a short period (usually hours to days) and tends to fluctuate during the course of the day.

D. There is evidence from the history, physical examination, or laboratory findings that the symptoms in criteria A and B developed during, or shortly after, a withdrawal syndrome.

Note: This diagnosis should be made instead of a diagnosis of substance withdrawal only when the cognitive symptoms are in excess of those usually associated with the withdrawal syndrome and when the symptoms are severe enough to warrant independent clinical attention.

Code (specific substance) withdrawal delirium:

291.0 alcohol   292.81 sedative, hypnotic, or anxiolytic
                          other (or unknown) substance

Use of hallucinogens such as LSD (lysergic acid diethyl amide) and DMT (dimethyl-tryptamine) and use of other classes of drugs, such as the arylcyclohexylamine (PCP), cannabis, or hashish oil, may be associated with hallucinations, panic, and loss of control. These toxic effects are sometimes associated with an impairment of judgment severe enough to qualify as a psychosis. Features unique to the management of toxic reactions to specific drugs are discussed in the relevant chapters, but there are general principles of management that are presented here. When the diagnosis of a toxic psychological reaction to a drug, now known formally in DSM-4 as a drug induced disorder (e.g., drug induced psychosis), is established, proceed as follows:

1. *Try to establish a relationship with the patient.* Introduce yourself and see if you can get a dialogue going with the patient. This is the centerpiece to successful resolution of the drug toxic state and is as important as any other measure, including drug treatment.

2. *Control the effects of stimulation.* Usually this means to reduce stimulation, but it also means to make stimulation predictable and meaningful. Ideally, the "bad trip" should be treated in a dimly lit room with minimum stimuli. Toxicity from phencyclidine, the most common form of PCP, may represent the only departure from this rule, in that some clinicians advocate as complete a reduction in stimuli as is possible (e.g., throwing a blanket over PCP-toxic patients and leaving them alone). Such extreme measures are not usually necessary; continued experience with PCP-toxic patients has indicated that many are not as difficult as early experience found them to be. In any event, your treatment plan has to be guided by your clinical findings rather than by preconceived definitions of drug specific behaviors. If you can establish rapport with a patient, violence is not likely, regardless of the drug or drugs involved.

3. *Reassure the patient:* "You're feeling out of control because you took some drugs. We've got the situation in hand and will give you something to calm you if you want. We'll check on you again in ten minutes."

4. *Orient the patient in time, place, and rationale for being in a treatment situation:* "You took some drugs at a party, and you are having a bad trip." "You're in a hospital emergency room and we expect you to be OK in a little while." "It's Tuesday, April 12, and it's about 2 o'clock in the morning. You've been in the hospital two hours now." Create order in the situation; for example, if possible, have the same people come back at regular time intervals that are identified to the patient.

5. *Introduce familiarity into the situation if you can.* Ask the patient if there is someone he or she would like to have present. Observe how the patient reacts to friends or family. If it is clear the patient wants the friend or family member in the room and that the relationship is not increasing the patient's agitation or other symptoms, permit that person to stay. Ask the patient if he or she would like to watch TV or listen to music he or she likes on the radio. Usually, patients respond to familiar programs, music, and so forth by reintegrating, but on occasion delusional thinking may be stimulated. If this is the case, the radio, or TV, reading ma-

terial, or whatever is triggering the delusion must be taken from the patient's environment.

6. *Use tranquilizers, but for explicit purposes only.* Anxiety and/or agitation may be severe and unresponsive to psychological management. Use of benzodiazepines, such as diazepam, is indicated when this is the case. Administer a usual dose (10 to 20 mg) and observe the effects; for example, if there is no reduction in agitation after 10 mg of diazepam in 20 minutes, give another 10 mg and again monitor the effect. With incremental doses, you should begin to bring symptoms under control. Benzodiazepines are preferred drugs because they are effective against the usual target symptoms of agitation or anxiety; in addition, they have anticonvulsant properties, which may be crucial if the dose of the stimulant or hallucinogen was high enough to produce a risk of convulsions.

    Hallucinations, violence (real or threatened), or delusions may require the use of butyrophenones; phenothiazines are contraindicated because they may intensify anticholinergic effects of commonly used street drugs and because they may induce hypotension.

7. *Monitor the patient for possible violence.* Violence can occur without warning, but in some instances there are many indicators that a patient's impulses are about to break through. Any of these should trigger management techniques designed to forestall violence: extremely fearful reactions to hallucinatory experiences, particularly in a patient whose immediate past behavior indicates that he/she does not recognize the therapeutic intentions of the medical personnel attending her/him; verbal threats, gestures, intense sweating, extreme agitation, scars from past violence, or recent bruises and cuts.

    If violence occurs, if possible, use people to restrain the patient. Making a show of force by assembling as many people as you can may prevent violence. If the patient sees that he is outnumbered, he will sometimes feel secure in that even if he loses control, the situation is such that he is not going to do something he does not want to do. Agitation may lessen as a consequence. If violence occurs, staff should be trained to respond with defensive measures only. Wrapping the patient in a blanket, holding down all four limbs, and the like are indicated safe measures. Clinical experience has repeatedly suggested that most violence in a hospital is preventable.

8. *Don't contradict the patient's delusions.* If delusions are part of the clinical picture, identify them as drug effects; tell the patient they will become less important as the management program is implemented.

9. *If touching a patient appears to be reassuring, touch the patient when you are making orienting remarks.* If a patient is suspicious or extremely fearful, it is best not to touch, because the patient may not be able to sort out your intentions and may respond with violence.

10. *Monitor the patient regularly.* Use your visits to introduce regularity into the situation: "I'm going to come back in 15 minutes to check on your progress" or, "The nurse is going to check on you every 10 minutes. She'll call me if there's a problem. I'll see you again in an hour." Try to return when you say you will. Your

behavior may be important in helping the patient reorder experience in time and with people.

11. *Your behavior and the behavior of staff is "infectious" to the patient.* Crisis studies indicate that people in crises are suggestible and internalize attitudes of the dominant persons in the environment. It is important, therefore, to be calm and to take time when communicating; it may be frustrating for a drug toxic patient to try to communicate with you because drug effects block or slow thinking. Taking time means that you do not add an iatrogenic component to an already complicated problem.

12. *Review with the patient the measures being taken to overcome the toxic state.* Try to enlist the patient's participation in the program by asking the patient to tell you if panic or violent impulses are becoming unmanageable.

13. *Finally, go over these principles with the entire team of individuals involved in managing the drug toxic state.* Periodic review of progress with the team and the patient, if the patient can be enlisted, will provide confidence and control.

MANAGEMENT OF TOXIC EFFECTS IN PATIENTS GIVEN A DRUG WITHOUT THEIR KNOWLEDGE

Over the years, I have seen a number of young patients who reported having been given drugs without their knowledge. Some of these patients may have made up the story of unknowing ingestion to avoid parental anger, but in most instances the lack of any premorbid or postmorbid history suggests their stories are genuine. Usually on a Friday or Saturday night at a party, they drink wine or beer that subsequently turns out to have been laced with LSD, PCP, or some other hallucinogen. They experience intense panic at being unable to understand or to control hallucinations and/or intense feelings. In some instances, perceptual problems such as "light trails" are particularly disturbing. Patients report that when they try to shift gaze, light sources appear to move in trailwise fashion. In other instances, the inability to think straight is intensely disturbing.

These patients can usually be managed at home by frequent brief orienting contacts on the part of family members together with sedatives or diazepam and assurance of your availability. There are families, however, in which fear of drug effects is so strong that home management may not be possible.

If psychiatric hospitalization is indicated, it is important to orient the patient by showing the patient the ward, introducing the patient to ward personnel, and preparing the patient for the aberrant behavior sometimes seen on psychiatric wards. Lay people have little or no experience with such behavior and if not properly oriented may become frightened or depressed. The patient should be oriented to the need for 24-hour-a-day supervision with the availability of helping persons should the need arise.

Patients with perceptual problems such as light trails should be told not to attend to these distracting experiences and to try to engage in normal pursuits. Usually, energy levels are low, apparently because of the energy needed for constant vigilance as a defense against hallucinations, perceptual distortions, and/or intense affects. Patients should be oriented to these facts and instructed to avoid activities requiring a lot of energy. Low-dose diazepam (2 to 5 mg, 2 to 3 times per day) may be tried as an adjunct to the basic plan of orientation and assurance of external control. In extreme cases, butyrophenones may be required to control severe toxic effects not controllable by the measures just described. Alcohol, cannabis, and other psychoactive substances should be avoided completely, as they make symptoms worse.

MANAGEMENT OF HALLUCINATION PERSISTING PERCEPTUAL DISORDERS OR "FLASHBACKS"

Flashbacks usually occur suddenly and are brief. Part of a drug induced hallucinatory experience is reexperienced days, weeks, or months after the initial episode. Sometimes the flashbacks consist of fully formed visual hallucinations, but some flashbacks may consist of perceptual distortions such as light trails.

Hallucinogens, PCP, and cannabis have been associated with the occurrence of flashbacks. Patients commonly report that fatigue and a variety of drugs usher in such experiences. In some patients, flashbacks are not troublesome, but in others they are associated with anxiety and may occur frequently enough to interfere with study or work.

The basic treatment consists of reassurance; patients should be told that clinical experience indicates that flashbacks diminish in frequency and intensity with time. The time for decrease or cessation is usually weeks, occasionally months. Additional measures that have been useful to patients include training the patient to focus not on the flashbacks but on "regular thinking," such as studying or TV. Low-dose diazepam 2 mg b.i.d. or t.i.d. may also be tried in refractory cases. Street drugs should be avoided completely.

COUNSELING THE SUBSTANCE ABUSER

Physicians are counselors, whether or not they consciously guide their clinical behavior by a set of counseling principles. Counseling should be distinguished from psychotherapy. Both have common elements—a nonjudgmental attitude and unconditional acceptance of the humanity of the patient—but psychotherapy is guided by a theory of human behavior, requires extended training for its practitioners, and utilizes the doctor-patient relationship in an interpretive way. Counseling, by definition, does not attempt to interpret dependent, aggressive, or sexual aspects of a given relationship with a patient. Psychotherapy aims at the resolution of emotional conflict, while counseling consists of aiding a patient in decision making. "You have gout; there are a number of treatments available, but no one with superiority over the other" is a statement that generates a counseling interaction. In counseling, information is exchanged for the purpose of decision making.

A physician may be asked to counsel substance abusers or persons close to substance abusers for varied reasons: "What does it mean that my 14-year-old daughter smokes marijuana once a month?" "Where are treatment programs for heroin addicts in this community?" "I'm very heavy, I know, but I can't stop eating"—all of these statements generate counseling exchanges. Counseling principles are as follows:

1. *Clarify your role with respect to the problem.* For example, "I'm not a psychotherapist, but maybe I can assist you in trying to understand your son's drug taking. Let's meet for an hour or two to see if we can understand better what the problem is." Note the time commitment, however. Before you commit to counseling, make sure you have time. Frequently, attempts at counseling founder because of the pressures of surgical, medical, or obstetrical practice.

2. *Clarify the question to be resolved.* "You seem to have many fears about your daughter's use of marijuana, but I don't know specifically what they are" and "Your son was hoping he would die when he overdosed. It was a suicide attempt. He needs help from a psychiatrist. I'm not qualified to deal with his depression" are statements that illustrate proper clarification of a problem and of a physician's role.

3. *Avoid giving advice.* The response to a question such as "What should I do?" should be, "What are some of the things you have thought of doing?" and/or "What have your friends (or children or parents) suggested?" Advice giving, in either counseling or psychotherapy, is always inappropriate with respect to major life decisions that express the uniqueness of the individual. "Should I have another baby?" "Should I divorce my husband?" are questions that no one but the individual asking them can answer. Good counseling assists the process of decision making by including the physician, but it is an error, possibly with serious medicolegal consequences, to preempt the individual's ultimate decision by prescribing abortion, divorce, marriage, children, etc.

   Clinical experience strongly suggests that attempts on the part of one partner in a marriage to change a substance abuser's behavior also engaged in by the other partner are fruitless unless both partners are treated. Proper counseling consists of presenting this fact of professional experience to the patient. Divorce or separation or an abortion are options that might be discussed in counseling, but the prescription of any of these actions by the counselor is outside the bounds of a good counseling relationship.

   The "Don't advise" principle should be applied broadly. To tell a teenager, "Don't take drugs or alcohol" is good advice; it's a good "doctor's order," but it isn't good counseling. To report your experience that the drug abusers and alcoholics you've seen have not been fulfilled people can promote communication without preempting the individual's need to decide. Advice and/or exhortation usually bring closure to a particular segment of a communicative exchange. In general, closure should be carried out by a patient who has made a decision based on the counseling process. A good counselor leaves closure to the patient.

4. *Set time limits as a fundamental element of the counseling relationship.* "Let's meet once a week for 30 minutes for the next 2 months" expresses the time limits in a counseling relationship. Limits are important in managing the emotional aspects of a counseling relationship for both physician and patient and should be reinforced in every session. Substance abusers tend to have many experiences of loss

and conflict in close relationships. They need structure to manage their tendency to want to intensify a rewarding counseling relationship and then give it up when it has run its course. The time structure and conscious repetition of its reality also aids the physician in managing what may be intense feelings about the patient.

5. *Focus the counseling exchange on here-and-now problems.* If a patient wants to examine childhood experiences as a way of understanding a substance abuse problem you have mutually contracted to concentrate on, you might try to assist in the attempt; but after a time, unless childhood exploration is clearly contributing to resolution of current problems, it is best to return to focus on the here and now. If the counseling sessions consistently return to such issues as childhood experiences, referral for psychotherapy should be considered with the patient.

6. *Project confidence.* A program can change things. We are able to achieve high rates of success if we can catch problems early. Medical education, historically, has tended to identify substance abusers by the most extreme cases, but in the last decade, in both public and private programs, we have been seeing people before they reach such extremes. Knowledge and experience create power. Patients commonly feel powerless, and if they sense that the physician is potent, they have a stimulus to try again.

7. *Model the decision-making process for the patient.* In making a decision, there is an analysis phase, which consists of identifying relevant facts and then interpreting these facts. This is followed by a decision phase consisting of selecting the most appropriate from several possible strategies. Periodic summarization is one technique to illustrate the process to the patient: "Last time we talked about your feelings of depression when you see your parents argue; you brought out that you drink more beer and smoke more pot when you have these feelings" sets the stage for further counseling, as well as modeling part of the decision-making process. As counseling progresses, encourage the patient to take on the job of summarizing. This helps in the psychological problem of separation when the counseling is over; hopefully, this skill will be internalized by the patient for use with life problems in the future.

8. *When parents undermine each other consistently, the fact of reciprocal undermining is what deserves mention by a counselor.* To join one partner in negative labeling of the behavior of the other is not good counseling. Your role with individuals and with families is to foster communication and to summarize as a method of improving decision making.

9. *Use simple words, phrases, and questions.* Examine your technique for content. Questions like "What happened next?" "How did you feel?" "What did you think about then?" are open-ended and lead to increased communication. Avoid questions like "Did that make you feel bad?" "Did you think about going home?" because they can be answered with a yes or no answer, which tends to bring closure to a given communication sequence. It is instructive to tape an interview— with the patient's permission—and then to study your counseling technique.

The comments above on counseling are based on clinical experience, but there are carefully controlled studies showing that the interest in helping patients and skill in counseling are potent agents of change.[6, 7] How a counselor approaches the job of counseling can make an important difference in the effectiveness of referral and treatment.

COUNSELING PARENTS OF TEENAGERS CONCERNING SUBSTANCE ABUSE

Parents may turn to a physician for guidance when they discover that their teenager or preteen child has experimented with and/or is using marijuana, alcohol, or other drugs. If the physician lacks time, experience, or interest in this kind of problem (and effective management requires all three), the family should be referred to another physician or to a social worker or psychologist who is experienced with these problems. To respond to the family's request, management principles are as follows:

1. *Try to assist the family to define its questions and fears.* Sometimes parental response is highly emotional, and parents do not formulate their concerns clearly. "My daughter is using marijuana" expresses, for some parents, a fear of ultimate heroin addiction, for others it expresses undefined anxiety, while for others it may express a realistic fear of the possible consequences of the long-term smoking of marijuana (e.g., pulmonary problems). The physician's job is to clarify these concerns and then attempt to respond to them. If parental concerns are clear and focused, they can be responded to by referral to appropriate practitioners or agencies.

2. *Try to understand what role the drug use has in the context of the young person's life.* If, for example, there is maintenance of adequate school performance, normal participation in social life, no impairment of appetite, sleep, energy levels, or the like, you may conclude that the child is engaging in drug experimentation, which, from a statistical point of view, is normative at this time in history. You may counsel the family to learn about the short-term and long-term consequences of drug use so that they may discuss intelligently the child's decision to use it. The parents should communicate clearly to the child their position and the consequences of the child's failure to respect their position.

   If the child points out that alcohol, a drug with many dangers, is used by the parents, the parents should be counseled to admit that this is so. One good solution for a family is for parents and children together to decide to eliminate or decrease their use of intoxicants, legal or illegal.

   What is at issue in most families is intoxication. Telling a young person that intoxication from alcohol is OK but intoxication from other drugs is not plays into the hands of the counterculture and leads nowhere. It is probably best to point out that intoxication is overvalued in our culture and that most of what is said about intoxicants, both legal and illegal, is false and is best understood by inverting what is said. Alcohol, for example, is sometimes sold by making it appear that its use is masculine, but a dose of alcohol sufficient to produce intoxication usually causes a decrement in sexual performance. Hallucinogens are sometimes promoted as substances whose use provides psychological insight, but insight takes work by a mind functioning fully.

3. *Have the parents talked with the child?* In almost all cases, it is desirable for the parents to communicate their concerns to the child. The more rational the communication the better, but in some families discussion of even trivial negative concerns is accompanied by such emotion that communication cannot occur. In such instances, it may be best to work with the child alone.

4. *If there are decrements in school performance or problems with mood, energy, sleep, or appetite, or if there is social withdrawal, the child and/or the family should be referred for therapy.* Again, the basic principle is that there must be change. In one instance, after learning that the teenage son of a family was heavily involved with drugs and had also become enmeshed with a vicious street gang, I concurred with the other family members that moving to a new city was the best course of action.

5. *Know sources of information.* Following the bibliography for this chapter, there are addresses and telephone numbers for the National Institute on Alcoholism and Alcohol Abuse and the National Institute on Drug Abuse. Both have excellent pamphlets and other materials on alcohol and drugs. The National Clearing House telephone number is 1–800–729–6686. In addition, each state has a single state agency that usually also has valuable information.

REFERENCES

1. Kessler RC, McGonagle KA, Zhao S, et al. Lifetime and 12 month prevalence of DSM-3-R psychiatric disorders in the United States. *Arch Gen Psychiatry* 51:8–19, 1994.
2. *Substance Abuse: The Nation's Number One Health Problem.* Princeton, NJ, prepared by the Institute for Health Policy, Brandeis University, for The Robert Wood Johnson Foundation. Princeton, NJ, October 1993, pp 33–35.
3. Novick DM, Joseph H, Croxson TS, et al. Absence of antibody to human immunodeficiency virus in long-term, socially rehabilitated methadone maintenance patients. *Arch Intern Med* 150:97–99, 1990.
4. Schuckit MA. *Drug and Alcohol Abuse: A Clinical Guide to Diagnosis and Treatment.* ed 4. New York, Plenum, 1995, pp 299–300.
5. American Psychiatric Association. *Diagnostic and Statistical Manual of Mental Disorders,* ed 4. Washington, DC, American Psychiatric Association, 1994.
6. McLellan AT, Woody GE, Luborsky L, et al. Is the Counselor an Active Ingredient in Substance Abuse Rehabilitation? *Journal of Nervous and Mental Disorders* 176(7):423–430, 1988.
7. Luborsky L, McLellan AT, Woody GE, et al. Therapist Success and its Determinants. *Arch Gen Psychiatry* 42:602–611.

ADDITIONAL READINGS

Miller WR, Rollnick S. *Motivational Interviewing: Preparing People to Change Addictive Behavior.* New York, Guilford Press, 1991.

Senay EC. Diagnostic Interview and Mental Status Examination. *Substance Abuse: A Comprehensive Textbook.* ed 3. Baltimore, Williams and Wilkins, 1997.

WEB SITES

National Institute on Drug Abuse (NIDA): http://www.nida.nih.gov

American Society of Addiction Medicine (ASAM): http://www.asam.org

National Institute on Alcohol Abuse and Alcoholism (NIAA): http://www.niaa.nih.gov

2. Diagnosis, Multiaxial Assessment, Negotiation over Treatment Assignment, and Patient Placement on the ASAM/JCAHO Continuum of Care

INTRODUCTION

Criteria-based diagnosis, recorded specifically in the chart (e.g., "Patient met criteria 1, 2, 3, and 7 for cocaine dependence"), is mandatory for both clinical and financial reasons in this era of managed care. In addition, the chart needs a number code, in this example 304.20, Cocaine Dependence. The criteria and number codes for various diagnoses are presented in DSM-4; this manual defines the official language for the near-term future. This chapter is focused on these DSM-4 diagnostic criteria and attempts to improve understanding of them and their use in clinical life. In addition, this chapter describes the negotiation over treatment assignment between doctor, patient, third-party payers, families, and others now frequently part of clinical interaction. It ends with a discussion of the assignment of the patient to a treatment unit on the continuum of care described by ASAM[1] and JCAHO.[2]

STRUCTURE OF DSM-4 WITH RESPECT TO SUBSTANCE RELATED DISORDERS

Substance Related Disorders is the general description of drug and alcohol diagnostic criteria, and it is an independent line on a rank with Schizophrenia, Mood Disorders, and other classes in DSM-4. Substance Related Disorders is then broken down into Substance Use Disorders and Substance Induced Disorders. The first of these two terms describes the criteria necessary to make a diagnosis of Dependence or Abuse; and the second, the criteria necessary to diagnose disorders such as intoxication, withdrawal, and a number of psychiatric syndromes such as dementia, psychoses, delirium, mood disorders, and others that are caused by effects of intoxicants, either direct or in withdrawal.

DSM-4 embeds Substance Induced Disorders along with the syndromes they cause. For example, Substance Induced Dementia is described in the section on Dementia; Substance Induced Mood Disorder is described in the Mood Disorders section. Note that DSM-4 no longer describes organic brain syndromes because of the growing indications from neuroimaging and other lines of evidence that all psychiatric syndromes have organic/biologic determinants or consequences.

THE ASAM CONTINUUM OF CARE AND PATIENT PLACEMENT CRITERIA

A complete substance abuse history obtains information that permits diagnosis and placement of the patient on the ASAM/JCAHO continuum of care. Before reviewing the specific criteria for diagnosis, it is important to understand the placement criteria and how they interrelate with the diagnostic criteria.

PATIENT PLACEMENT ON THE CONTINUUM OF CARE ACCORDING TO THE ASAM CRITERIA

The ASAM continuum of care disposes of the historically incorrect notion that these disorders could be conceived of and treated as single episodes of care, delivered by a provider with a fixed treatment menu for all. As noted in chapter 1, most of the people meeting criteria for a diagnosis have careers of episodes of dependence interspersed with periods of abstinence. Any episode of dependence may have quite different severity and involvement of important life domains from other episodes in the career. The ASAM continuum of care recognizes and incorporates these facts and provides for changing needs in any given episode of care. For example, after treatment for potentially life-threatening withdrawal from alcohol, the patient can then be moved to intensive outpatient, then to less intensive outpatient, and finally, perhaps, solely to self-help care.

The basic principles underlying the ASAM placement criteria are:

1. *Objectivity.* Clinical decision is always based on clinical experience informed by research. The ASAM criteria are objective wherever possible to increase to the fullest degree possible the clarity and rationality of clinical choices.
2. *Choice of treatment levels.* The ASAM criteria describe four basic levels of care: outpatient, intensive outpatient, residential, and intensive inpatient.
3. *Continuum of care.* The ASAM criteria recognize that the four levels of care are points on an underlying continuum. This permits the system to respond to variation both for a single patient and between patients with respect to treatment needs at different times in a career.
4. *Treatment failure.* ASAM discourages using treatment failure as a criterion for placement based on clinical experience that so doing bars patients from a level of care they need to prevent progression of the disorder. Assigning patients to levels of care based on clinically determined need should avoid this problem and also avoid the problem of failing to recognize that a treatment failure may not have been linked to the patient's needs but to inadequate assignment procedures.
5. *Length of stay.* Note that the ASAM criteria do not specify length of stay in any level. This absence reflects experience with some managed care organizations in which such criteria were used inflexibly, thus preventing some patients from getting vitally important extended care. These patients had much more severe problems than those of the average patient, at a given level of care.

6. *Twelve step/mutual self-help recovery groups.* ASAM recognizes the importance of spiritual dimensions in all levels of care but does not prescribe this dimension at any particular level of care. Most providers at all levels include self-help because they recognize its importance.

It is important to understand that the ASAM scheme does not describe any currently existing set of services. At this time, there is an almost complete separation of theory and practice. The ASAM continuum of care is the way it should be, not the way it is. The reader needs to be aware that the field will be changed by the ASAM continuum of care. Current programs will have to adapt by changing program structure and staffing to adapt to the ASAM model. How managed care organizations will respond to these changes is also not clear. Obviously, the clinician with the best understanding of these systems will be in the best position to negotiate for the patients.

The definitions of the various levels of care should be read across the top line of the following tables. These tables are adapted from the ASAM manual. They link level of care with the six underlying dimensions of decision making, which are explained below. These dimensions are present in the tables if one reads from top to bottom on the left side of the table. The tables relate the levels of care to the underlying dimensions in general terms. I have presented these same relationships for a specific level of care in the table describing Opioid Maintenance Therapy, which follows the general tables. The reader should be aware that in the ASAM scheme there are both general and specific criteria relating level of care with the six principles of assignment to care. The entire ASAM manual is many pages long, but if the reader reviews the two axes presented here, the basic structure of the ASAM patient placement manual will be clear.

Placement on the ASAM continuum of care is determined by consideration of six underlying dimensions:
1. Withdrawal status
2. Biomedical status
3. Psychiatric status
4. Readiness for treatment
5. Relapse potential
6. Recovery environment

After these six dimensions are considered, the patient can be placed on the continuum of care according to need. If, for example, a patient is in acute alcohol withdrawal and has a history of seizures in previous withdrawal episodes, placement would be appropriate in the most intensive level of care, level 4, medically managed intensive inpatient, with full ability to respond to a range of medical/psychiatric and/or surgical emergencies such as arrhythmias, cardiac arrest, and status epilepticus. If, on the other hand, the patient has no withdrawal or threat of withdrawal and has stable medical and psychiatric status, an outpatient placement would be in order.

As noted above, there are specific ASAM criteria for various types of treatment. Those for Opioid Maintenance Therapy are presented below.

Adult Admission Criteria: Crosswalk of Level 0.5 through IV

	Levels of Service				
Criteria Dimensions	Level 0.5 Early intervention	OMT Opioid Maintenance Therapy	Level I Outpatient services	Level II.1 Intensive outpatient	Level II.5 Partial hospitalization
Dimension 1: Alcohol intoxication and/or withdrawal potential	No withdrawal risk	Patient is physiologically dependent on opiates and requires OMT to prevent withdrawal	I-D Ambulatory detoxification without extended on-site monitoring	Minimal risk of severe withdrawal	II-D Ambulatory detoxification with extended on-site monitoring
			Minimal risk of severe withdrawal		Moderate risk of severe withdrawal
Dimension 2: Biomedical conditions and complications	None or very stable	None or manageable with outpatient medical monitoring	None or very stable	None or not a distraction from treatment and manageable in level II.1	None or not sufficient to distract from treatment and manageable in level II.5
Dimension 3: Emotional/ behavioral conditions and complications	None or very stable	None or manageable within outpatient structured environment	None or very stable	Mild severity, with potential to distract from recovery; need monitoring	Mild to moderate severity, with potential to distract from recovery; need stabilization
Dimension 4: Treatment acceptance/ resistance	Willing to understand how current use may affect personal goals	Resistance high enough to require structured therapy to promote treatment progress but will not render outpatient treatment ineffective	Willing to cooperate but need motivating and monitoring strategies	Resistance high enough to require structured program but not so high as to render outpatient treatment ineffective	Resistance high enough to require structured program but not so high as to render outpatient treatment ineffective

Adult Admission Criteria: Crosswalk of Level 0.5 through IV (continued)

Criteria dimensions	Level 0.5 Early intervention	OMT Opioid Maintenance Therapy	Level I Outpatient services	Level II.1 Intensive outpatient	Level II.5 Partial hospitalization
			Minimal risk of severe withdrawal		Moderate risk of severe withdrawal
Dimension 5: Relapse/ continued use potential	Needs understanding of, or skills to change, current use patterns	High risk of relapse or continued use without OMT and structured therapy to promote treatment progress	Able to maintain abstinence or control use and pursue recovery goals with minimal support	Intensification of addiction symptoms, despite active participation in level I; high likelihood of relapse or continued use without close monitoring and support	Intensification of addiction symptoms, despite active participation in level I; high likelihood of relapse or continued use without monitoring and support
Dimension 6: Recovery environment	Social support system or significant others increase risk for personal conflict about alcohol/drug use	Supportive recovery environment and/or patient has skills to cope with outpatient treatment	Supportive recovery environment and/or patient has skills to cope	Environment unsupportive, but, with structure and support, the patient can cope	Environment is not supportive but, with structure, support and relief from the home environment, the patient can cope
Dimensions	Residential services	Intensity residential services	Intensity residential services	Inpatient services	Inpatient services
Dimension 6: Recovery environment	Environment is dangerous, but recovery is achievable if level III.1 structure is available	Environment is dangerous; patient needs 24-hour structure to learn to cope	Environment is dangerous; patient lacks skills to cope outside of a highly structured 24-hour setting	Environment dangerous for recovery; patient lacks skills to cope outside of highly structured 24-hour setting	Problems in this dimension do not qualify the patient for level IV services

Adult Criteria: Opioid Maintenance Therapy

Characteristic	Opioid Maintenance Therapy
Examples	Methadone maintenance and L-alpha-acetyl-methadol (LAAM) therapy
Setting	Any licensed setting with permanent free-standing clinics, community mental health centers, community health centers, hospitals, medication units, satellite clinics, or mobile units attached to a permanent clinic site.

Support Systems Support systems include:
   a) Linkage with or access to psychological, medical, and psychiatric consultation
   b) Linkage with or access to emergency medical and psychiatric affiliations with more intensive levels of care, as needed
   c) Linkage with or access to evaluation and ongoing primary medical care
   d) Ability to conduct or arrange for appropriate laboratory and toxicology tests
   e) Availability of physicians to evaluate, prescribe, and monitor use of methadone or LAAM, and/or nurses and pharmacists to dispense and administer methadone or LAAM
   f) Ability to provide or assist in arrangements for transportation services for patients who are unable to drive safely or who otherwise lack transportation

Staff Staff includes:
   a) An interdisciplinary team of appropriately trained and credentialed addiction professionals, including a medical director, counselors, and the medical staff delineated in (b) below. The team includes social workers and licensed psychologists, as needed. They must be knowledgeable in the assessment, interpretation, and treatment of the biopsychosocial dimensions of alcohol/other drug dependence. Staff members receive supervision appropriate to their level of training and experience.
   b) Licensed medical, nursing, or pharmacy staff who are available to administer medications in accordance with the physician's prescriptions or orders. The intensity of nursing care is appropriate to the services provided by an outpatient treatment program that uses methadone and LAAM.
   c) A physician who is available during medication-dispensing and clinic operating hours, either in person or by telephone

Therapies Therapies offered include:
   a) Interdisciplinary individualized assessment and treatment
   b) Medication: assessing, prescribing, administering, reassessing, and regulating dosage levels appropriate to the individual; supervising detoxification from opiates, methadone, or LAAM; overseeing and facilitating access to appropriate treatment, including medication for other physical and mental health disorders, provided as needed.
   c) Monitored urine testing
   d) Counseling: range of cognitive, behavioral, and other addiction focused therapies, reflecting a variety of treatment approaches, provided to the client on an individual, group, or family basis
   e) Case management: case management, including medical monitoring and coordination of on-site and off-site treatment services, provided as needed. Case managers also assure the provision of or referral to educational/vocational counseling, treatment of psychiatric illness, child care, parenting skills development, primary health care, and other adjunct services as needed.
   f) Psychoeducation, including HIV/AIDS and other health education services

Assessment/ treatment plan review

Elements of the assessment and treatment plan review include:
a) A comprehensive medical history, physical examination, and laboratory tests, provided or obtained in accordance with federal regulations. The tests must be done on admission and reviewed by a physician as soon as possible and no later than 14 days after admission (FDA 21 CFR Part 291)
b) An individual biopsychosocial assessment
c) An appropriate regimen of methadone or LAAM (as required by FDA regulation), established by a physician at admission, monitored carefully until the individual is stable and an adequate dose has been established, and then reviewed as indicated by the client's course of treatment
d) Continuing evaluation and referral of any serious biomedical problems
e) An individualized treatment plan, including problem formulations, treatment goals, and measurable objectives, as well as activities designed to meet those objectives
f) Treatment plan reviews conducted at specific times, as noted in the treatment plan and whenever a significant event occurs

Documentation

Documentation includes:
a) A biopsychosocial assessment, including all laboratory reports and the individualized treatment plan, recorded in the patient record
b) Progress notes, recorded in the patient record at the time of each face-to-face contact, that clearly reflect implementation of the treatment plan as well as the patient's response to treatment
c) Documentation of each dose of methadone or LAAM administered
d) A physician's orders for methadone or LAAM

In the following paragraphs, the verbatim criteria from DSM-4 are presented and then discussed for Substance Use Disorders. Substance induced disorders are described in the drug specific chapters; for example, alcohol induced dementia is described in the chapter on alcohol, where the diagnostic criteria are reviewed and then followed by treatment guidelines.

SUBSTANCE USE DISORDERS

SUBSTANCE DEPENDENCE

DSM-4 criteria for the diagnosis of substance dependence

A. A maladaptive pattern of substance use, leading to clinically significant impairment or distress, as manifested by three or more of the following, occurring at any time in the same 12-month period:
1) Tolerance, as defined as either of the following:
   a) a need for markedly increased amounts of the substance to achieve intoxication or desired effect
   b) markedly diminished effect with continued use of the same amount of the substance
2) Withdrawal, as manifested by either of the following:
   a) the characteristic withdrawal syndrome for the substance (refer to criteria A and B of the criteria sets for withdrawal from the specific substances)
   b) the same (or a closely related substance) is taken to relieve or avoid withdrawal symptoms

3) The substance is often taken in larger amounts or over a longer period than was intended

4) There is persistent desire or unsuccessful efforts to cut down or control substance use

5) A great deal of time is spent in activities necessary to obtain the substance (e.g., visiting multiple doctors or driving long distances), use the substance (e.g., chain smoking), or recover from its effects

6) Important social, occupational, or recreational activities are given up or reduced because of substance abuse

7) The substance abuse is continued despite knowledge of having a persistent or recurring physical or psychological problem that is caused or exacerbated by the substance (e.g., current cocaine use despite recognition of cocaine induced depression; or continued drinking despite recognition that an ulcer is made worse by alcohol consumption)

Specify if:
With physiological dependence: evidence of tolerance or withdrawal (i.e., either item 1 or 2 is present).
Without physiological dependence: no evidence of tolerance or withdrawal (i.e., neither item 1 nor 2 is present).

DSM-4 then provides for current status of the dependence by one of four Course Specifiers. These are paraphrased as:

1. Early full remission: no criteria for abuse or dependence have been met for at least one month but not more than 12 months.
2. Early partial remission: one criterion for abuse or dependence has been met for at least one month but not more than 12 months.
3. Sustained full remission: no criteria for abuse or dependence have been met for more than 12 months.
4. Sustained partial remission: some criteria for dependence have been met but not enough for a diagnosis.

Two additional Course Specifiers are available. The first, On Agonist Therapy, is defined as no criteria present for abuse or dependence for at least one month, but the person is taking methadone, LAAM, or analgesics on a prescribed and controlled basis. The second, In a Controlled Environment, is defined for a person who is in an environment with no access to drugs, such as a therapeutic community or a locked psychiatric ward.

SUBSTANCE ABUSE

DSM-4 criteria for the diagnosis of substance abuse

A. A maladaptive pattern of substance use, leading to clinically significant impairment or distress, as manifested by one or more of the following:

1) Recurrent substance use, resulting in a failure to fulfill major obligations at work, school, or home (e.g., repeated absences or poor work performance related to substance use; substance related absences; suspensions or expulsions from school; neglect of children or household)

2) Recurrent substance use in situations in which it is physically hazardous (e.g., driving an automobile or operating a machine when impaired by substance use)

3) Recurrent substance related legal problems (e.g., arrests for substance related disorderly conduct)

4) Continued substance use despite having persistent or recurrent social or interpersonal problems caused or exacerbated by the effects of the substance (e.g., arguments with spouse about consequences of intoxication, physical fights)

B.   The symptoms have never met the criteria for substance dependence for this class of substance

---

This diagnosis would then be followed by appropriate Course Specifiers.

It may be useful to point out that there are three major underlying dimensions in the syndrome of dependence:
1.   Receptor-mediated changes, as a consequence of sustained exposure to a drug. Criterion 1, "tolerance," and criterion 2, "withdrawal," of the dependence syndrome define this dimension.
2.   Loss of control, as it is defined by criterion 3, "took more than intended," and 4, "tried to cut down or stop."
3.   Salience; drug taking displaces activities and people in the hierarchy of importance to the person affected. Drug taking and drug seeking come to be more important than children, spouse, money, self-esteem, loss of bodily functions or parts, and the like. It is defined by criterion 5, "time spent on drugs"; criterion 6, "important activities given up for drugs"; and criterion 7, "continued use despite negative consequences."

In the abuse syndrome, criterion 1, "recurrent drug use" impairing role performance; criterion 3, drug related legal problems; and criterion 4, "use despite negative consequences," all can be thought of as expressions of salience. Criterion 2 of the abuse syndrome, "hazardous use," is for Driving Under the Influence (DUI) and/or operating dangerous equipment while impaired by drugs. It is a separate and lone dimension. Receptor-mediated pathology (tolerance or withdrawal) is not a part of the abuse category.

It is easier to remember the three underlying dimensions when taking a history, and if clinical inquiry covers all three, it is likely that you will be able to make a judgment about the seven specific criteria. If you do a lot of drug abuse workups, you will have memorized the seven criteria for dependence and the four for abuse. If you go over each of them when you are summarizing with the patient toward the end of the interview, it will sharpen your diagnosis and prepare you for writing your workup in the chart; or in the event that a computer program prepares your clinical records, it will prepare you to critique this draft.

Additional points of importance in the history:
1.   Recent pattern of use. If there has been no drug use in the past two to three weeks, then neither criterion 1, "tolerance,"–nor 2, "withdrawal," from the DSM-4 criteria of dependence is met at the time of admission; it is also clear that the first ASAM dimension, "withdrawal status," will not require an intensive level of care.
2.   What drugs or, more properly, classes of drugs should be considered in a basic substance abuse history? It is important to note that you must ask specifically about each class of drugs to obtain a good history. Frequently, patients do not think it important to tell you they are taking drugs like Valium, "because it's a

medical drug and can't hurt anybody," or cannabis, "because pot isn't a drug, it's an herb," or alcohol, "because I only drink beer, and people can't get into trouble with beer." One should ask specifically about dosage, frequency, consequences, and route of administration of the following classes of drugs:

- Alcohol—wine, beer, hard liquor
- Nicotine—cigarettes, cigars, pipes, chewing tobacco
- Cannabis—pot, hashish
- Central nervous system depressants—barbiturates, benzodiazepines, methaqualone (Ludes), ethychlorvinyl (Placidyl), glutethimide (Doriden), methyprylon (Noludar), meprobamate (Milltown, Equanil).
- Stimulants—amphetamines, cocaine, crack cocaine, sympathicomimetic-amines, MDMA, etc.
- Tranquilizers and antidepressants—phenothiazines, butyrophenones, monoamine oxidase inhibitors, etc.
- Inhalants—glue, paint, gasoline, aryl and butyl nitrites, nitrous oxide, etc.
- Arylcyclohexylamines—phencyclidine (PCP)
- Opioids—heroin, morphine, methadone, meperidine, codeine
- Hallucinogens—lysergic acid diethylamide (LSD), 2,5-dimethoxy-4-methy-lamphetamine (STP), etc.

3. Is there a history of hallucinations, confusion, delirium, overdoses with attendant coma, delusions, or mood changes in association with runs of drug use? It is important to know whether a patient has a psychosis and is using drugs or is a drug abuser with psychotic symptoms only in association with drug use. Psychiatric drugs might be required in the first instance but might not be required in the second. Frequent drug use, particularly as dose rises, is sometimes associated with impairment of energy levels and motivation; many daily marijuana users and PCP users report decreased energy. This is important information in assessing the psychiatric status of the patient, which is one of the dimensions required by ASAM for proper placement.

4. Assessment of medical problems is straightforward and should usually be performed after the substance abuse history has been taken.

5. Is there a history of convulsions? Did convulsions precede the onset of drug abuse? Patients frequently do not associate convulsions with drug or alcohol use, so it is important to know whether a patient is a drug abusing epileptic or whether the patient's convulsions are solely attributable to drug use. A history of a few convulsions occurring after heavy drug or alcohol consumption began in life strongly suggests drug related convulsive states. A history of adult onset of convulsions should raise suspicion of drug abuse. This is important information in assessing the withdrawal status of the patient, as a history of seizures mandates the most intensive level of care for withdrawal treatment, medically managed intensive inpatient.

6. Assessment of the relapse potential and recovery environment can be split into external factors and internal factors. Answers to the questions "Who do you live with? Do they use drugs/drink? Who do you work with? Do they use

drugs/drink? Who do you socialize with? Do they use drugs/drink?" should provide information on relapse potential and the recovery environment. It should be stressed that recovery cannot be sustained when a patient spends time with active drug users in any sphere; as noted previously in this text, if a person hopeful for a robust recovery is married to an active user and the active user will not enter treatment, there must be a separation if recovery is to occur.

Internal factors important in relapse can be assessed by asking if various mood states trigger relapse. The wisdom in the self-help community is that a recovering person should never get too hungry, lonely, angry, or tired, as these can be triggers for relapse for many people. It is important in taking a history to explore previous relapses to uncover relapse triggers for the individual.

7. Why is the patient coming for assessment now? Because he or she wants to reduce the strength of a heroin habit? Because a spouse has threatened to leave unless the patient does something about his or her alcohol use? Or because the patient wants a clean bill of health from you, regardless of clinical findings, which he or she can then use in arguments with family members, employers, or the like? Is there legal pressure? Is the patient concerned about the damage to his or her body from drug abuse? It is important to know what motivation for treatment the patient has and to know the origin of the pressure for change. "What made you decide to seek a medical opinion at this time?" is a question which, in one form or another, should be asked of every patient. This is important information for assessing relapse potential and the recovery environment.

Answers to the "Why treatment now?" question assist in determining the patient's readiness for treatment. As noted in chapter 1, the psychology of substance abuse is one of ambivalence, and it is common for patients to be ambivalent about treatment. In general medical practice, one should expect to see persons who are in the "precontemplative" phase, in that they can't admit that they have a problem either to themselves or to others. These patients need the physician's nonjudgmental statement that a problem is present and needs action to move them from the precontemplative to the contemplative phase of readiness for treatment. Other patients are in the contemplative phase but are not yet ready to take action.

8. What is the period of heaviest lifetime use? In terms of dose per unit time, knowledge of when the greatest lifetime use has occurred may be useful in judging how drugs have fit into the life of the patient. For example, some female alcoholics and heroin addicts use most heavily when involved romantically with an alcoholic or heroin abuser, and when not in a relationship do not use at all or use in a much more controlled pattern. This data is important in the estimation of the relapse potential.

9. What was the age of first use? In general, the younger the age of first use, the more likely one is to find pathology from both biological and psychological viewpoints. It is part of the assessment of the relapse potential of the patient. Someone who is now thirty-five and started daily intoxication at age nine, which has lasted for most of the next twenty-six years, probably has a worse progno-

sis—greater relapse potential—than someone who started daily intoxication at age thirty and is now thirty-two.

10. What does the patient get from the drug? It is surprising how many people derive no pleasure from long-standing use of drugs that are powerful reinforcers. It is not unusual to encounter heroin addicts who state that they take heroin solely to stop withdrawal, and that it has been many years since they experienced a high. Asking directly about this point sometimes may not elicit useful information, but during the interview the physician should listen for relevant information. This information is also important in assessing relapse potential.

11. Are drug and alcohol histories valid? Abundant clinical experience with a variety of substance abusers suggests that if the addict or alcoholic sees the physician as a helping person, the history given will be as valid as that given by patients in general. If there is uncertainty in the substance abuser's mind about confidentiality or about who the physician serves (as might be the case for a physician working for an institution such as a jail or the military or a government agency), or if the physician is seen by the patient as working for the interests of others, such as family members or a corporation, the history may reflect such uncertainties. There are patients who consciously misrepresent dosage in an attempt to influence the physician's prescribing of tranquilizers, methadone, and the like, but, my experience, in general, indicates that drug and alcohol histories are as valid as histories in any other branch of medicine.

As reviewed in chapter 1, the diagnosis should be presented to the patient nonjudgmentally, and it will fit the first part of the clinical paradigm of "Here's the problem—here's the solution." The second part of this paradigm is the prescription: "You need to be detoxified in a hospital because there is risk to your life from the probable withdrawal from alcohol and the sedative drugs you have been taking," or, "You appear to know the risks from continuing to smoke cigarettes. Most people are helped by getting formal treatment, and I want you to go the behavioral health clinic at the hospital for treatment."

MULTIAXIAL ASSESSMENT

DSM-4 requires descriptions on five dimensions because of recognition that the context in which a disorder occurs is often powerfully influenced by the disorder and, in turn, may powerfully influence the disorder. Both scientific and clinical communities appear to agree on this, so it is becoming formalized in diagnostic paradigms. The five dimensions are:

1. Clinical disorders
2. Personality disorders
   Mental retardation
3. General medical conditions
4. Psychosocial and environmental problems
5. Global assessment of functioning

The DSM-4 term *disorder* is not a repudiation of the view of many that some drug and alcohol problems are diseases; it is simply a higher-order concept which acknowledges that the disease cannot be isolated from its interaction with the context in which it occurs. It is in no sense contradictory to the self-help concept of a disease; it is more general for scientific purposes, and directs attention to the important relationship between context and disease. Hypertension is a disease, but it is more generally a biopsychosocial disorder in that social, cultural, nutritional, and psychological factors are important in its detection, treatment, and course.

NEGOTIATION WITH THE PATIENT, THE FAMILY, THIRD-PARTY PAYERS, AND TREATMENT UNITS CONCERNING TREATMENT ASSIGNMENT

In the research community, this process is known as patient treatment matching, but clinically, it is often a negotiation concerning what is potentially helpful for the patient and what is acceptable, available, accessible, and affordable. The implication in patient treatment matching is that the clinician moves the patient like a checker on a checkerboard of possibilities. It is something the doctor does to the patient—for the patient's benefit, to be sure—but it misses the central fact of clinical life that most people with drug problems are competent adults who often have strong opinions about treatment options. With or without such opinions, they are entitled to know the range of possibilities for the treatment of their drug problem and to be a full partner in negotiating what is ultimately their choice of treatment. The process of patient assignment is active on both sides, and a good clinician knows and integrates this posture into clinical life.

There are some circumstances in which the patient has no choice. The addicted physician, for example, is often mandated to see a certain physician and have a particular mode of therapy. To keep a medical license, the physician must go along with the mandate. Frequently, there is strong pressure from family, employers, courts, or other sources of coercion. The clinician still owes the patient the same careful review of the options available within the framework of the coercion; in other words, the clinician must not rely on the coercion to supplant any part of the job of building a relationship with the patient. Most patients are ambivalent about the coercion; in keeping with general ambivalence about drug taking, they recognize the need and potential for good in the coercion, but they also have expectable feelings of resentment and anger. The clinician needs to be sensitive to both sides of the ambivalence.

Patients without coercion often have strong feelings about what treatment they want and will have made up their minds well in advance of their workup. If you judge that they are making a serious error, you should tell this to the patient with a summary of your reasons. You can refuse to go along with what the patient wants, but you owe the patient a full explanation. I saw a nurse who was using over thirty sleeping pills a day. Her intake of drugs was impairing her work, and she wanted help before she did something that would harm somebody or herself. She was living with an active drug user who would not come in for treatment and who would not be part of her recovery. She wanted me to treat her while she continued to live with her drug taking boyfriend. I told her there was no point in wasting her time under such a condition, as it would be totally fruitless. When she was adamant, I told her I would be glad to refer her to another therapist, but that if she wanted to work with me, she had to move away from the boyfriend immediately. Reluctantly, she did. Later, when she was in stable recovery, she thanked me for insisting on her move. She, like many in recovery, had come to realize that irrational thinking—so-called stinking thinking—is part of a drug problem.

Relationships with third-party payers can be problematic. There was a time not too long ago when there was just the doctor-patient relationship, but today one can speak of a doctor, patient, third-party payer, lawyer, undercover reporter, quality-control relationship, which can be complex indeed. When your clinical judgments are not supported or are only partially supported by the managed care provider, it complicates the relationship with the patient; other parties are part of clinical life to a degree never before encountered. A patient can well wonder about your judgments if they are questioned by a powerful third party. It is an added problem for both patient and clinician. But one should avoid denigrating anyone who is important in the process of patient assignment. Respect for both patient and for the third-party payer needs to be maintained. What this problem requires is for your work to be careful and complete. The more it is based on specific DSM-4 criteria and the assignment conforms to the ASAM placement criteria, the more likely you will be able to persuade a third-party payer to allow you to exercise your best judgment. Denigration, anger, resentment, and other negative emotions need to be minimized, because they can interfere with proper relationships with patients even when they appear to be justified and compelling to the clinician. In addition to the above-described problems with negotiation of treatment assignment, there may be absolutely contradictory laws governing different treatment options. The classic illustration is that of the pregnant woman whose drug use defines her as a criminal. State law may mandate that she be reported to a state agency. But there is a federal law forbidding one from disclosing the fact of drug dependence to anyone under penalty of fine and imprisonment without written specific permission to do so. In such a case, I sought legal counsel and was told that there was no clear solution and that "it would have to be played out in court."

What to do in dilemmas like this? The answer is to focus on what is good patient care. Questions such as "What is best for this patient? Are others going to be harmed by this course of action? What is best for the baby?" should be reviewed and answered. The answers will indicate a course of action. Obviously, one cannot operate a service for pregnant drug users if they feel that you are forced to report them to a criminal justice agency. It is in the interests of everyone for a pregnant woman to get the prenatal care she needs. After review of the above questions, I opted not to report—to obey the federal instead of the state law—and was ready to accept the consequences. Fortunately, there were none. The underlying principle is that in confusing legal/ethical situations, you should consult with others, but ultimately you have to make a personal decision and then be ready to live with it.

REFERENCES

1. American Society of Addiction Medicine. *Patient Placement Criteria for the Treatment of Substance Related Disorders*, ed 2 (ASAM PPC-2). Chevy Chase, MD, The Society, 1996.
2. Joint Commission on Accreditation of Healthcare Organizations (JCAHO). *MHM: Accreditation Manual for Mental Health, Chemical Dependency and Mental Retardation/Developmental Disabilities Services*, vol 1, Standards; vol 2, Scoring Guidelines. Oakbrook Terrace, IL, 1995.

3. Alcohol

If alcohol were a new drug, its behavioral toxicity, teratogenicity, and carcinogenicity would prevent it from getting to the Investigational New Drug (IND) stage of development. The power of custom, however, continues to give alcohol a public health impact of enormous proportions. Family problems, accidents in cars, trains, planes, boats, and factories, loss of productivity, fires, homicides, suicides, perinatal morbidity and mortality, and a long array of other medical and psychiatric problems form only a partial account of the total cost of the social acceptance and commercialization of alcohol induced intoxication.[1]

There are a number of office screening instruments, such as the CAGE,* the MAST (Michigan Alcoholism Screening Test), the ASI (Addiction Severity Index), and others, but there can be no substitute for a high index of clinical suspicion. The CAGE and the MAST, for example, do not ask about drugs such as cocaine, heroin, or nicotine; given the current pattern of multiple concurrent drug and alcohol use, this is an important deficit. There is no substitute for a detailed, sensitive clinical examination in which the clinician hears and sees the patient's responses on multiple levels. Judgments about the presence and depth of denial and of how to present the results of the workup are more effective if based on a clinically conducted examination involving interaction with the patient.

For some clinicians, this process is facilitated by the use of screening instruments, but there is no unanimity on whether they should be used. Instruments tend to be valid; they offer norms for measuring treatment progress, and some patients may feel more confident if treatment is based on established norms. The use of instruments can also help the clinician cover domains that may not receive sufficient attention in a regular clinical interaction with a patient. Gallant's detailed discussion of instruments and their use will be helpful to the interested clinician.[2]

Vaillant's work on the natural history of alcoholism was the first to point out the career aspect of abuse/dependence—the alternation, over decades, between abstinence and active drinking.[3] He also pointed out the difference between heavy social drinking without negative consequences and the progression, in some, from heavy

* CAGE is an acronym for answers to four questions: Have you ever tried to Cut down your drinking? Have you ever been Annoyed by criticism of your drinking? Have you ever felt Guilty about your drinking? Have you ever used alcohol as an Eye opener in the morning (that is, drinking to relieve withdrawal)? One or more positive answers leads to suspicion of an alcohol problem and should trigger a complete workup to determine whether a full, formal diagnosis can be made. If not, the patient should be advised this behavior puts him or her at high risk for the development of a problem.

social drinking to abuse and then to dependence. Cloninger's typology of alcohol problems seems almost self-evident in clinical life, particularly type 2.[4] He found that people meeting criteria for alcohol problems of abuse and dependence fall into two groups. Members of the type 1 group have an onset of problems with alcohol after age twenty-five, have less severe physical dependence, are not predominately male, may not have a family history positive for alcoholism, and are characterized by high harm avoidance and low novelty-seeking personality characteristics.

Members of the type 2 group have an onset before age twenty-five, are more likely to be male, have a heavier intake of alcohol leading to severe withdrawal, tend to have a family history positive for alcoholism, and are characterized by high novelty seeking and low harm avoidance. Type 2 subjects are more likely to be aggressive and perhaps to have antisocial personality disorder. Type 2 also appears to have a worse prognosis than type 1. These typologies may prove to be like those of Jellinek, in that they may appear to be reflected in clinical experience but cannot be demonstrated in rigorous testing. Gallant has reviewed this question in relation to the failure of Schuckit to confirm the typology developed by Cloninger with respect to type 2 subjects.[5]

PHYSICAL AND LABORATORY FINDINGS SOMETIMES ASSOCIATED WITH ALCOHOL ABUSE AND DEPENDENCE

Tremors, acne rosacea or other skin conditions causing facial erythema, cigarette burns, bruises, contusions and/or fractures from falls during intoxication, hepatomegaly, tachycardia, hypertension, obesity or excessive weight loss, and arcus senilis in males under sixty years of age[6] are sometimes associated with but are not diagnostic of alcohol abuse or dependence. Their presence should raise clinical suspicion that alcoholism is present. Complaints of heartburn or other upper gastrointestinal complaints, morning cough, insomnia, and arrhythmias (the so-called holiday heart syndrome) should lead the physician to suspect alcohol abuse or dependence.

There is evidence, reviewed by Goodwin,[7] that sustained alcohol intake, at the level of two drinks per day or more, is sometimes associated with an increase in the mean corpuscular volume (MCV) of red cells; elevation of high-density lipoprotein cholesterol (HDL); elevation of gamma glutamyl transpeptidase (GGT); elevation of blood uric acid levels; and an increase in the blood levels of carbohydrate-deficient transferrin (CDT).[8] CDT may be used to monitor drinking in known alcoholics, as it has a half-life of around fourteen days. These so-called markers for alcoholism appear to reflect consumption levels and should be used only to indicate that a workup is necessary. They are not diagnostic of alcohol abuse and dependence. They are not always positive in alcoholics and may be positive in those who drink but are not alcoholics. The clinician needs to be careful not to diagnose from these markers, because premature and/or incorrect labeling of people can be quite harmful. A positive diagnosis should be made only on the basis of a complete examination, ideally together with information from the spouse or family members.

Blood alcohol concentration (BAC) may also be useful if available. Concentrations exceeding 10 mg percent define intoxication legally in many jurisdictions. If BACs of 100 to 150 mg percent are present without intoxication, there is unquestionably tolerance. If liver disease is present, it is reflected in elevation of liver transaminases and/or other enzymes.

MANAGEMENT OF ALCOHOL ABUSE AND ALCOHOL DEPENDENCE

When the results of a history and physical examination indicate that a patient has a diagnosis of alcohol abuse or alcohol dependence, a number of important questions are raised. Whether to tell the patient, how to tell the patient, and what, if anything, to tell the family are common clinical problems. The consensus among clinicians is clear. The physician should tell the patient; indeed, the physician has an obligation to do so. But how the patient is told should be determined by the clinician's sense of what the patient will tolerate. Too blunt a presentation may lead to a lost patient. Too soft a presentation may reinforce the patient's denial. Telling a family member before telling the patient, or perhaps instead of telling the patient, is not a good idea, as it will probably lead only to useless conflict. Sooner or later the clinician has to confront the patient, and if this results in patient denial and breaking off the medical relationship, the clinician should take comfort in the fact that an ethical obligation has been met. The clinician should review the sequence of events to see if there might have been another way to manage the problem, or perhaps seek consultation with an addiction medicine specialist.

Because some patients react with denial and varying degrees of anger to being told that they have a problem, a physician may increase clinical effectiveness by reviewing the principles of confrontation described in chapter 1.

Most workers in the field also agree that the spouse should be made aware that the patient has been confronted. Ideally, the spouse should be present during the workup, and the relationship between patient and spouse should be carefully examined. In some instances, the spouse plays an important role in maintaining the pathology in the situation (the "co-alcoholic" or "enabler"). A cautionary note should also be sounded about diagnosing prematurely, thus labeling without a full examination, based on the construction of a therapeutic alliance with the family member and sustained evidence that enabling is present. The posture of many current programs is that the family should be counseled on how to help the alcoholic; if, in this process, there is clinical evidence of enabling, then it is responded to, but not until a therapeutic alliance has been established that permits examination of these possibilities, and not before there is solid evidence. Referral to Al-Anon may be indicated for a spouse in any event. Family therapy may also be elected. Some therapists feel that treating the family unit is the best method, but this is not always possible. For a review of these important questions see Steinglass.[9]

If the patient agrees to treatment, you will want to consider the following elements of a treatment program.

REFERRAL TO ALCOHOLICS ANONYMOUS (AA)

A physician should recognize that not all patients can accept referral to self-help groups or use them successfully. The physician should become familiar with local AA groups so that a match can be made between the patient's needs and the sometimes unique service capabilities of some AA groups (e.g., in some cities there are AA groups for doctors, lawyers, and workers in other occupations). A physician should inquire carefully about the patient's attitude toward these groups. Of those who are willing to try AA, many profit greatly, but some do not. A frequent basis for rejection of AA is that it is "religious," and some find this unacceptable. The physician should try to educate the patient to the fact that while AA is spiritual, it is not religious in the sense of promoting any particular form of spirituality. The physician may suggest that connecting or perhaps reconnecting with spiritual dimensions in life can be very important. The physician should pressure the patient to try AA, Narcotics Anonymous (NA), or a similar program but should not abandon the patient if this element in the management plan is not acceptable, feasible, or effective.

ASSISTANCE FROM RECOVERING SUBSTANCE ABUSERS

The alcoholic commonly expresses profound hopelessness with respect to communicating with people who would normally be expected to be in close and frequent contact with him or her. The spouse is, of course, the most frequent object of such feelings. People in the alcoholic's environment may be quite willing to try to help, although they usually feel equally hopeless because of long-standing problems in communication. A neutral person who has "been there" is uniquely able to say, "I had this problem and I'm no longer isolated, I'm coping." This can be very important in reversing the isolation and demoralization that is almost invariably experienced by alcoholics.

In the culture of AA, each member has a "sponsor" who has worked the Twelve Steps successfully and whose personal recovery is enhanced by helping fill this important need of the newcomer to AA.

CAREFUL REVIEW OF THE PATIENT'S HISTORY FOR AFFECTIVE DISORDERS

Detecting affective disorders may require special psychiatric evaluation. Alcohol may be a self-prescribed "therapeutic" drug for persons experiencing major affective disorders. If these disorders are untreated or improperly treated, the entire treatment plan may fail. This subject is reviewed further in the chapter on dual diagnosis.

INVOLVEMENT OF THE FAMILY

The physician should discuss with the patient the pros and cons of family members becoming full partners in the management plan. As noted, reducing the almost universal sense of isolation experienced by the patient is the strategic center of treatment. Finding out that the spouse, parents, or close friends are concerned and willing to offer support can be an important source of hope for the patient. Successfully treated persons with alcoholism often cite reunification with family members as one of the most beneficial effects of treatment.

IDENTIFICATION OF PSYCHOLOGICAL DYNAMICS

The physician should listen carefully to the patient's description of his or her problems with a view toward identifying major sequences of behavior. Sooner or later patterns should emerge. For example, the patient begins to feel hopeless about his marriage and stops working on it; the resulting demoralization causes reversals at work, and the hopelessness intensifies. The patient changes from a pattern of heavy social drinking to pathologic drinking—high doses in a short period of time, "gulping" drinks instead of sipping them.

MEDICAL EVALUATION AND TREATMENT OF MEDICAL PROBLEMS

A complete history and physical examination with relevant laboratory tests and treatment are an important part of the management plan.

USE OF DISULFIRAM

The physician should acquaint the patient with the benefits and risks attendant on the use of disulfiram (Antabuse). It is a treatment element that may be helpful for some patients for time-limited use in a management plan. Disulfiram, however, should not *become* the management plan. For benefits to occur, both the physician and the patient must have clear objectives, and the disulfiram should be one element of a comprehensive treatment program.

The usual dosage of disulfiram is 0.5 g for a few days as a loading dose, then 0.25 g daily as maintenance. Some use disulfiram only three to five days per week. If the patient drinks alcohol—or, in some instances, uses such preparations as mouthwashes or aftershave lotions containing alcohol—a severe dysphoria with hypotension, flushing, dyspnea, nausea, vomiting, intense headaches, and blurred vision may result. The treatment of this syndrome usually consists of rest, in the Trendelenberg position, for a few hours. The administration of 95 percent oxygen, 5 percent carbon dioxide (carbogen) together with treatment for shock may be necessary. The stress of this reaction may aggravate heart disease, diabetes, or other medical problems; consultation may be necessary to treat these underlying conditions.

Occasional side effects of disulfiram include skin rash, sedation, confusion, optic neuritis and polyneuritis, hepatitis, and, in some patients, psychosis. Rainey, on the basis of observations in both animals and humans, believes the infrequent neurologic and behavioral side effects of disulfiram are attributable to the buildup of carbon disulfide, one of the major metabolites of disulfiram, in the body.[10] The side effect of sedation can be managed by dose reduction. The more severe side effects may require cessation of disulfiram therapy. Disulfiram may potentiate the effects of coumarin derivatives, phenytoin, and isoniazid. Patients should have a complete medical workup before being placed on disulfiram. Persons with heart disease, epilepsy, diabetes, and renal disease should receive disulfiram only under medical supervision by a physician certified by the American Society of Addiction Medicine.

Bourne and Fox reported on an experience with many patients with coronary disease, diabetes, cirrhosis, and other chronic conditions who were treated without incident by keeping the disulfiram dose low.[11] Allergies to the drug have been reported. Gitlow and Peyser state that the only contraindications to the use of disulfiram are hypersensitivity (which is rare), pregnancy, and inability of a patient to understand why the drug is being used, such as might be the case with patients with active psychoses.[12] Some clinicians in the alcoholism treatment community reject the use of disulfiram because of their belief that any pharmacologic support is detrimental to the long-term welfare of the alcoholic.

Patients should be abstinent from alcohol for at least five days before being placed on disulfiram. An occasional alcoholic drinks while taking disulfiram in an attempt at self-injury. Other patients plan ahead by not taking the disulfiram for a few days so that they can drink. Patients should be advised that one to two weeks without disulfiram are required to be sure they will not have a reaction. Before taking disulfiram, every patient should be indoctrinated thoroughly and given a written sheet describing side effects, as well as a card to carry in case of emergency. These materials should be available from the pharmacy.

I was taught, and clinical experience has confirmed, that disulfiram was not useful for many, if not most, alcoholics, particularly those in most need of additional help. Disulfiram is most useful for high-functioning people with alcohol problems undergoing some stressful event in life, such as a divorce or job change, where its use for a few months to a year can be of great assistance. A study by Fuller and colleagues is often cited as demonstrating that disulfiram has very modest effects, if any at all, as relapse rates in subjects receiving placebo doses did not differ from those in subjects receiving 250 mg per day.[13] The Fuller study did not place subjects on any scale that could be used to judge whether subjects met the criteria for "high functioning," but the study appears to be biased in that direction by the many exclusion criteria, such as living alone, affective disorders, difficult behavior, and so forth.

When research findings appear to conflict with clinical experience, one needs to examine both sources of information carefully and then be guided by the results of the examination. In this instance, I am not persuaded that there is sufficient generalizability to "high functioning" recovering alcoholics in the Fuller study; for me, "high functioning" means, for instance, holding a steady job, maintaining a relationship with a nondrinking spouse, being free of mood disorders, and no longer being motivated by drug culture values. We do not know whether such subjects were included and evenly distributed among Fuller's three study groups. In this instance, therefore, I will not reject clinical experience, but I will follow research on this question closely.

I have always suspected that disulfiram worked as an "active" placebo and have almost always used it that way (in low doses, e.g., 125 to 250 mg per day, only four or five days a week). Side effects are unusual with such regimens, and there appear to be useful effects.

USE OF NALTREXONE

In two studies, naltrexone, a pure opioid antagonist, reduced recidivism rates at 12 weeks following alcohol detoxification treatment by 50 percent.[14, 15] Some subjects reported that the naltrexone changed their experience of the alcohol high so that it did not drive their behavior. They were able to manage brief episodes of drinking so that slips or lapses did not become relapses, a return to alcoholic drinking patterns.

Mode of action. Naltrexone is a chemical analog of naloxone and is without agonist effect, but it displaces opioids from receptor sites, causing withdrawal. If no opiates are present, it selectively occupies these sites in preference to all known opioids, thus preventing euphoria or the relieving of withdrawal by use of heroin or other opioids. The inhibition of drinking by naltrexone versus placebo was first discovered in animals who had been bred to prefer alcohol; this finding led to its exploration in human populations.

Dose. The usual dosing regimen is naltrexone 50 mg daily.

Side effects. Some patients experience nausea, which can be counteracted by taking with milk or other types of food. It is not usually a side effect that deters subjects from the basic regimen.

Drawbacks. If a patient on naltrexone needs analgesia, opioids are not effective, and other agents may have to be used.

Procedures. The patient must be opiate free for at least 10 days before administering naltrexone for treatment of any sort.

Effectiveness. As noted, administration of naltrexone reduces recidivism rates in detoxified alcohol dependent persons by 50 percent. One problem for some patients is cost; currently patients pay about $5 a day for the naltrexone dose. There are anecdotal reports of occasional patients who have repeatedly failed in every other type of treatment, but when on naltrexone made dramatic improvement.

MONITORING ALCOHOL AND DRUG USE

As described in chapter 1, urine and breath tests are important elements in a treatment program. The chapter on toxicology presents additional information on monitoring.

GENERAL ELEMENTS OF A SUBSTANCE ABUSE TREATMENT PLAN

The general elements of a substance abuse treatment plan were discussed in chapter 1.

DIAGNOSIS AND TREATMENT OF ALCOHOL INDUCED DISORDERS

ALCOHOL INTOXICATION 303.00

DSM-4 criteria for the diagnosis of Alcohol Intoxication

A.   Recent ingestion of alcohol

B.   Clinically significant maladaptive behavioral or psychological changes (e.g., inappropriate sexual or aggressive behavior, mood lability, impaired judgment, impaired social or occupational functioning) that developed during, or shortly after, alcohol ingestion

C.   One (or more) of the following signs, developing during, or shortly after, alcohol use:
1) slurred speech
2) incoordination
3) unsteady gait
4) nystagmus
5) impairment in attention or memory
6) stupor or coma

D.   The symptoms are not due to a general medical condition and are not better accounted for by another mental disorder.

Treatment. Intoxicated individuals can be "talked down" according to the clinical guidelines described in chapter 1. Occasionally in severely intoxicated individuals, a sedative may be helpful. Diazepam 5 or 10 mg orally or lorazepam 0.5 mg parenterally is effective, but it may be necessary to repeat or increase the dose. The use of pharmacologic agents in alcoholic populations should be limited to brief periods for specific objectives, such as to assist in control of potentially violent, acutely intoxicated patients. If intoxication is severe and accompanied by increasingly severe ataxia, dysarthria, or other signs of increasing intoxication, sedatives or tranquilizers would not be indicated because of possible synergism with danger of a lethal outcome. Physical restraints may have to be employed in these cases.

ALCOHOL WITHDRAWAL 291.8

Gitlow and Peyser believe that one drink of alcohol may begin a sequence of psychobiologic effects that culminates in a mild withdrawal syndrome.[12] As intake increases, the withdrawal syndrome becomes correspondingly more severe and persistent. With high levels of intake (a fifth of whiskey, gin, etc.) per day over many days, weeks, or months, cessation of intake or marked reduction of the volume consumed per day results in the onset of the alcohol withdrawal syndrome. This syndrome is manifested primarily by tremors, nausea, sweating, tachycardia, agitation, and dysphoric mood.

DSM-4 criteria for the diagnosis of Alcohol Withdrawal

A. Cessation of (or reduction in) alcohol use that has been heavy and prolonged

B. Two (or more) of the following, developing within several hours to a few days after criterion A:
1) autonomic hyperactivity (e.g., sweating or pulse rate greater than 100)
2) increased hand tremor
3) insomnia
4) nausea and vomiting
5) transient visual, tactile, or auditory hallucinations
6) psychomotor agitation
7) anxiety
8) grand mal seizures

C. The symptoms in criterion B cause clinically significant distress or impairment in social, occupational, or other important areas of functioning.

D. The symptoms are not due to a general medical condition and are not better accounted for by another mental disorder.

Specify if:
With perceptual disturbances: This specifier may be noted when hallucinations with intact reality testing or auditory or visual or tactile illusions occur in the absence of delirium. Intact reality testing means that the person knows that the hallucinations or illusions are induced by the substance and do not represent external reality. When hallucinations occur in the absence of intact reality testing, a diagnosis of Substance Induced Psychotic Disorder with hallucinations should be considered.

An illusion is a misinterpretation of a real external stimulus. For example, footsteps in the hall may be reported as low rumbling voices that the patient experiences as threatening. Classically, psychiatric diagnosis has classified the "psychosis" that accompanies severe alcohol withdrawal as delirium. The above paragraph seems to suggest a change in this practice, but if the syndrome is of short duration and is clearly triggered by a reduction or cessation of alcohol intake, the syndrome should be diagnosed as a delirium.

ALCOHOL WITHDRAWAL DELIRIUM 291.0

DSM-4 criteria for the diagnosis of Alcohol Delirium

A. Disturbance of consciousness (i.e., reduced clarity of awareness of the environment) with reduced ability to focus, sustain, or shift attention

B. A change in cognition (such as memory deficit, disorientation, language disturbance) or the development of a perceptual disturbance that is not better accounted for by a preexisting, established, or evolving dementia

C. The disturbance develops over a short period of time (usually hours or days) and tends to fluctuate during the course of the day.

D. There is evidence from the history, physical examination, or laboratory findings that the symptoms in criteria A and B developed during, or shortly after, a withdrawal syndrome.

MANAGEMENT OF WITHDRAWAL AND WITHDRAWAL DELIRIUM

The reader should review the general principles described under management of toxic drug effects in chapter 1. Psychological management is crucial to successful treatment of this condition. Whitfield and co-workers found that they could manage 92 percent of 1,114 patients in what the authors termed "non drug" detoxification centers.[16] Management in these centers is based on the creation of a therapeutic relationship by expression of concern, use of nonthreatening surroundings with provision of food, radio, TV, and so forth; with medical consultation, there may be a pharmacologic component in the program. The environment of these nonhospital detoxification centers differs markedly from that of the average hospital, where the surroundings and staff attitudes of indifference or frank hostility to alcoholics may serve to worsen and/or prolong the alcohol withdrawal syndrome.

Persons with a history of seizures should be observed closely for the development of "rum fits," alcohol withdrawal seizures. Proper use of benzodiazepines should prevent seizures from developing. Benzodiazepines should be given if tremulousness is increasing, or deep tendon reflexes (DTR's) are consistently hyperactive, or patients report persisting, intense restlessness and/or uneasiness.

When the alcohol withdrawal syndrome is associated with clouding of consciousness and hallucinations (usually visual but sometimes tactile and/or auditory), the diagnosis of alcohol withdrawal delirium should be made.

The placement of a person in alcohol withdrawal is best based on the Clinical Institute on Alcohol Withdrawal scale. ASAM guidelines suggest certain scores to match different levels of care; for example, a CIWA-Ar score of 8 suggests placement in a social setting detoxification center, whereas a score of 10 or above suggests the need for medication, with higher scores, of course, indicating a higher level of care. There are 10 items on the CIWA-scale: sweating, anxiety, tremor, auditory disturbances, agitation, nausea, tactile disturbances, headache, and orientation. All except orientation are scored on a scale from 0 to 7, while orientation is scored from 0 to 4.[17] Clinical care will increasingly depend on criteria and scales rather than on general nonspecific clinical diagnoses.

Clinical experience indicates that one should have different treatment goals for management of alcohol withdrawal delirium depending on the presence or absence of complications. If alcohol withdrawal delirium is uncomplicated (that is, it is not accompanied by a major illness such as pancreatitis, a long bone broken, or pneumonia), then the therapeutic objective should be to resolve the delirium within 24 to 48 hours. The physician could administer 20 mg of diazepam and observe the effects on specific target symptoms. If there is no impact on any of the symptoms, particularly tremor and restlessness, by 20 to 30 minutes, then another dose of 20 mg should be administered, and so on until there is observable reduction in tremors and restlessness. In most cases, the desired effects are achieved after one or two doses; then the total dose that had an effect (e.g., 40 mg of diazepam, derived by adding two separate doses of 20 mg) is administered every four to six hours with close monitoring. Repeated observation is required to ensure that stabilization of symptoms is not accompanied by too much sedation.

In uncomplicated cases, the patient will sleep after a few doses and will wake with a clear sensorium. The benzodiazepines then can be reduced in dose and frequency of administration over a three- to five-day period, or longer if the dose required to control the patient was high. If delirium tremens is complicated—that is, accompanied by an infection, gunshot wound, head injury, or the like—the physician cannot expect resolution in 24 to 48 hours, but in this period control over severe agitation, terror from hallucinations, should be achieved. The key to this control consists of monitoring carefully the effects of doses of benzodiazepines given and increasing or decreasing the dose according to the observations. The course of complicated alcohol withdrawal can take a week or two to resolve completely, and benzodiazepine therapy may need to be prolonged. When no longer needed, benzodiazepines should be withdrawn slowly with monitoring for possible tremors, hyperactive DTR's, and so on. As noted in chapter 1, good psychologic management—that is, construction of a therapeutic bond with the patient, use of frequent orientation, introduction of familiarity, observation of effects of high-stimulus versus low-stimulus periods of the day on orientation—can be as potent as pharmacologic agents in control of this condition.

If delirium occurs in a patient with severe liver disease, lorazepam should be used instead of diazepam or chlordiazepoxide, as discussed by Schuckit.[18] Lorazepam is metabolized in the kidney rather than in the liver and therefore may be a safer benzodiazepine. Some experts use lorazepam routinely because it is well absorbed after parenteral use, whereas diazepam and chlordiazepoxide are not, and in very delirious patients or in those with vomiting, the oral route of administration is not available. Other experts use oxazepam for all the above conditions because they feel it is not as rewarding as diazepam or other benzodiazepines and is therefore less likely to be abused post treatment.

As reviewed by Gallant, a number of other agents such as clonidine, beta-blockers, and carbamazepine have therapeutic effects on the severe alcohol withdrawal syndrome.[19] For the nonspecialist, these more experimental drugs should be avoided. Beta-blockers, for example, do not have antiseizure effects; clonidine has some potential for producing a withdrawal syndrome when used for over two weeks in a row; carbamazepine can have occasional effects on the bone marrow. For the physician without special training working in most hospital settings, benzodiazepines should be used because they are safe, well established, and effective. Carbamazepine may ultimately prove to have the advantages of preventing death from subsequent

Addiction Research Foundation
Clinical Institute Withdrawal Assessment for Alcohol, Revised (CIWA-Ar)

Patient: Date: Time:
Pulse or heart rate, taken for 1 minute: Blood pressure:

Nausea and vomiting: Observation:
Ask, "Do you feel sick to your   0. No nausea and no vomiting
stomach? Have you vomited?"   1. Mild nausea with no vomiting
                                                   2.
                                                   3.
                                                   4. Intermittent nausea with dry heaves
                                                   5.
                                                   6.
                                                   7. Constant nausea, frequent dry heaves and vomiting

Tactile disturbances: Observation:
Ask, "Have you any itching, pins and   0. None
needles sensations, any burning, any   1. Very mild itching, pins and needles, burning,
numbness, or do you feel bugs crawling   or numbness
under your skin?"   2. Mild itching, pins and needles, burning,
                                                      or numbness
                                                   3. Moderate itching, pins and needles, burning,
                                                      or numbness
                                                   4. Moderately severe hallucinations
                                                   5. Severe hallucinations
                                                   6. Extremely severe hallucinations
                                                   7. Continuous hallucinations

Tremor: Observation:
Arms extended and fingers spread apart   0. No tremor
                                                   1. Not visible but can be felt fingertip to fingertip
                                                   2.
                                                   3.
                                                   4. Moderate, with patient's arm extended
                                                   5.
                                                   6.
                                                   7. Severe, even with arms not extended

Auditory disturbances: Observation:
Ask, "Are you more aware of sounds   0. Not present
around you? Are they harsh? Do they   1. Very mild harshness or ability to frighten
frighten you? Are you hearing   2. Mild harshness or ability to frighten
anything that is disturbing to you? Are   3. Moderate harshness or ability to frighten
you hearing things you know are   4. Moderately severe hallucinations
not there?"   5. Severe hallucinations
                                                   6. Extremely severe hallucinations
                                                   7. Continuous hallucinations

Addiction Research Foundation
Clinical Institute Withdrawal Assessment for Alcohol, Revised (CIWA-Ar) Continued

Paroxysmal sweats:

Observation:
0. No sweat visible
1.
2.
3.
4. Beads of sweat obvious on forehead
5.
6.
7. Drenching sweats

Visual Disturbances:
Ask, "Does the light appear to be too bright? Is the color different? Does it hurt your eyes? Are you seeing anything that is disturbing to you? Are you seeing things you know are not there?"

Observation:
0. Not present
1. Very mild sensitivity
2. Mild sensitivity
3. Moderate sensitivity
4. Moderately severe hallucinations
5. Severe hallucinations
6. Extremely severe hallucinations
7. Continuous hallucinations

Agitation:

Observation:
0. Normal activity
1. Somewhat more than normal activity
2.
3.
4. Moderately fidgety and restless
5.
6.
7. Paces back and forth during most of the interview, or constantly thrashes about

Orientation & clouding of sensorium:
Ask, "What day is this? Where are you? Who am I?"

Observation:
0. Oriented and can do serial additions
1. Cannot do serial additions or is uncertain about date
2. Disoriented for date by no more than 2 calendar days
3. Disoriented for date by more than 2 calendar days
4. Disoriented for place and/or person

Score: (maximum possible score = 67)

Note: This scale is not copyrighted and may be used freely.

episodes of withdrawal*; of having fewer sedative effects in withdrawal, thereby permitting patients to participate in recovery programs earlier; and of reducing psychiatric symptoms more than other agents. Until there are more studies, however, I believe the average physician should stay with the more established benzodiazepines.

The use of thiamine parenterally should be routine in all alcohol withdrawal syndromes, and multivitamins, including folic acid with minerals such as zinc and magnesium, are indicated on a daily basis.

HYDRATION

Examining the question of hydration, Beard and Knott studied patients in withdrawal and found that alcohol is only a diuretic while its concentration is rising; after the concentration of alcohol stabilizes, body water begins to be retained.[20] The person with delirium tremens may be overhydrated, and intravenous fluid loads are therefore contraindicated. In uncomplicated cases, give oral fluids ad libitum. If the patient has severe sweating, vomiting, and/or diarrhea, determine the hydration status by blood analysis and clinical observation; treatment is given as indicated by these data.

AMETHYSTIC AGENTS

The discovery of a safe amethystic agent—a drug that speeds the metabolism of alcohol—would revolutionize the care of persons with alcoholic coma and delirium. In social use, levels of intoxication might be reduced before driving and a host of negative consequences from alcohol intoxication avoided. To date, a few compounds are known to speed the metabolism of alcohol. One of them, fructose, increases the rate of metabolism of alcohol by about 30 to 35 percent. Unfortunately, use of fructose leads to hyperuricemia and lactic acidosis, both dangerous developments in managing delirium tremens. Other amethystic agents are being studied by industry, but none is safe for general use. The physician should also be aware that alcoholic intoxication cannot be affected by stimulants, walking around, or similar measures. An alert intoxicated person may be more dangerous than a sleepy one because he or she may insist on driving and/or on more drinking. Stimulants do not affect blood alcohol concentrations, nor do they reverse impairment of judgment or coordination.

CONTROL OF SEIZURES

One of the primary objectives of treatment of delirium tremens is prevention of seizures. Seizures usually occur within 24 to 48 hours after the onset of withdrawal. They usually occur once only, but status epilepticus does occur occasionally. Benzodiazepines are effective both to prevent and to treat withdrawal seizures. Diphenylhydantoin is usually said to be ineffective because there is not time for it to

* By preventing "kindling," or setting the threshold for seizures much lower than normal. Kindling is discussed further in the chapter on cocaine.

reach therapeutic blood levels in the alcohol withdrawal syndrome before seizures occur. One study, however, suggests that concurrent use of benzodiazepines and diphenylhydantoin is helpful.[21] Diphenylhydantoin should be given orally or intravenously because the parenteral form is not well absorbed. Most texts in the field do not advocate diphenylhydantoin for the prevention of seizures in alcohol withdrawal.

Alcohol withdrawal delirium in its most severe form may not be manageable and may culminate in death. Heroic measures such as administration of intravenous alcohol, intravenous diazepam, or rectal paraldehyde may be considered in cases that do not respond to the measures described.

OTHER ALCOHOL INDUCED DISORDERS

Alcohol dependence and abuse can result in a range of syndromes in addition to those identified above. Most of these, such as mood disorders and alcohol induced anxiety disorders, are discussed in the chapter on dual diagnosis, but the alcohol induced syndromes of amnesia and dementia are presented here.

DSM-4 criteria for the diagnosis of Alcohol Induced Persisting Dementia

A. The development of multiple cognitive deficits manifested by both
1) memory impairment (impaired ability to learn new information or to recall previously learned information)
2) one (or more) of the following cognitive disturbances:
a. aphasia (language disturbance)
b. apraxia (impaired ability to carry out motor functions despite intact motor function)
c. agnosia (failure to recognize or identify objects despite intact sensory function)
d. disturbance in executive functioning (i.e., planning, organizing, sequencing, abstracting)

B. The cognitive deficits in criteria A1 and A2 each cause significant impairment in social or occupational functioning and represent a significant decline from a previous level of functioning.

C. The deficits do not occur exclusively during the course of a delirium and persist beyond the usual duration of Substance Intoxication or Withdrawal.

D. There is evidence from the history, physical examination, or laboratory findings that the deficits are etiologically related to the persisting effects of substance use (e.g., a drug of abuse, a medication).

The code for alcohol in this connection is 291.2.

DSM-4 criteria for the diagnosis of Alcohol Induced Amnestic Disorder

A. The development of memory impairment as manifested by impairment in the ability to learn new information or the inability to recall previously learned information

B. The memory disturbance causes significant impairment in social or occupational functioning and represents a decline from a previous level of functioning.

C.   The memory disturbance does not occur exclusively during the course of a delirium or a dementia and persists beyond the usual duration of Substance Intoxication or Withdrawal.

D.   There is evidence from the history, physical examination, or laboratory findings that the memory disturbance is etiologically related to the persisting effects of substance use (e.g., a drug of abuse, a medication).

The code for alcohol for this diagnosis is 291.1.

It is important to diagnose these conditions carefully, as they are definitive diagnoses. They have no specific treatments, and once established, they have a downhill course. A structured program of social and recreational activities with good nutrition and nursing care can reduce the negative impact of the disorder on the quality of life for the afflicted individual.

MEDICAL PROBLEMS ASSOCIATED WITH ALCOHOL ABUSE

A few common clinical problems associated with alcohol abuse that are both medical and behavioral are discussed here. There is a host of alcohol effects of great medical significance that are beyond the experience and expertise of this author. This text, therefore, does not describe the many pathologic effects of alcohol on the neurologic, gastrointestinal, cardiovascular, reproductive, pulmonary, and immune systems, to name just a few of the many systems of the body on which alcohol can have devastating effects. The reader is referred to a recent publication that presents a careful, comprehensive, and scholarly review of these effects.[1] Another outstanding resource is the Project Cork slide series.[22]

ALCOHOLIC COMA

Alcoholic coma can be induced in a naive user—usually a teenager—with as little as a quarter to one-half a fifth of 80-proof whiskey (that is, if the history of alcohol intake in these unusual cases can be trusted). Alcoholic coma in a long-term abuser of alcohol is also unusual, and if observed should trigger a search for causes other than or in addition to alcohol. The commonest of these would be combined use of alcohol and other drugs such as benzodiazepines or methaqualone. In all cases of coma with the odor of alcohol on the breath, blood for blood alcohol concentration, blood glucose, and a drug screen should be drawn.

In alcoholic coma, head injury (e.g., subdural hematoma), diabetes, meningitis, pneumonia, and septicemia should be ruled out specifically. Coma involving alcohol and other drugs most frequently represents a suicide attempt. Some believe in "accidental overdoses," in which a patient becomes intoxicated to a point sufficient to impair judgment. The patient is then said not to be able to appreciate the probable consequences of taking a handful of pills and/or a water glass full of Scotch. In my experience with such cases, clear current suicidal intent was present, past suicide attempts had been made, and there were histories of severe loss, depressive affects, and so forth, so I am skeptical of the "accidental overdose" theory.

Treatment of alcoholic coma consists of maintaining an airway, with an endotracheal tube if necessary. The patient should be placed face down with feet slightly elevated to avoid problems with aspiration. Shock, if present, should be treated with routine measures. The bladder should be catheterized and fluid intake and output monitored. Analeptics are contraindicated. As noted earlier, the use of fructose to speed the metabolism of alcohol should not be attempted because of the danger of inducing acidosis and hyperuricemia. Good nursing care (turning the patient, frequent suctioning, etc.) is essential. Alcoholic coma usually resolves successfully.

WERNICKE'S SYNDROME

Alcoholics and nonalcoholics (such as prisoners of war) enduring nutritional deprivation may develop a progressive opthalmoplegia that initially presents as horizontal nystagmus; if untreated, the nystagmus is complicated by weakness of lateral gaze. Its full expression is paralysis of all eye movements. Ataxia and polyneuropathy may also be present. Thiamine 100 mg daily is the treatment of choice.

KORSAKOFF'S "AMNESTIC CONFABULATING" PSYCHOSIS

Korsakoff's syndrome, originally intended to describe a severe memory impairment and not a psychosis, is usually preceded by Wernicke's syndrome. Learning is severely affected, and the patient may confabulate. Common confabulations are seen in response to the mental status question asked of a hospitalized patient. In response to the query, "Where are you?" hospitalized patients with Korsakoff's may reply that they are in a railroad station, army barracks, or a relative's house, or will give evidence of some other dramatic impairment in orientation to place; but confabulation is not necessary to the diagnosis. Severe memory and learning impairments, sometimes but not always ushered in by a confabulating state, are essential to the diagnosis. If Wernicke's syndrome progresses to the Korsakoff's stage, reversal is unusual, and institutional care may have to be provided. In DSM-4, Korsakoff's psychosis should probably be identified as alcohol amnestic disorder or alcohol induced dementia.

PREGNANCY AND ALCOHOL

Alcohol passes the placental barrier and has the same plasma concentration for the fetus as it has for the mother. The detrimental effects of alcohol on pregnancy were observed by the ancients. In modern times we have come to recognize that even low daily doses of alcohol are associated with increased perinatal morbidity and mortality for both mother and child.[1] It should be emphasized that no one contests the relationship between alcohol use and an increased risk of perinatal morbidity and mortality. A causal relationship between maternal alcohol intake and the production of a specific set of fetal abnormalities, the fetal alcohol syndrome (FAS), is still debated, however.

FAS is usually described as follows: facial abnormalities include short palpebral fissure, low nasal bridge, epicanthic folds, indistinct philtrum, short nose, small chin, flat midface, and narrow upper lip. Sometimes ptosis, strabismus, and minor malformations of the external ear are also observed. Minor joint anomalies, altered palmar crease patterns, and cardiac and genital anomalies sometimes accompany the syndrome. Infants are small at birth and do not "catch up" in the first year. FAS newborns may be tremulous and hypotonic and may have hyperacusis and weak sucking ability. Hyperactivity, mental retardation, slow development, and perceptual motor disturbance are frequently seen in FAS. Children of alcoholic mothers may show a variety of abnormalities without an accompanying FAS, such as low birth weight, low IQ, and abnormal EEG.

Prospective studies have established that maternal alcohol consumption is unquestionably associated with low birth weight, stillbirths, congenital malformations, and neonatal behavioral effects. The precise role played by alcohol is not clear, for there are many factors involved, such as exposure to other drugs, including nicotine; poor nutrition; variation in individual metabolism of alcohol; and other toxins in alcoholic beverages. The preponderance of evidence appears to be overwhelming that maternal alcohol consumption in the so-called social range—that is, a few drinks per day—is associated with substantial risk of producing some undesirable consequences for both mother and child, if not a full-blown FAS. Women who are pregnant or at high risk for becoming pregnant should be advised not to drink alcohol.

Rosett and colleagues demonstrated that treatment of alcohol using mothers which resulted in a decrease in alcohol use or complete abstention in the third trimester, while not eliminating risk, resulted in fewer abnormalities than were seen in mothers who continued to drink heavily.[23] This study suggests that every effort should be made to influence pregnant women who drink to stop or to reduce drinking.

SELF-HELP GROUPS

ALCOHOLICS ANONYMOUS (AA)

A physician should have some exposure to the culture of Alcoholics Anonymous, because it has been useful to a great many people with alcohol problems. AA, as should be clear from the description below, exerts no pressure on people to stay in it; they do so because of their perception that it helps them. I have never seen any harm from it, so I wonder at the sometimes derogatory comments that AA has not proved its worth. AA is free, it works for those who work it, and it has no side effects.

In 1935 an alcoholic surgeon, Dr. Bob, and an alcoholic businessman, Bill W., founded Alcoholics Anonymous, or AA. AA has devoted itself exclusively to the rehabilitation of alcoholic persons and now has tens of thousands of chapters all over the world, with a U.S. membership of one-quarter to one-half million. Although a key tenet of AA invokes God "as we understand Him," AA is not religious in an institutional sense, meaning that the individual AA member, not AA as an organization, defines God. AA has no property and no paid offices. Chapters are founded by people wishing to form chapters. AA defines alcoholism as a disease and strongly advocates abstinence as the goal of treatment.

Some AA group meetings are open to interested parties, while other meetings are closed. Meetings sometimes focus on the Twelve Steps of AA and sometimes on the AA "bible," a book of personal histories of AA members, while other meetings may be devoted to personal testimonies of AA members.

There is no better way to describe AA than to present the Twelve Steps and the Twelve Traditions. They constitute the basis of the culture of AA.

The Twelve Steps

1. We admitted we were powerless over alcohol—that our lives had become unmanageable.
2. Came to believe that a Power greater than ourselves could restore us to sanity.
3. Made a decision to turn our will and our lives over to the care of God as we understood Him.
4. Made a searching and fearless moral inventory of ourselves.
5. Admitted to God, to ourselves, and to another human being the exact nature of our wrongs.
6. Were entirely ready to have God remove all these defects of character.
7. Humbly asked Him to remove our shortcomings.
8. Made a list of all persons we had harmed, and became willing to make amends to them all.
9. Made direct amends to such people wherever possible, except when to do so would injure them or others.
10. Continued to take personal inventory and when we were wrong promptly admitted it.
11. Sought through prayer and meditation to improve our conscious contact with God as we understand Him, praying only for knowledge of His will for us and the power to carry that out.
12. Having had a spiritual awakening as the result of these steps, we tried to carry this message to alcoholics, and to practice these principles in all our affairs.

The Twelve Traditions of AA

1. Our common welfare should come first; personal recovery depends upon AA unity.
2. For our group purpose there is but one ultimate authority—a loving God as He may express Himself in our group conscience. Our leaders are but trusted servants; they do not govern.
3. The only requirement for AA membership is a desire to stop drinking.
4. Each group should be autonomous except in matters affecting other groups or AA as a whole.
5. Each group has but one primary purpose—to carry its message to the alcoholic who still suffers.
6. An AA group ought never endorse, finance, or lend the AA name to any related facility or outside enterprise, lest problems of money, property, and prestige divert us from our primary purpose.
7. Every AA group ought to be fully self-supporting, declining outside contributions.
8. Alcoholics Anonymous should remain forever nonprofessional, but our service centers may employ special workers.
9. AA, as such, ought never be organized; but we may create service boards or committees directly responsible to those they serve.

10. Alcoholics Anonymous has no opinion on outside issues; hence the AA name ought never be drawn into public controversy.
11. Our public relations policy is based on attraction rather than promotion; we need always maintain personal anonymity at the level of press, radio, and films.
12. Anonymity is the spiritual foundation of all our Traditions, ever reminding us to place principles before personalities.

An interested physician should visit local AA groups to facilitate referrals and to gain an understanding of how this approach achieves its remarkable results.

AL–ANON

While AA provides a resource for the alcoholic, Al-Anon offers an important resource for the families of alcoholics. Referral to Al-Anon is indicated for the family member of an alcoholic who will not seek treatment. In the best-case scenario, the participation of this family member "pulls in" the alcoholic, who then joins AA, and both parties do very well. Even if the alcoholic family member is not pulled in, at a minimum the nonalcoholic family member gets some measure of support and usually learns from others with the same problem. I have never seen any downside from making referrals to Al-Anon.

Many families live for years with a severely alcoholic parent or child without seeking help. The basic advice to members of such families is that there must be change. I advise family members to generate and keep pressure on the alcoholic person to seek treatment, and to stop rescuing the alcoholic from the negative consequences of alcoholic behavior. Families frequently bail alcoholics out of jail for driving while intoxicated or do not tell other relatives about the deterioration taking place, knowing that these relatives will take action or will not deny their anger in relation to the alcoholic behavior. There are many ways families facilitate the alcoholic problem in the long term by mitigating negative consequences of substance abusing behavior in the short term. I regularly advise families with an alcoholic member who won't seek treatment to get together and form a common plan known to all family members, including the alcoholic, if possible. The focus of this plan is to get the alcoholic to join AA, to see a physician, and so on. The family, ideally, should resolve not to continue to support the alcoholic and to keep the pressure on to get help.

Involvement of the family in treatment is complicated and requires special training. In general, the better treatment centers engage families in treatment successfully, and they do so without labeling them as co-alcoholics or by making them feel guilty. They assess the needs of family members and try to respond to these needs. This builds a therapeutic alliance in which negative behaviors can be approached. Steinglass[9] and Galanter[24] have excellent articles discussing this most important area.

Families Anonymous is another resource for families with a drug or alcohol-afflicted individual who denies having a problem. Involvement of the non drug using family members "pulls in" the drug or alcohol using family member exactly as in the scenario with Al-Anon. Al-a-Teen is for children of substance abusing parents who are in denial. All these resources are in the Yellow Pages of the phone book and thus are easily accessible for most people.

ALCOHOLISM TREATMENT PROGRAMS

Most large cities in the United States have a number of alcoholism treatment programs. They range from outpatient programs to nonmedical detoxification facilities, halfway houses, and hospital detoxification wards. Some are privately funded, some publicly funded, but almost all depend on third-party payment of some kind. In these facilities, alcoholism counselors deliver individual and group therapy. In addition, patients may have activity therapy, educational services, and, for younger patients, regular school classes. Families are usually strongly urged or required to participate in the treatment process.

Some facilities require the alcoholic to initiate the contact with the unit and refuse any other kind of referral. A physician should learn about the characteristics of community programs. The best method is by visiting. By federal mandate, each state has a single state agency charged with coordinating treatment and prevention in the state. These agencies usually keep an updated roster of the facilities available. They too are accessible from the phone book.

INDUSTRIAL PROGRAMS

Many large industrial concerns now attempt formally to assist employees with alcohol and drug problems by creating employee assistance programs (EAP's). Usually the company pays for staff to counsel affected employees and to make appropriate referrals; in-company treatment is not usual.

Experience has taught companies to focus on job performance; that is, a supervisor does not try to diagnose alcoholism or substance abuse, but rather evaluates whether the employee is performing adequately. Absenteeism or inadequate job performance provides the supervisor with the occasion for action. The supervisor then requires the employee to visit the employee assistance counselor as a condition of continued employment. Success rates under these circumstances are high.

CHANGES IN THE LEGAL DEFINITION OF INTOXICATION

The work of the Toronto group, which demonstrated that almost 95 percent of public inebriates could be detoxified in nonmedical facilities without the use of drugs, was a public health advance of great importance. This work set the stage for legislation that has redefined the problem of public inebriation. In many states in the United States (and provinces of Canada), public intoxication is now legally defined as a medical and not a legal problem. Police, therefore, have sanction to bring inebriates to nonmedical detoxification facilities or to hospitals instead of to jail.

One of the problems with this approach is that it takes resources to implement. Many legislative bodies are unwilling to create the resources, so these legal changes do not have much on-line impact. The public inebriate in many jurisdictions is, as a consequence, not treated better than he or she was under the old laws.

BEHAVIOR MODIFICATION AND ALCOHOL RELATED PROBLEMS

Contingency contracting, chemical aversion (but not electrical aversion), blood alcohol level discrimination training, and broad-spectrum behavioral approaches all show promise as treatment methods for persons with alcohol and other substance abuse problems. A physician should recognize that these techniques are sufficiently complex to preclude use by anyone without training. If there are experienced practitioners in the community, these approaches should be explored as a potential element in the general treatment program. For an excellent review of relapse prevention and alcoholism, the reader should consult Marlatt and Barrett.[25]

NEUROBIOLOGY OF ALCOHOL

Alcohol is metabolized at a rate of roughly 0.85 of a drink per hour. This is a zero-order transformation; that is, the rate of degradation is independent of the concentration of alcohol in the blood. Alcohol has complex effects. It changes membrane lipid characteristics so the flow of Na, Ca, and K is altered; it has stimulant effects at N-methyl-d-aspartate (NMDA) receptors; and it has depressant effects at the gamma-amino butyric acid (GABA) receptor. Its final effects are the results of a complex interaction between actions at these receptor sites and complex effects on neurohormonal systems.[26] Females have a later onset of alcoholism than males, and this is probably related to social factors; but the biology of alcohol is different in females than in males. Females have higher blood levels than males after equivalent doses because they have more fat relative to water in the body and therefore have a relatively smaller volume of water to dilute the alcohol; alcohol is much more soluble in water than in fat. In addition, females do not have the same level of alcohol dehydrogenase in their gastric mucosa as males, which means that less alcohol is broken down in the stomach of females. Since absorption of alcohol is mainly in the intestinal tract, females have a greater proportion of alcohol going into their bloodstream than do males. The gastric enzyme level in females is further reduced by sustained alcohol use. The end result is that in females, there is little difference between oral peak levels of alcohol and those that would occur if there were intravenous administration of alcohol.[27]

Some Asian populations have more active forms of liver acetaldehyde dehydrogenase, so they have higher levels of acetaldehyde in the bloodstream after equivalent doses of alcohol. This may account for the lower levels of alcohol problems in these populations relative to Western populations. Family, twin, and adoption studies reveal a four times greater risk of alcoholism in children with a parent positive for the disease, regardless of home environment during maturation. The monozygotic concordance for alcoholism is greater than dizygotic concordance. Children of alcoholic parents respond to a series of tests as if they were born tolerant to alcohol effects, such as alcohol augmentation of body sway, intoxicating effects, and so forth.[28]

CHILDREN OF ALCOHOLICS

Children of alcoholics are at risk of developing alcoholism and should be so counseled, but having alcoholism in one or more parents does not doom an offspring; studies indicate that while rates of alcohol problems are higher in family history–positives, more than half never develop a problem with alcohol. Studies of these relationships are very difficult to conduct because of problems in sampling and imprecision in diagnosis, as well as the fact that hundreds of variables must be controlled.[29] On a clinical level, family history–positives should be advised that their responses to alcohol may be harder to control than the responses of family history–negative persons, and they therefore should use alcohol cautiously, if at all. In particular, they should avoid establishing a pattern of repeated alcohol intoxication.

REFERENCES

1. *Alcohol and Health: Eighth Special Report to the U.S. Congress*, 1993.
2. Gallant D. *Alcoholism: A Guide to Diagnosis, Intervention and Treatment.* New York, WW Norton, 1987, pp 47–62.
3. Vaillant GE. *The Natural History of Alcoholism.* Cambridge, MA, Harvard University Press, 1983.
4. Cloninger CR. Neurogenetic adaptive mechanisms in alcoholism. *Science* 236:410–416, 1987.
5. Gallant D. The type 2 primary alcoholic? In *Alcoholism Clin Exp Res* 14:67, 1990.
6. Ewing JA, Rouse BA. Corneal arcus as a sign of possible alcoholism. *Alcoholism* 4:104, 1980.
7. Goodwin DW. Alcohol: Clinical aspects, in Lowinson JH, Ruiz P, Millman RB, et al (eds), *Substance Abuse: A Comprehensive Textbook.* Baltimore, MD, Williams & Wilkins, 1992.
8. Xin Y, Lasker J, Rosman AS, et al: Isoelectric focusing/Western blotting: A novel and practical method for quantification of carbohydrate deficient transferrin in alcoholics. *Alcoholism Clin Exp Res* 15:814–821, 1991.
9. Steinglass P. Family therapy, in Galanter M, Kleber HD (eds), *Textbook of Substance Abuse Treatment.* Washington, DC, American Psychiatric Press, 1994, pp 315–329.
10. Rainey, JM. Disulfiram toxicity and carbon-disulfide poisoning. *Am J Psychiatry* 134:371, 1977.
11. Bourne PG, Fox R. *Alcoholism: Progress in Research and Treatment.* New York, Academic Press, 1973.
12. Gitlow SE, Peyser HS. *Alcoholism: A Practical Treatment Guide*, ed 2. New York, Grune & Stratton, 1988.

13. Fuller RK, Branchey L, Brightwell DR, et al. Disulfiram treatment of alcoholism. JAMA 256:1449–1455, 1986.
14. Volpicelli JR, Alterman AI, Hayashida M, et al. Naltrexone in the treatment of alcohol dependence. *Arch Gen Psychiatry* 49:876–880, 1992.
15. O'Malley SS, Jaffe AJ, Chang G, et al. Naltrexone and coping skills therapy for alcohol dependence. *Arch Gen Psychiatry* 49:881–887, 1992.
16. Whitfield CL, Thompson G, Lamb A, et al. Detoxification of 1024 alcoholic patients without psychoactive drugs. *JAMA* 239:1409–1410, 1978.
17. Sullivan JT, Sykora K, Schneiderman J, et al: Assessment of alcohol withdrawal: The revised clinical institute withdrawal assessment for alcohol scale (CIWA-Ar). *Br J Addiction* 84:1353–13576, 1989.
18. Schuckit M. *Drug and Alcohol Abuse*, ed 4. New York, Plenum, 1995, pp 97–115.
19. Gallant D. Alcohol, in Galanter M, Kleber HD (eds), *Textbook of Substance Abuse Treatment*. Washington, DC, American Psychiatric Press, 1994, pp 67–89.
20. Beard JD, Knott DH. Fluid and electrolyte balance during acute withdrawal in chronic alcoholic patients. *JAMA* 204:135, 1968.
21. Sampliner R, Iber FL. Diphenylhyantoin control of alcohol withdrawal seizures. *JAMA* 230:1430, 1974.
22. Streisguth AP, Little RE. *Alcohol Use and Its Medical Consequences*, ed 2, 1994 (available through Milner Fenwick Inc, 2125 Greenspring Drive, Timonium, MD 21093).
23. Rosett HL, Weiner L, Zuckerman B, et al. Reduction of alcohol consumption during pregnancy with benefits to the newborn. *Alcoholism: Clinical and Experimental Research* 4:178–184, 1980.
24. Galanter M. Network therapy for the office practitioner, in Galanter M, Kleber HD (eds), *Textbook of Substance Abuse Treatment*. Washington, DC, American Psychiatric Press, 1994, pp 253–262.
25. Marlatt GA, Barrett K. Relapse prevention, in Galanter M, Kleber HD (eds), *Textbook of Substance Abuse Treatment*. Washington, DC, American Psychiatric Press, 1994, 285–299.
26. Tabakoff B, Hoffman PL. Alcohol: Neurobiology, in Lowinson JH, Ruiz P, Millman RB, et al (eds), *Substance Abuse: A Comprehensive Textbook*. Baltimore, MD, Williams & Wilkins, 1992, pp 152–185.
27. Blume SB. Alcohol and other drug problems in women, in Lowinson JH, Ruiz P, Millman RB, et al (eds), *Substance Abuse: A Comprehensive Textbook*. Baltimore, MD, Williams & Wilkins, 1992, pp 794–807.
28. Antonelli RM, Schuckit MA. Genetics, in Lowinson JH, Ruiz P, Millman RB, et al (eds), *Substance Abuse: A Comprehensive Textbook*. Baltimore, MD, Williams & Wilkins, 1992, pp 39–50.
29. Children of alcoholics: Are they different? Rockville, MA, Alcohol Alert, National Institute on Alcohol and Alcohol Abuse (NIAAA) No.9 PH288, Rockville, MA, July 1990.

ADDITIONAL READINGS

Orford J, Edwards G. *Alcoholism.* New York, NY, Oxford University Press, 1977.

Friedman L, Fleming NF, Roberts DH, et al. *Source Book of Substance Abuse and Addiction.* Baltimore, MD, Williams & Wilkins, 1996.

Kinney J. *Clinical Manual of Substance Abuse.* St Louis, MO, CV Mosby, 1996.

Mendelson JH, Mello NK. *Medical Diagnosis and Treatment of Alcoholism.* New York, McGraw Hill, 1992.

Winger G, Hofman FG, Woods JH. *A Handbook on Drug and Alcohol Abuse: The Biomedical Aspects.* New York, Oxford University Press, 1992.

4. Opioids

Many people who experiment with heroin entrain themselves inexorably to the worst-case scenario of physical and psychological dependence, progressing to severe deterioration in personal, family, and social domains, including criminal involvement and/or death.[1] There are some who use heroin once or twice, then reflect on the probabilities of a worst-case scenario and stop heroin without further use and with no negative consequences. But some who experiment like the experience enough to use heroin again, and some of these become casual or occasional users. In parallel with the first group, some decide that heroin does not presage a bright future and stop permanently.[2-4]

But many occasional/casual users advance their frequency and quantity of heroin use until they satisfy criteria for dependence or abuse according to DSM-4. Some of those who meet the criteria for diagnosis are able to reflect rationally on the probable consequences, decide to stop, and do so successfully without treatment of any kind. But most of the group meeting criteria for abuse/dependence are not able to do this, and they then enter on a decades-long career centered on heroin.

Making broad statements about the paths described above is risky, because one has to look at the entire process with a time frame of decades in mind. For some heroin dependent individuals, heroin dependence is self-limited. The Vietnam experience is a case in point.[5] In Vietnam, there was high availability of heroin, and many servicemen became dependent, but when they returned to the United States they stopped heroin use. It is possible that they continued on careers centered on intoxication from other drugs, but the evidence is substantial that most of them stopped heroin.

Another form of self-limited heroin dependence is the "maturing out" phenomenon.[6] Social science research establishes that as a population ages, there is a diminution in the number of members who engage in a variety of delinquent behaviors. With respect to this hypothesis for heroin dependence, on a clinical level, it appears to be true. One hears stories of relatives or friends of heroin dependent persons who "kicked cold turkey" and never used again. But there are many who "mature in." We examined the age of first heroin use for the first 9,000 admissions to the Illinois Drug Abuse Program and found that 500 had a first use of heroin after the age of 30. Zinberg and Jacobson identified a group of 96 "chippers," occasional controlled users of heroin, who indulged without apparent progression.[7]

What the studies briefly reviewed in these paragraphs mean to the clinician is that there is a progression to heroin dependence that is quite complex, is different for many individuals, and has quite varied outcomes. Platt provides the best and most comprehensive review of the career aspect of drug dependence.[8] In this connection, it is important to note that iatrogenic opiate dependence occurs but is unusual in populations coming for treatment.

Heroin dependent people coming for treatment may ultimately mature out, but the clinician's job is to help keep them alive until they can test whether or not they will enjoy one of these possible, but not probable, outcomes. For most who meet criteria for abuse/dependence, there is a career, which daily clinical experience indicates can be life-long, if the opiate use does not cause premature death. Death from overdose, the violence in the drug scene, and a wide range of severe medical consequences of heroin use—unsterile needle use and HIV, hepatitis, bacterial endocarditis, and so forth—are real possibilities for the average heroin dependent individual.

DIAGNOSTIC CONSIDERATIONS

Abuse and dependence are diagnosed according to the general criteria for these conditions presented in chapter 2. An additional diagnosis of importance is:

Opioid Intoxication

A. Recent use of an opioid

B. Clinically significant maladaptive behavioral or psychological changes (e.g., initial euphoria followed by apathy, dysphoria, psychomotor agitation or retardation, impaired judgment, or impaired social or occupational functioning) that developed during or shortly after opioid use

C. Pupillary constriction (or pupillary dilation due to anoxia from severe overdose) and one (or more) of the following signs, developing during or shortly after opioid use:
1) drowsiness or coma
2) slurred speech
3) impairment in attention or memory

D. The symptoms are not due to a general medical condition and are not better accounted for by another mental disorder.

This syndrome may be seen in emergency rooms, where it may be an element in a complex syndrome of intoxication induced by use of multiple drugs. Opioid intoxication is sometimes followed by negative feeling states—"initial euphoria followed by apathy, dysphoria" in criterion B above. DSM-4 criteria do not present the variation in intensity of these negative states. For some, usually high-dose users, there is intense dysphoria; users feel very depressed, and there is no relief. To rid themselves of these negative feelings, those affected may use stimulants such as cocaine, either concurrently or sequentially. The stimulants relieve the dysphoria, or, when taken concurrently in "speedballs"—the combination of heroin and cocaine—the dysphoria is prevented.

DSM-4 criteria for the diagnosis of Opioid Withdrawal

A. Either of the following:
    1) cessation of (or reduction in) opioid use that has been heavy and prolonged (several weeks or longer)
    2) administration of an opioid antagonist after a period of opioid use

B. Three (or more) of the following, developing within minutes to several days after criterion A:
    1) dysphoric mood
    2) nausea or vomiting
    3) muscle aches
    4) lacrimation or rhinorrhea
    5) pupillary dilation, piloerection, or sweating
    6) diarrhea
    7) yawning
    8) fever
    9) insomnia

C. The symptoms in criterion B cause clinically significant distress or impairment in social, occupational, or other important areas of functioning.

D. The symptoms are not due to a general medical condition and are not better accounted for by another mental disorder.

The diagnosis of opioid withdrawal is important clinically. Urine tests for the presence of opioids can assist in the diagnosis, although they are not formally part of the criteria. In general, morphine is detected in the urine of heroin users for one to two days following use. Other opioids have similar windows of detectability. A negative urine for morphine in someone claiming to have used heavily on the day of the examination and/or in the days leading up to the examination would raise suspicion of some form of malingering. A later chapter in this book on drug detection introduces the reader to the techniques and the varying times of detection for the different classes of drugs. Here it is important to note that opiates tend to be detectable for one to two days after use, depending on dose.

Physical examination may reveal: hyperpigmentation above veins; "fresh" and "old" needle tracks (that is, puncture areas with fresh blood in the center, "fresh"; or with a brown, crusted-over center, "old"); hepatomegaly; hyperemia of the nasal mucosa, if the opioid was "snorted"; brawny edema of the extremities (sometimes this form of edema is unilateral and involves the forearms and/or an entire lower extremity); abscesses; and circular depressed scars from "skin popping," injecting heroin into the skin (these may be found almost anywhere on the body but predominantly on the extremities). All these findings can be seen in users of many classes of drugs other than opioids and are related simply to unsterile needle use.

Laboratory findings in most addicts are as follows:

Liver function tests. Total protein is commonly elevated, with an elevation of both albumin and globulin, globulin elevation being the more pronounced. Serum glutamic oxaloacetic transaminase (SGOT) and serum glutamic pyruvic transaminase

(SGPT) are frequently elevated, as are immunoglobulins. Bilirubin and alkaline phosphatase also tend to be elevated. Improvement of these values occurs in a few patients during narcotic substitution treatment, but generally they tend to remain elevated despite cessation of the use of unsterile needles. What is puzzling about these changes is their relative lack of clinical meaning. Many addicts have chronic subclinical hepatic disease that does not appear to flare up often. Hepatitis A and hepatitis B antigen levels are elevated in addicts over those observed in the general population.

Serologic test for syphilis. Because opioids induce false-positive results, nonspecific serologic tests for syphilis in addicts are of no value. The fluorescent *Treponema* antibody (FTA) test is required to diagnosis this disease. The FTA test is not affected by narcotics, but it is positive in addict populations more frequently than in nonaddict populations.

Lymphocytes and polymorphonuclear leukocytes. These are elevated in many addicts. Usually, repeated attempts to locate silent infections are fruitless. Levels of these cells tend to remain elevated during treatment even if addicts refrain from using unsterile needles. If there is fever, which there usually is not, workup should proceed as in the non opioid dependent person.

Hemoglobin levels. In some addicts, hemoglobin levels are elevated. Again, workup does not usually disclose a treatable disease, and in treatment hemoglobin levels tend to become normal after months or years.

Blood urea nitrogen. BUN is elevated in some addicts, but again most frequently without clinical meaning. BUN levels tend toward normal during treatment.

ASSESSING THE DEGREE OF OPIOID DEPENDENCE

Naloxone, a narcotic antagonist, has occasionally been used diagnostically in treatment programs to precipitate withdrawal. It is definitive when positive, but it is least useful where most needed; that is, in the milder degrees of dependence. Challenge with narcotic blocking agents, in addition to frequently yielding equivocal results, is time-consuming and in some instances induces substantial distress. Most workers in the field, this writer included, do not use precipitated withdrawal as a diagnostic tool, preferring to make a diagnosis on the basis of the history, physical examination, and laboratory data.

The clinical history is usually reliable enough to permit accurate estimation of the degree of dependence on opioids.[9] If a heroin addict relates that he or she has been using only once or twice a day for a two-week period before coming to treatment and that the quality of the heroin is poor, the degree of dependence is usually minimal, if it exists at all. As the quality of the heroin is rated more highly by the addict and as the number of uses per day increases, so does the degree of dependence.

Estimation of the number of milligrams per day used by an addict is possible by extrapolating from the cost. For example, if the street price of heroin is $4 to $5 per milligram and the addict is spending approximately $100 a day, the habit would be in the 15 to 25 mg/day range, a frequent level today in major American cities.

Reference to a pharmacology text enables the clinician to estimate the degree of dependence on other opioids by using potency ratios (e.g., heroin is about three times more potent than morphine). It is important to keep in mind that most text-books express relative potencies in terms of analgesic effects (e.g., for analgesia, 1 mg of heroin equals approximately 2 mg of methadone equals approximately 3 mg of morphine), but for suppression of the narcotic withdrawal syndrome, clinical experience strongly suggests that heroin and methadone are equipotent. The basic point is that one can usually estimate level of dependence accurately, but one must give a dose of a substitute opioid, usually methadone, and monitor the effect on the specific symptoms of clinical concern; clinical monitoring of this type is essential to good management.

MANAGEMENT OF OPIOID DEPENDENCE/WITHDRAWAL IN GENERAL PRACTICE OR HOSPITAL SETTINGS

General principles. Establish a relationship with the addict that is clear and known to all members of the treatment team. Discuss with the addict what you are going to do (e.g., maintain on methadone), what you plan for analgesia, and also what the limits are (e.g., no use of drugs in the hospital). Then make sure all members of the treatment team know what the plan is.

It is important to define roles with the patient. I tell a hospitalized addict that I will visit regularly and will make sure he or she does not suffer unnecessarily. The addict's role is to relate symptoms to me and ask whatever questions he or she feels are important. If methadone is being used to treat a patient, some clinicians feel strongly that the addict has a right to know the dose. I try to make dose a nonissue and do not mention it unless the patient raises the question. If an addict insists on knowing the dose, I tell him or her. What is crucial in the treatment plan is the evidence that the physician is making every attempt to provide good care. In essence, this demonstration rests on periodic visits, the projection of an attitude of concern, and the projection of competence.

Addicts are no more or less manipulative than any other class of patients, but they can become management problems. An addict may, of course, manipulate the various factions on a ward in masterful fashion. If this happens, it may be necessary to have a ward meeting in which a specific plan is worked out. On occasion there are addicts who are unmanageable, but most addicts respond to clarity, firm control, and good care. The ward team should not hesitate to bar visitors, institute room searches, limit areas of ward access, use security guards, and take whatever other measures are necessary to achieve responsible control. If the manipulative addict knows that the treatment team is serious and will take whatever steps are necessary, including transfer or legal action, manipulative behavior will stop. In rare instances (e.g., repeated smoking in dangerous areas or repeated drug use in the hospital), the institution may have to transfer the patient to another institution, or, with legal consultation, to discharge the patient to home care.

Do not sum stresses. If an addict has a gunshot wound, a long bone broken, a diabetic crisis, or the like, he or she has enough stress to adapt to, and to add the stress of detoxification is not sound. Drug dependence on opioids should be maintained until the medical or surgical problem is resolved. Withdrawal is properly considered at that point.

Analgesic needs and narcotic maintenance needs are independent. Clinical experience teaches that narcotics given to substitute for street narcotics to maintain drug dependence have little or no analgesic effect. If a patient comes into a general hospital taking methadone from a licensed program, the best course of action is to maintain the same dose of methadone in the hospital as given chronically in the outpatient methadone program. Analgesics in usual doses and frequency are indicated for pain relief for such patients, in addition to regular doses of the maintenance methadone.

If the patient comes into the hospital with a so-called street habit, then methadone maintenance is indicated at least during the period of medical or surgical stress. With rare exception, addicts can be managed in the hospital on maintenance doses much smaller than they take on the street. This is because the dose required to intoxicate is greater than the dose necessary to control withdrawal. In my experience, almost every street addict can be managed in the hospital on 30 mg of methadone a day or less. Dividing the daily dose into two or three parts, administration orally or parenterally, is also effective in the event that once-a-day administration does not control the withdrawal symptoms.

In actively dependent addicts, the use of drugs for analgesia such as pentazocine (Talwin), which has narcotic antagonist as well as agonist effects, should be avoided, because the antagonist effects are strong enough to produce sometimes severe withdrawal symptoms. Newer drugs with mixed agonist/antagonist effects such as buprenorphine, butorphanol, and nalbuphine are also contraindicated for analgesia in an active addict.

In the general hospital, establish a regimen for the street addict. Give a 5 or 10 mg dose of methadone and observe the effects at 30 minutes and one hour. If there is no effect, double the dose and observe at 30 minutes and one hour. If the psychological management of the addict is sound, the second dose usually brings the situation under control. The total dose administered can then be given in one dose the next day or in divided doses as discussed above.

If an addict complains that analgesics are not controlling pain, observation of the effects of a given dose of an analgesic over a 30-minute to two-hour period can be decisive in determining whether or not the addict is manipulating or has true unmet analgesic needs. The appearance of sedation and/or relaxation from the analgesic signals that analgesia is probably present and that the addict wants an intoxicating dose rather than a pain-suppressing dose.

Determine what the addict wants with respect to next steps. Once the medical or surgical crisis is over, most street addicts elect to return to the street rather than to stay in the hospital to try to achieve abstinence. It is perfectly sound to discharge a street addict back to the street if this is what he or she wants. Attempts to detoxify such patients without their cooperation are bound to come to grief, with a loss of time and money. In addition, most surgical or medical wards have no programs for opioid treatment and are not good environments in which to withdraw people. If an addict wants to attempt to detoxify, then one should try to obtain some estimates of how much time the addict is thinking of investing in the attempt. Objectives should be clear in such situations and reviewed for achievability, because, as noted in chapter 1, addicts commonly have unrealistic attitudes concerning withdrawal.

In the event that an addict is enrolled in a methadone program, the program should be contacted and asked to participate in planning next steps.

Federal law prohibits physicians from prescribing narcotics, including methadone, to treat narcotic dependence unless the patient is part of a federally licensed treatment program or is in a hospital for a primary medical, surgical, or obstetric problem.[10] Any physician can prescribe opioids, including methadone, for analgesia, cough control, and the like in addicts if there are clinical indications. In a hospital setting, as noted, when an addict has a medical or surgical problem, a physician should maintain the opioid dependence, usually with methadone, until the medical or surgical problem is resolved.

In opioid withdrawal, mental functions such as alertness, orientation, and cognition are almost always intact; in extreme cases, addicts report an altered state of consciousness characterized as dreamlike, "the yen." The presence of hallucinations, marked tremors, delusions, or other serious psychiatric or neurologic signs or symptoms should strongly suggest a diagnosis in addition to opioid withdrawal. Since multiple use of drugs including opioids is so common, mixed withdrawal syndromes must be suspected in every case.

"COLD TURKEY" IS NOT HUMANE AND HAS NO BENEFITS

The experience of clinicians in all parts of the world over many decades is that "cold turkey" withdrawal does not teach the addict anything and is an inhumane procedure. It is a universal observation that the experience of even severe, repeated withdrawal symptoms does not have any effect on recidivism. Every physician working with opioid dependent persons has encountered at least a few addicts who have gone cold turkey by themselves and have achieved many years of abstinence. These are atypical cases. As noted above, recidivism rates for most addicts are substantial following attempts to withdraw either with or without treatment.

Detoxification assisted by alpha-adrenergic agonists such as clonidine is a common practice at present.[11] Clonidine is an alpha-2 adrenergic agonist used in the treatment of hypertension. It blocks many of the symptoms of opioid withdrawal (bone aches, insomnia, and craving are not touched by clonidine) by agonist actions on alpha-2 adrenergic receptors, which inhibit outflow from the locus ceruleus, a center hypothesized to be central to the production of the opioid withdrawal syndrome.

The ordinary hypertensive dose is 0.25 mg three times per day. For reduction of opioid withdrawal, the usual dose is 0.1 mg three times on the first day, building up daily to 1.5 mg in a six- or seven-day period. Clonidine must then be tapered over another six- to seven-day period, because longer periods of use are associated with withdrawal symptoms from clonidine, which are opioidlike.

Hypotension and sedation can occur, but with good clinical monitoring these problems are infrequent. Hallucinations occur rarely.

When opioid dependence of mild or moderate degree is in question, then clonidine is quite effective in assisting addicts to detoxify. When opioid dependence is severe, most clinicians reduce the habit before using clonidine. Like all detoxification methods, it has not demonstrated effects on recidivism rates, which are high in opioid dependent persons detoxified with any method.

Gradual reduction of an opioid with concurrent use of clonidine may be problematic, as clonidine and opioids may potentiate each other's sedative properties. In an unpublished study in which we used clonidine and concurrent tapering doses of methadone, we found potentiation of sedative effects severe enough to prevent some study subjects from working.

Clonidine may have some effects in alcohol and nicotine withdrawal; use for these indications is being explored at present.

OPIOID OVERDOSE

DIAGNOSIS

Pinpoint pupils, depressed respiration (e.g., 2 to 4 per minute or not detectable), and shallow coma (coma from which the patient can be roused, but into which the patient falls back without continued stimulation) form the classic triad of opioid overdose. Opioid overdose from meperidine may present with dilated pupils. Dilated pupils may also be observed when anoxia has been severe or if phenothiazines have been involved. Pulmonary edema is a frequent expression of the opioid overdose syndrome. It may be complicated by attempts on the part of the addict's friends, who may administer coffee, milk, salt solutions, and the like, thereby inducing an aspiration pneumonia. In differentiating between pulmonary edema and an aspiration pneumonia, respiratory rate is important. In pulmonary edema it is depressed or perhaps normal; in aspiration pneumonia it is elevated.

TREATMENT

The treatment of choice for opioid overdose is naloxone. Naloxone is administered intravenously in a dose of 0.4 mg. Failure to observe a prompt improvement in respiratory rate after administration of naloxone suggests that opioids are not responsible for the overdose.

Naloxone should be administered slowly to avoid too rapid a return to consciousness with the possibility of disorientation, hyperactivity, extreme dysphoria, and possible violence. If the overdose is from propoxyphene, higher doses of naloxone may be needed, because propoxyphene acts predominantly at kappa and sigma receptors rather than at the mu receptor, and these receptors are much less sensitive than the mu receptor to naloxone. Naloxone has its antagonist effects for one to two hours. If the overdose is from a long-acting opioid such as methadone, a period of 24 hours of observation is mandatory, with the probable need for repeated naloxone if the patient initially cleared by naloxone becomes obtunded again.

The next sections of this chapter describe the most common treatment methods for opioid dependent persons. They are intended to provide the community-based physician who needs to refer opioid abusing patients with an understanding of what these programs involve.

METHADONE MAINTENANCE PROGRAMS

Dole and Nyswander, in the middle and late '60s, pioneered the use of methadone as a narcotic substitution therapy for heroin addicts.[12] Results of their early studies indicated that 80 percent of the patients stopped criminal activities, reduced or eliminated illicit drug use, and became legitimately employed. Such unprecedented success in treating heroin addicts led to rapid expansion of this method across the country. Methadone maintenance grew rapidly in the early '70s, with an enrollment at times of approximately 100,000 addicts. Current estimates place the number of patients in maintenance programs in the neighborhood of 115,000.

Results have not continued to be as favorable as those obtained in the '60s, probably because the early studies screened out medically and/or psychologically disabled patients. But the results of many studies in the last decade indicate that methadone maintenance continues to be successful in reducing illicit drug use and criminality. It also is successful, but in less pronounced fashion, in improving employment rates and social and community functioning. In recent years we have come to appreciate the prevention aspect of methadone maintenance, as a number of studies have shown that rates of HIV infection are dramatically lower in methadone maintained patients than in out-of-treatment populations. With the possible exception of psychotherapy, probably no human service modality has been as much evaluated as this sometimes-controversial treatment; the evaluations, some encompassing tens of thousands of addicts studied for years, are positive.

The statistics on methadone maintenance programs can be misleading. These programs treat some of the most severely disadvantaged people in our society, and in the face of this, the programs accumulate from one-third to one-half of a patient load consisting of people who have made a real and positive change in their lifestyle. The progress of this third is sometimes canceled out statistically by another third of patients who do not change from criminal lifestyles centered on intoxication. Critics of methadone programming usually focus on the third of patients not doing well, missing the point that before methadone programming there was no method for generating the third who do well.

There are poorly managed methadone programs, and the uninitiated can characterize the entire national treatment effort by such failures. I am convinced, based on a review of the now-global database, a knowledge of the treatment systems of many of the major cities around the world, and close to 30 years of clinical experience, that this method is useful for many heretofore unreachable opioid dependent persons.

OPERATING PROCEDURES OF METHADONE MAINTENANCE PROGRAMS

Methadone is the logical narcotic for substitution therapy because it is effective orally and suppresses abstinence symptoms for 24 to 32 hours with one dose a day. Properly prescribed methadone eliminates withdrawal without euphoria or sedation. This is an important point. Methadone is not substituting one "high" or "buzz" for another. When properly dosed, methadone maintained patients are, in their words, "normalized"; they are not dysphoric from withdrawal, and they are not euphoric or "high" from the methadone. Their sensorium is clear, and they are able to focus normally on work or other pursuits. Driving records of methadone maintained patients are unremarkable, and sophisticated tests demonstrate no major problems with cognition or judgment.[13]

Methadyl acetate or L-alpha-acetyl-methadone (LAAM), a methadone congener, is also effective orally and suppresses the opioid withdrawal symptoms for 48 to 72 hours. Detailed descriptions of the clinical use of these drugs are given in the next chapter, which is focused on the physician working in a treatment program using methadone, LAAM, or other legal opioids for maintenance or detoxification.

The ordinary methadone maintenance program has a case load of approximately 100 to 300 patients. It is staffed by a part-time physician, with a nurse, LPN, and/or pharmacist, and an ex-addict counseling staff. Generally, the ratio of counselors to patients is 1:20 to 1:50, depending on resources. Clinics usually have a part-time mental health consultation capability with a psychiatrist, psychologist, or social worker. Programs have varied structures for administration, with the physician, psychologist, social worker, or ex-addict counselor frequently serving an administrative function in addition to holding clinical responsibilities.

NALTREXONE: A PURE OPIOID ANTAGONIST

Naltrexone is a chemical analog of naloxone and is without agonist effect, but it displaces opioids from receptor sites, thus causing withdrawal. If no opiates are present, it selectively occupies these sites in preference to all known opioids, thus preventing euphoria or relieving withdrawal by use of heroin or other opioids. In contrast to methadone, naltrexone can be used by any physician to treat opioid related problems.[14] A community-based physician might encounter a heroin addict wanting to be treated privately by a physician so as to escape notice. Such a patient could be placed on prescribed naltrexone by any licensed physician. If a physician decides to try this treatment, it would be a good idea to establish some working relationship with whatever drug treatment facilities are available in the community to assist in dealing with failure of naltrexone and a full-blown relapse. If there is an ASAM-certified physician, then the physician not so certified could obtain a consultation if problems occur.

Before placing an addict on naltrexone, there must be a period of no heroin use as demonstrated by repeated negative urine screens or by the administration of naloxone with no precipitated withdrawal. Then the patient can be started on naltrexone 50 mg Monday and Wednesday and 75 mg on Friday. This regimen blocks the effects of ordinary doses of heroin or other opioids.

Experience to date indicates that street populations get little benefit from naltrexone, because they will not take it. The effectiveness of naltrexone is enhanced by the presence of some form of coercion, such as in drug dependent nurses or physicians who must ingest the naltrexone under observation in a clinic in order to maintain their licenses.

Patients may experience nausea from taking the drug. In this case it should be taken with food. There are no other side effects from naltrexone. The prescribing physician should also be mindful that opioid analgesics are not going to be effective for 24 or more hours. In the event of a need for analgesia, other drugs or, perhaps, anesthetics must be used.

The patient should attend a self-help group, or be in some kind of therapy if self-help groups are not available or acceptable, and the community-based physician should obtain periodic urine screens to monitor for use of drugs other than opioids. In some cases family members can be charged with giving the naltrexone, thus introducing a form of control. The patient's consent, of course, must be obtained.

THERAPEUTIC COMMUNITIES

As in the case of methadone treatment, this chapter presents material that should orient the community-based physician not working in drug treatment to general aspects of the programs to which, hopefully, the physician is referring drug dependent and drug abusing patients.[15-17] The next chapter presents a more detailed review for the physician working in a therapeutic community.

Therapeutic communities were pioneered by Charles Diederich in the late 1950s and early 1960s. In Synanon, the original therapeutic community, addicts were viewed as needing fundamental resocialization. This was accomplished by immersing them in an authoritarian, hierarchical social structure in which rewards such as social status, better jobs, and so forth were contingent on conformity to the rules of the community's group life. Diederich rejected "professionals" and, in particular, the concept of an unconscious; thus addicts were expected to know what was in their minds and to be able to report mental content clearly. Anything else was viewed as dishonest and a continuation of "street games." Synanon demanded repeated verbal commitments to its program before admission. Applicants were sometimes required to demonstrate their commitment to change by being forced to come back several times, sometimes over a span of days or weeks, before being admitted.

Once admitted to Synanon, the addict went "cold turkey" for a few days before beginning one of the most menial jobs in the community. In addition to long hours of work, addicts might be "pulled up," or confronted for any aspect of their behavior. Attendance was mandatory at "Synanons," or encounter groups based on direct and, often, harsh confrontation. Since Synanon rigidly excluded professionals, former addicts were the group leaders of Synanons. In some instances the entire community might participate in decisions, such as putting addicts out of the community for behavior involving violence, threats of violence, use of drugs, or "conning." The early therapeutic communities also used demeaning techniques such as shaving the heads of community deviants and/or forcing clients to wear signs that described their delinquent behavior.

As addicts progressed in the community, they were charged with increasingly important administrative and clinical tasks. The ultimate goal of the program was not clear when Synanon started. Some in Synanon felt that an addict could go back to the community once he or she had learned honesty. Others felt an addict was vulnerable and that society would overwhelm him or her again if he or she were exposed. This latter view prevailed in Synanon. At present, it has its own schools, and Synanon philosophy holds that an addict must maintain strong lifelong ties with Synanon to continue drug free living. The Synanon model was effective, and in the middle '60s it was much imitated.

Major modifications of the Synanon model have been made without impairing effectiveness. The goal of most modern therapeutic communities, for example, is a return to community living; confrontation, particularly in therapeutic communities operated for teenagers, is no longer utilized, and professionals now have prominent places both administratively and clinically in many therapeutic communities. Phoenix House and Odyssey House in New York City, and Gateway House and Interventions in Chicago, are prominent examples.

Basically, the use of live-in social dynamics to effect change in behavior should be applicable to problems other than drug dependence. To date, however, we have not systematically studied such applications. As with methadone maintenance, therapeutic communities have been evaluated intensively during the last decade. Samples of thousands of clients have been studied, and the conclusion is that therapeutic communities are effective in changing the behavior of drug dependent persons, although dropout rates are high, from 75 to 90 percent. Studies indicate that length of time in a therapeutic community, after a threshold period of approximately one to three months, is associated with greater degrees of post-treatment success. The number of therapeutic communities has increased steadily, and the method is now a worldwide movement.

MULTIMODALITY PROGRAMMING

Dr. Jerome Jaffe pioneered the concept of the multimodality program, in which addicts were presented with information about methadone maintenance, detoxification, or therapeutic communities or variants thereof, and then could choose the treatment from these alternatives.[18] Jaffe found that a single administrative structure could offer all the known effective treatments, and that such an arrangement had substantial clinical and economic advantages. In many cities today, an addict applying for one modality does not learn about the potential of any of the other modalities. A chronic heroin addict with an active relationship with his or her family and a legitimate and desirable job is not a prime candidate for a therapeutic community; it is unlikely that such a patient could take a year or two from work and not jeopardize his or her job. Similarly, an itinerant addict without employment or family ties is better treated in a therapeutic community than in maintenance. Multimodality programming facilitates the match between such patients and appropriate treatments. From a public health point of view, the community is better served, because administrative costs can be reduced and standard assessment procedures can facilitate evaluation of all modalities. Jaffe's multimodality program is the forerunner of the ASAM continuum of care, which provides for patients' right to know treatment alternatives and to be embraced by a system of care that can be adapted to varying needs in a career of recovery rather than a career of addiction.

IATROGENIC OPIOID DEPENDENCE

Opioid dependence acquired during the course of opioid use for analgesia for a nonchronic medical/surgical condition rarely leads to a career of opioid dependence. Once the need for analgesia has passed, withdrawal is easily accomplished by gradual reduction of dose over a few days to a week if large amounts of opioids were involved. Sometimes opioids are stopped abruptly, and patients suffer needlessly. A daily reduction in dose of 10 to 20 percent in the beginning, with a 5 to 10 percent daily reduction toward the end of the detoxification, affords a smooth, relatively trouble-free regimen.

Long-term iatrogenic opioid dependence occurs in patients with chronic diseases such as ulcerative colitis or arthritis. Sometimes these patients may behave like street addicts, but most such patients take narcotics for analgesia every day for decades without increasing the dose and without serious disruption of their ability to work and to relate to other people. They do not ordinarily experience euphoria from the doses used. In some instances, after the physician who has prescribed the opioid moves away or dies, the physician taking over the case may misinterpret current laws. I have consulted on a few cases in which misunderstandings of FDA regulations caused patients severe problems. Physicians assuming the care of these chronic situations believed that they were adhering to the law by forcing the patients to withdraw. The chronic disease flared; patients turned to sedatives and/or alcohol for relief, and did so in ways that were destructive.

My counsel in these cases was to reinstitute narcotics and to use them as long as there was need for analgesia. With participation from the single state agency, patients' needs can be met without legal problems. The principle is clear: opioids can be used for analgesia for as long as there is clinical need. What is forbidden by law is the use of narcotics to treat addiction on a chronic basis. I do not advocate the use of narcotics for analgesia in chronic medical conditions such as rheumatoid arthritis or ulcerative colitis, but if use is long established, the dose is stable, and the patient is doing reasonably well, my belief is that such situations are best left alone. If, for whatever reason, detoxification is attempted in chronic disease complicated by opioid dependence, it should be accomplished slowly. Sudden withdrawal will almost certainly exacerbate the underlying disease. Slow withdrawal regimens, over six to eighteen months, in such cases can be carried out on an outpatient basis, perhaps accompanied by inpatient treatment to overcome the usual difficulty with the last few milligrams of methadone.

In Asia, one frequently sees long-term opioid dependence in people with severe chronic diseases such as dysentery or tuberculosis. In these cases, narcotics provide symptomatic relief. Frequently such patients live in areas where there are no physicians or medicines. As with their counterparts in the West, withdrawal is difficult even with adequate treatment of the underlying condition.

MEDICAL COMPLICATIONS OF OPIOID ABUSE AND DEPENDENCE

This section is a brief overview of some areas of interest in clinical practice. The best and most comprehensive review of medical aspects of opioid dependence is by Karch.[19] Opioid abusers are vulnerable to infection, principally because of their repeated use of unsterile needles and diluents. This exposes the body to foreign proteins, assorted chemicals, and repeated attacks by virulent organisms. Reticuloendothelial hyperplasia is a frequent postmortem finding in chronic users of unsterile needles. Direct introduction of pathogens to the interior of the body, poor nutrition, concurrent use of alcohol, nicotine, and other drugs, poor medical care, and suppression of the cough reflex by opioids all interact to produce infectious disease in addict populations. The preponderance of evidence indicates that the chronic use of opioids, if taken in sterile fashion and in a dose low enough to avoid severe respiratory depression, has remarkably little effect on health; although opioids may have some immunosuppressive effects, the clinical significance of these effects, if any, is not known.

ENDOCARDITIS

We do not have accurate figures concerning the incidence and prevalence of endocarditis in addicts, but most hospitals servicing low-income populations usually have one or more cases in the hospital at any given time. Addicts with endocarditis, in contrast to others with the disease, usually do not have rheumatic heart disease or valve deformities. According to a number of authors, the organisms involved in endocarditis in addicts are different than in nonaddicts, and the clinical presentation is also different. Addicts may present without a murmur and are more likely to have acute endocarditis with a fulminating course. Addicts have more tricuspid valve involvement, with or without repeated pulmonary emboli, than nonaddicts and may present with repeated episodes of dyspnea and/or pulmonary infections. *Staphylococcus aureus* is the organism most frequently involved, but unusual organisms such as Candida may be observed. Therapy in such cases may have to be aggressive with early surgical intervention. Multiple pathogens involving more than one valve can also occur.

HEPATITIS

Hepatitis in drug abusers is usually not fatal and occurs in 80 percent of cases within the first two years of unsterile needle use. Subclinical hepatic disease probably accounts for the high rates of elevation of SGOT, SGPT, and Australia antigen in opioid abusing populations. Alcohol abuse, which occurs frequently in opioid abusers, undoubtedly also contributes to these findings. Substance abuse should be suspected and carefully ruled out in any case of hepatitis.

SKIN, SOFT TISSUE, MUSCLE, AND JOINTS

Common skin problems in addicts are old and fresh needle tracks; circular, depressed scars from "skin popping," or subcutaneous injection of opioids; edema of the hands; edema of the feet; severe cellulitis; abscesses; infections of the fascia of the hand; necrosis secondary to intraarterial injection of drugs; contracture of the fingers secondary to repeated injections in the hand; and pyomyositis and carbon deposits in skin secondary to heating needle tips in an effort to achieve sterility, with resultant deposition of intradermal carbon. Pentazocine and tripelennamine, so-called T's and Blues, appear to have sclerosing effects, which complicate the foregoing conditions. T's and Blues users have more severe soft tissue pathology than heroin addicts.

Thrombophlebitis is frequent in addicts and may involve the entire superficial venous system. Venipuncture in such cases is impossible, and femoral puncture or a cut-down may be required.

TETANUS

Most cases of tetanus involve drug abusers. Females are more frequently infected than males; they "skin pop" more frequently than males because of their relatively poor venous development. In so doing, they deposit *Clostridium tetani* in poorly vascularized areas, which are ideal for the development of anaerobic infections. When tetanus occurs, the prognosis is guarded.

MALARIA

Most recently, malaria was seen in California following the return of infected soldiers exposed in Asia during the Vietnam War, but since then I have not heard of a case. Needle sharing caused a small outbreak that was quickly contained. In areas like Chicago and New York, where quinine was used as a diluent, malaria in addicts was a rarity. I include some comments about malaria because it might be significant once again in parallel with a disease like tuberculosis. The use of quinine as a diluent probably can be traced to the 1930s, when there was an outbreak of malaria in New

Orleans among sailors who had contracted the disease in North Africa and spread it by needle sharing. Addicts recognized that quinine might prevent the spread, and thus quinine became a regular part of heroin use in many major cities of the country.

RESPIRATORY TRACT

Sinusitis, bronchitis, upper respiratory infections, and pneumonia occur more frequently in opioid abusers than in the general population. Since the advent of HIV, there has been a resurgence of tuberculosis, and specifically of treatment-resistant strains. The medical treatment of current tuberculosis is outside the purview of this text, but interactions with drugs such as rifampin should be known by all methadone maintenance program medical staff. Opioids suppress the cough reflex and may have primary immunosuppressive effects. Opioid abusers tend to smoke nicotine and cannabis and to drink alcohol heavily, and their nutrition is not good. In addition, opioid abusers, as well as patients on methadone maintenance programs, may have problems with sweating and with control of body temperature. Whatever the role of such factors, the incidence of infection of the respiratory system is unquestionably high in opioid users in comparison to the general population.

Microcrystalline inclusions in the lungs of opioid abusers may result from the talc and/or starch used as diluents. T's and Blues (pentazocine and tripelennamine) abusers have frequent pulmonary problems (angiothrombotic pulmonary hypertension) from such inclusions. In some abusers, large numbers of bacteria are seeded throughout the lungs. The resulting pneumonia may be difficult to treat.

NEUROLOGIC SYSTEM

There are many, but fortunately rare, neurologic complications of opioid use such as transverse myelitis. The causes are not known. Some feel that heroin or its diluents can cause hypersensitivity reactions. In some instances, quinine may be the toxic agent.

Postanoxic syndrome following overdose. Occasionally, an addict overdoses and remains comatose for days. Following this episode, a variety of syndromes may occur, such as partial paralysis, deafness, Parkinson's disease, occlusion of the middle cerebral artery, and hemiballismus.

Optic effects. Blindness, probably a toxic effect of quinine, has occurred in opioid abusers. Field defects attributable to talc emboli in retinal vessels have also been observed.

Peripheral nerve lesions. Direct injection of a nerve or plexus may produce neuropathy distal to the injection site.

Muscle disorders. Following an opioid induced stupor, an addict may sleep with all of his or her weight on an extremity. A "crush syndrome" may occur, which may manifest itself in rhabdomyolysis and/or myoglobinuria. If the myoglobinuria is severe enough, renal failure may occur. Chronic myopathies, probably secondary to repeated direct injections into muscle, can also be observed in addicts.

Renal disorders. Use of opioids has been implicated in the production of the nephrotic syndrome. Immunoglobulins have been detected in renal tissue, leading to the speculation that opioid use has a relationship to immune disease. Glomerulonephritis from septic emboli has also been observed in opioid abusers.

Allergic reaction. Urticaria, pruritus, and anaphylaxis occasionally occur in opioid abusers. Pruritus is a regular part of the heroin experience. Heroin releases histamine in the skin, which accounts for the pruritus and the warm tingling sensations reported by many addicts.

Osteomyelitis. Osteomyelitis, involving the lumbar vertebrae, sacrum, hip, clavicle, and other bones of the body, has been observed in addicts. The etiology is obscure but presumably is related to the injection of bacteria along with the opioids.

MULTIPLE SIMULTANEOUS DEPENDENCE INCLUDING OPIOID DEPENDENCE

Occasionally, an addict enters the hospital dependent concurrently on two or more classes of drugs. One addict I saw in consultation entered the hospital with a gunshot wound in the chest. His girlfriend stated that he was using "pure" heroin intravenously six times a day and had been so using for many months. He was also drinking a fifth or more of liquor daily and using 2 to 3 grams of barbiturates a day. Cannabis and cocaine use was frequent but not daily. On admission, he was tremulous, with hyperactive deep tendon reflexes. He began to hallucinate within hours of admission. Based on the principle of replacing each class of drugs the patient is dependent on with a drug from that class, my management of the case included methadone 30 mg per day in three divided doses, phenobarbital 200 mg q6h while awake, and chlordiazepoxide (Librium) 100 mg q6h while awake.

In the case under discussion, the patient had hallucinations and tremors and apparently was undergoing simultaneous withdrawal from alcohol, heroin, and barbiturates. He was maintained on the regimen described above for many weeks while his chest wound was treated successfully. Withdrawal of barbiturates and chlordiazepoxide was then accomplished simultaneously over a three-week period, and he was discharged back to the street with a 30 mg/day methadone intake. He did not want to attempt detoxification from methadone and stated that he was confident he could get enough heroin to be comfortable.

Some authors suggest a withdrawal regimen for concurrent dependence on alcohol and CNS depressants utilizing one drug, but in my experience, admittedly limited to a handful of cases, management appears to be smoother if one substitutes for each class of drugs involved (e.g., benzodiazepines for alcohol and Phenobarbital for barbiturates or other sedative-hypnotics such as methyprylon, glutethimide, and so on), but barbiturates can be used to cover both the alcohol and the sedative-hypnotic withdrawal.

MANAGEMENT OF PREGNANT ADDICTS

The opioid dependent pregnant woman creates a treatment dilemma.[20, 21] If she has a substantial degree of opioid dependence, attempts to detoxify her carry a real risk of causing fetal and perhaps maternal death. Opioid withdrawal for the human fetus, unlike the human adult, carries risk of death. Experience in different treatment centers in the United States has led to a policy of maintaining the pregnant opioid addict on daily doses of methadone as low as is consistent with reduction or elimination of heroin use through the pregnancy and delivery.

After clinical experience in the late '60s demonstrated that detoxification of pregnant addicts carried a high risk of fetal death, there was a change in clinical practice toward the use of high-dose methadone maintenance for pregnant addicts. Fetal death during term was avoided, but neonates were affected by severe withdrawal syndromes, and a few died. This experience led to the modern option of low-dose maintenance.

When opioid dependent pregnant women are maintained on low doses of methadone, 25 to 50 mg/day, the neonatal withdrawal syndrome is frequently mild and may be manageable by swaddling. Perinatal morbidity and mortality are not reduced to normal but are reduced by this approach as much as they can be.

It may be possible, with a highly cooperative pregnant opioid dependent patient, to lower the maintenance dose by reducing the methadone by 1 mg every few days. But the patient has to monitor the activity of the child carefully. Fetal activity is an index of the severity of its withdrawal. In many cases it is not possible to reduce the dose more than a few milligrams. Dose reduction should be attempted only by patients with high degrees of compliance with the prenatal care program, who are monitored carefully, and then only if they insist on attempting it and they are making the attempt with experienced personnel in an established center. There is a real risk of losing the fetus if the dose decreases are too large.

The pregnant addict who demands more methadone should be told that continued low doses of methadone will be increasingly successful in controlling withdrawal and to try to continue the dose for a few days. Clinical observation should determine if severe withdrawal is present. The patient should be counseled that raising the dose is associated with risks for the fetus. In the era of HIV, one must balance all the risks. I would use higher doses of methadone in a pregnant addict now than previously because the threat of acquiring HIV more than counterbalances the risk of higher degrees of dependence for the fetus/neonate. The opioid dependent pregnant woman has to be instructed on the risk of alcohol, nicotine, marijuana, or other drug use during pregnancy.

With low-dose methadone maintenance, many neonates have no withdrawal symptoms, but others have mild to moderately severe withdrawal syndromes, and a few have severe withdrawal. The neonatal abstinence syndrome consists of a variable subset of the following signs and symptoms: coarse or flapping tremors, high-pitched cry, sleep disturbance, sneezing, increased muscle tone, frantic sucking of the fist, vomiting, diarrhea, convulsions, elevated respiratory rate, hyperactive Moro reflex, frequent yawning, nasal stuffiness, fever, and dehydration. Neonatal withdrawal, probably because of immature development of the enzyme systems necessary for biotransformation of opioids, is more variable than it is in adults. The onset of withdrawal in neonates may be delayed for weeks after delivery, and the withdrawal syndrome may have a lingering course of many weeks. These facts mandate prolonged observation of addicted neonates and different expectations concerning length of withdrawal treatment than obtains in the adult.

Neonatal withdrawal varies more in its expression than in adults. It may present in neonates relatively confined to symptoms expressed in one system, such as gastrointestinal (e.g., vomiting); neurological (e.g., convulsions); failure to thrive, and the like; or it may be multisystemic, as in adults. Since multiple drug use has become common, it is necessary to monitor opioid dependent neonates for withdrawal from alcohol, sedatives, and other CNS-active drugs, and possibly from other drugs such as PCP. The withdrawal syndrome from multiple drug abuse cannot be discriminated from opioid withdrawal. Failure of usual management techniques of the opioid withdrawal syndrome should raise suspicion of multiple dependencies.

Because it is so variable in its form, the neonatal withdrawal syndrome can be mimicked by hypoglycemia, hypercalcemia, intracranial injuries, and meningitis. Rarely, hyperthyroidism may be encountered, but usually the mother has a known and active case of hyperthyroidism if it is encountered in a neonate.

If drug therapy is required, the regimen of choice is paregoric, with phenobarbital supplementation if neonatal withdrawal cannot be controlled by paregoric alone. The barbiturate covers the threat of seizures, which are an expression of withdrawal in a neonate, while rare in adults. Opioids do not treat this serious risk, and therefore a two drug regimen is necessary. Once the diagnosis of neonatal withdrawal is established, the dosage is paregoric 0.2 mL by mouth every 3 to 4 hours, increased by 0.05 mL per dose until symptoms are controlled or until the dose is at the 0.75 mL level, or until seizures occur. If the dose reaches 0.75 mL without control of symptoms or if seizures occur, phenobarbital should be added in a dose of 5 mg/kg/day in three divided doses.

Once control is achieved, Finegan recommends maintaining the regimen for 5 to 7 days, then decreasing each dose by 0.05 mL daily and monitoring symptoms.[21] If restlessness occurs, Finegan recommends reinstituting the previous day's dose level. The point is not to eradicate all symptoms, but rather to maintain feeding behavior, weight gain, and control of tremors. Mild symptoms should not cause the withdrawal process to stop as long as the infant is thriving.

Some experience has been recorded with chlorpromazine and diazepam in the treatment of the neonatal opioid withdrawal syndrome. Finegan believes these drugs should be avoided or, if employed, they should be used only with careful monitoring. Studies indicate that paregoric restores sucking behavior better than chlorpromazine or diazepam. Chlorpromazine is not an opioid agonist and is therefore not specific for withdrawal. Diazepam can lead to obtundation, and its benzoate diluent can inhibit bilirubin binding. In an infant with hyperbilirubinema, this could be damaging.

The opioid dependent mother can be withdrawn from her maintenance methadone if that is her wish, but she may be maintained on methadone, regardless of any other eligibility considerations, if clinically indicated.

ACUPUNCTURE

There would appear to be no question that acupuncture can relieve at least mild degrees of opioid withdrawal.[11] The best judgment I have, after reviewing the literature and talking to proponents of acupuncture in the Far East, is that it will relieve symptoms of opioid withdrawal but not on a predictable basis; in addition, its application is costly in terms of staff time. At this writing, acupuncture appears to be a phenomenon we may profit greatly from understanding, but it is not a technique we can use consistently in daily clinical life. Each day during withdrawal, an addict may receive one or more treatments requiring the presence of staff for 20 to 30 minutes. Most practitioners prefer decrements of methadone as a withdrawal technique, because its effects are constant, predictable, and less demanding in terms of resources.

REFERENCES

1. O'Donnell JA, Voss HL, Clayton RR, et al. *Young Men and Drugs*. National Institute on Drug Abuse, research monograph #5, Rockville, MD, 1976.
2. Robins LN. Addict careers, in Dupont RI, Goldstein A, Brown B. (eds), *Handbook on Drug Abuse*. National Institute on Drug Abuse, Rockville, MD, 1979.
3. Crawford GA, Washington MC, Senay EC. Careers with heroin. *Intl J Addict* 18:701–715, 1983.
4. Robins LN, Murphy GE. Drug use in a normal population of young Negro men. *Am J Pub Health* 57:1580–1596, 1967.
5. Robins LN, Helzer JE, Hesselbrock M, et al. Vietnam veterans three years after Vietnam: How our study changed our view of heroin, in Harris L (ed), *Annual Report of The Committee on Problems of Drug Dependence*. Richmond, VA, 1977.
6. Winick C. Maturing out of narcotic addiction. *Bull Narcotics* 14:1–7, 1962.
7. Zinberg NE, Jacobson RC. The natural history of "chipping." *Am J Psychiatry* 133:37–40, 1976.
8. Platt JJ. *Heroin Addiction: Theory, Research and Treatment,* vol 2. Malabar, FL, Krieger Publishing, 1995.
9. Maddux JF, Desmond DP. Reliability and validity of information from chronic heroin users. *J Psychiatr Res* 12:87, 1975.
10. Federal Drug Administration regulations (21 CFR 21). *Federal Register.* March 2, 1989.
11. Kleber HD. Opioids: Detoxification, in Galanter M, Kleber HD (eds), *Textbook of Substance Abuse Treatment.* Washington, DC, American Psychiatric Press, 1995, pp 191–208.

12. Dole VP, Nyswander ME. Methadone maintenance treatment: A ten year perspective. *JAMA* 235:2117, 1978.
13. Gritz ER, Shiffman SM, Jarvik ME, et al. Physiologic and psychological effects of methadone in man. *Arch Genl Psychiatry* 32:237–242, 1975.
14. O'Brien CP. Opioids: Antagonists and partial agonists, in Galanter M, Kleber HD (eds), *Textbook of Substance Abuse Treatment.* Washington, DC, American Psychiatric Press, 1995, pp 223–236.
15. DeLeon G. Therapeutic communities, in Galanter M, Kleber HD (eds), *Textbook of Substance Abuse Treatment.* Washington, DC, American Psychiatric Press, 1995, pp 391–414.
16. Yablonsky W. *Synanon: The Tunnel Back.* New York, Macmillan, 1965.
17. Densen-Gerber J. *We Mainline Dreams: The Odyssey House Story.* Garden City, NY, Doubleday, 1973.
18. Senay EC. Multimodality programming in Illinois: Evolution of a public health concept, in Lowinson JH, Ruiz P, *Substance Abuse: Clinical Problems and Perspectives.* Baltimore, MD, Williams & Wilkins, 1981.
19. Karch SB. *The Pathology of Drug Abuse*, ed 2. Boca Raton, FL, CRC Press, 1996.
20. Finegan LP. Perinatal substance abuse: Comments and perspectives. *Semin Perinatol* 15:331–339, 1991.
21. Finegan LP, Kaltenbach K. Neonatal abstinence syndrome, in Hoelkelman RA, Friedman SB, Nelson NM (eds), *Primary Care*, ed 3. St Louis, MO, CV Mosby, 1992, pp 1367–1378.

ADDITIONAL READINGS

Ball JC, Ross A. *The Effectiveness of Methadone Maintenance Treatment.* New York, Springer Verlag, 1991.
Hubbard RL. Evaluation and treatment outcome, in Lowinson JH, Ruiz P, *Substance Abuse: Clinical Problems and Perspectives.* Baltimore, MD, Williams & Wilkins, 1992.
Platt J. *Heroin Addiction: Theory, Research and Treatment,* ed 2, vols 1–3. Malabar, FL, Kreiger Press, 1986, 1995.
Sells S. *Evaluation of Treatments*, vols 1–5. Cambridge, MA, Ballinger Press, 1974–1976.

5. *Methadone Treatment and Therapeutic Communities*

This chapter reviews material relevant to the needs of a clinician working in a methadone treatment clinic or in a therapeutic community. It centers on common clinical problems; the reader's familiarity with the material in the preceding four chapters of this book is assumed.

METHADONE TREATMENT

PHARMACOLOGY

Methadone is an opiate (in current pharmacologic parlance, opioid) drug that acts at the mu, or morphine, receptor. Methadone, therefore, has pain-relieving and dependence-producing effects almost exactly like those of morphine. Methadone, like other members of the class of opioid drugs, such as heroin, codeine, meperidine, and so forth, produces dose dependent euphoria/intoxication, but the degree of this effect is significantly clinically different among these drugs. Heroin is di-acetyl morphine. More rapid and complete transfer of the acetylated morphine across the blood-brain barrier accounts for the difference in the rapidity of onset and intensity of euphoria between heroin and morphine, and for the fact that addicts do not put as high a value on methadone because its effects, like those of morphine, are not as rapid in onset and not as intense.

Pain relief from methadone has a time course identical with that of morphine, but suppression of opioid withdrawal by methadone lasts for 24 to 36 hours, in contrast with 3 to 6 hours for morphine. Methadone also differs from morphine in that it is effective when taken by mouth. The two characteristics of oral effectiveness and longer suppression of the opioid withdrawal syndrome make methadone a logical and effective drug for legal maintenance treatment of opioid dependent persons.

In addition to these advantages over other drugs, such as heroin, that might be selected for legal substitution therapy, methadone has a substantial margin between suppression of the opioid withdrawal syndrome and the production of intoxication. It is possible, therefore, to provide sustained relief from opioid withdrawal while avoiding intoxication or other behaviorally toxic effects that might impair a person's ability to operate a machine or to make reasoned judgments. It is important to stress that methadone maintained patients have pursued every occupation necessary to the functioning of urban life without problems from behavioral toxicity.[1, 2]

METHADONE STABILIZATION

While there is a lot of intraindividual and interindividual variability in methadone metabolism, for many patients body pools of the drug build up over days or weeks and reach a stabilization level that patients experience as being "normalized." This means that there is a time gap between original administration and optimal effect. It is important to educate patients about this delay so they accept that stabilization is not immediate. Over a period of weeks, withdrawal may be suppressed slowly, but patients may report mild withdrawal or mild withdrawal with craving, or perhaps craving without other withdrawal symptoms. If craving persists or leads to heroin use, then the dosage should be raised to whatever level eliminates the craving.

Patients on methadone are tolerant to the usual doses of street heroin (in most cases, between 5 and 20 mg), so there is not much point in a patient spending money on heroin when taking properly prescribed methadone.

STABILIZATION/MAINTENANCE DOSE

After a period of days or weeks, a pool of methadone is built up in the body. The size of this pool relative to the daily dose can be large, as it is common for patients who miss a daily dose not to experience any consequences whatsoever. This pool also accounts for the counterintuitive fact that methadone maintenance patients needing analgesia require additional analgesics (e.g., codeine, meperidine) in usual doses at the usual frequencies for analgesic effects to occur. Analgesic effects require some relatively substantial increase in plasma levels from a given dose, and this does not occur with methadone as it is used in maintenance.

RAPID METHADONE METABOLIZERS

There are occasional patients who biotransform methadone rapidly (i.e., 12 to 20 hours versus 24 to 36 hours). They can take a dose sufficient to suppress withdrawal in most patients, but they will not have full 24-hour effects because they metabolize methadone so quickly. The clinic can test such patients by giving an observed dose (while checking to ensure that the patient is not "cheeking," or sequestering some of the dose in the mouth) and then taking urine samples 24 hours later. Frequently, such patients are reported as negative but, in fact, have positive levels for methadone metabolites. These levels, however, are below the National Institute on Drug Abuse (NIDA) cut-off levels for positive, so it is important to ask the lab for the actual levels in these cases. Laboratories frequently only report positive or negative and do not give levels unless asked.

Assessment of these patients is complicated because physical and/or psychological stress, independent of any other factors, can speed the metabolism of methadone. Weather extremes, marital or job stress, concurrent illness and drug use—particularly alcohol and cocaine—all appear to have this effect. The assessment of these patients must include a search for all these factors. Trouble confined to weekends may suggest intoxicant use or family quarrels. Those who metabolize rapidly can, of course, have all the stresses other patients do. If the stress is job related (e.g., a patient gets a job in a dry-cleaning business and is suddenly exposed to sustained high temperatures), a dose increase is indicated. If the dose increase has to be higher than current FDA rules permit to achieve good suppression of withdrawal, as it often is (e.g., 120 mg/day), then the single state agency (SSA) should be contacted and an exception to the rules obtained. This requires a brief description of the problem with a justification for an exception to the regulations. The U.S. clinician should appreciate that in the European harm-reduction model, doses of methadone up to 300–500 mg per day are sometimes used, and are sometimes given intravenously.

If the stress is related to other drug use, then the level of treatment should be increased to reverse the stress without increasing the dose. If there are no stress factors or if all other measures fail, the patient may be a true rapid metabolizer, and the dose should be raised high enough to achieve the desired state of full suppression of withdrawal without sedation or euphoria. This may require doses in the range of 120 to 200 mg per day, and, in rare cases, higher.

Payte obtains blood levels of methadone in problem cases.[3] In general, blood ranges from 120 to 600 ng are associated with desirable effects. Payte states that the peak-to-trough ratio is the critical focus; when it is over 2 a rapid metabolizer is identified (e.g., peak of 500 ng, trough of 250 ng). Part of the problem clinically is that withdrawal complaints are not specific to opioid withdrawal; they may be related to drug interactions or to conditions such as HIV that cause sweating, nausea, and the like. Borg and colleagues[4] studied patients with four or more withdrawal complaints versus those with fewer symptoms and found a correlation between the withdrawal complaints and either low methadone plasma levels or the presence of some complicating medical condition such as Paget's disease, hypertension, or HIV positivity. Determination of plasma levels may be critical in determining the source of withdrawal complaints and in deciding on the proper dose level.

Methadone is an opiate and therefore has no role to play in the treatment of cocaine dependence. Cocaine is sometimes called a narcotic in legal documents, but cocaine is, of course, a stimulant drug and not an opiate.

SIDE EFFECTS

The side effects of methadone are identical to those of morphine—constipation, sweating, occasional nonmalignant edema in females (especially in the summer), and, occasionally, diminution or loss of libido. When these effects occur in maintenance treatment, they usually go away with time and/or dose reduction. Constipation can be troublesome for a few patients; this can be treated by giving stool softeners, advising patients to increase water intake, and reducing the dose if necessary. Sweating can be severe in a few patients, but in my experience, some patients do not want their dose lowered and prefer to accept the sweating. Others with this problem accepted dose reductions that resulted in diminishment or elimination of the problem.

There are four cases in the literature of severe edema from methadone.[5] Methadone had to be discontinued in these patients.

METHADONE EFFECTIVENESS

Methadone has been studied in thousands of addicts who have been followed for periods of as long as 12 years. The only legitimate question to ask about methadone is whether or not medically prescribed methadone decreases or eliminates the use of heroin or other opioids. We have massive data on this question, and there is no ambiguity in the results. Methadone reduces heroin use in many and eliminates it for a significant fraction of patients. Because addicts are heterogeneous and have a variety of problems, many of which are severe, different programs may have widely different success rates independent of their methods and quality of treatment due to their different populations of addicts. Methadone, for example, cannot alter antisocial personality disorder, but it can and does alter the use of heroin by addicts with this disorder. In relation to the reduction of heroin use, crime rates go down by a factor of eight when addicts are medically maintained. There are also modest gains in employment, psychological functioning, and health status.

Since results from this treatment are the classical one third (get better), one third (vacillate between better and worse), and one third (do not change lifestyle and continue to live for crime and drugs), one can see what one wants to see when looking at methadone programs. The subtlety is that before methadone treatment, there was no known method for generating either the third who do well or the third who vacillate between "street" and "straight."

In the age of AIDS, one effect of methadone deserves special mention: the provision of legal methadone reduces substantially the use and exchange of needles by heroin addicts, with the consequence that addicts who enter methadone programs and, particularly, those who do well on methadone have much lower rates of seropositivity for HIV than those who did not.[6, 7]

Both clinical and research streams of data confirm that heroin addicts tend to use treatment to abort episodes of heroin dependence, and that they often leave programs before they should. Relapse rates are high when this occurs. But there is no question that there is a significant amelioration of the morbidity and mortality of a treated versus an untreated career of heroin addiction. As the careers mature, heroin addicts tend to use methadone programs in preference to therapeutic communities, whereas at younger ages, more of them, relatively speaking, try residential treatment.

SAFETY

Even the most rabid methadone critics do not debate the safety of properly administered methadone. We have decades of experience, and it indicates that methadone is safe when used as prescribed. Because methadone is an opioid, it can cause death by respiratory depression in overdose, and the use of other drugs may increase the potential for respiratory depression. The press periodically publishes the results of coroners' reports about "methadone related" deaths, many of which were of patients who were in methadone maintenance programs at the time of their death. When one inquires as to the criteria that have to be met to make such a diagnosis, one finds that there are none. Indeed, in the usual case reported as methadone related, several other drugs are detected. Many of these drugs could cause death independent of any interaction with methadone (e.g., cocaine, alcohol, sedative/hypnotics with or without alcohol).

As discussed by Karch, levels of methadone in maintenance patients overlap the levels found in so-called methadone related deaths when no other drugs are detected.[8] Karch concludes, "It is difficult, if not impossible, to distinguish between overdose and maintenance dose on the basis of toxicology testing alone." In one case reported as a heroin-related death, I observed in the autopsy report that the patient had a bullet hole through the center of the forehead, in addition to having morphine in the urine screen. I wondered why the death was not called "bullet related." It may be necessary to educate the press about the questions to be asked when writing these kinds of reports.

PROCEDURES

Medical monitoring of methadone is governed by federal and state rules and regulations.[9] Only physicians in licensed (by the Food and Drug Administration [FDA], the Drug Enforcement Administration [DEA], and single state agencies [SSAs]) programs can prescribe methadone for treatment of opiate dependence, but any physician can prescribe methadone for pain if there are legitimate indications for such use. Eligibility requires at least one year of dependence except for pregnant addicts and addicts younger than age 18.

FEDERAL AND STATE ELIGIBILITY CRITERIA FOR METHADONE MAINTENANCE

Methadone can be used for analgesia by any licensed physician, but it can only be used for the treatment of opioid dependence by a physician working in a treatment facility licensed by the agencies cited above. States can have criteria more stringent than those established by the FDA, but they cannot have less-stringent criteria. States differ in eligibility criteria and in a variety of regulations on such matters as take-home methadone. By federal mandate, each state must have an single state agency (SSA) that licenses and coordinates drug treatment and prevention programs. If there are questions about eligibility criteria, these SSAs should be consulted. The FDA's eligibility criteria for methadone maintenance, which is defined as the use of methadone for the treatment of narcotic dependence for more than 90 days, are:

Current physiologic dependence on opioids. A one-year history of physiologic dependence on opioids must be present together with current physiologic dependence as demonstrated by positive urine for opioids, needle tracks, and signs and symptoms of opioid withdrawal. The regulations do not specify any particular subset of the foregoing criteria for current physiologic dependence; it is a medical judgment that physiologic dependence exists. The regulations require that the judgment be based on some of the criteria. An addict, for example, may never have used needles and can still have acquired a substantial degree of physiologic dependence by "snorting" or insufflating opioids. The physiologic dependence on opioids must have existed episodically or continuously for a one-year period. If the addict has a history of only six to seven months of dependence during a given year, the physician should request an exception to the rules from the SSA before beginning a treatment regimen of methadone maintenance.

Persons from penal institutions. A person who has been in a penal institution is eligible for methadone maintenance after a period of incarceration without current physiologic dependence on opioids if eligibility criteria were met before entering the penal institution.

Pregnant patients. Pregnant patients can be placed on methadone maintenance if they are currently physiologically dependent on opioids. There is no stipulation that the dependence must have existed for one year in the case of the pregnant addict, simply that physiologic dependence is current. A physician can place a pregnant addict who has been opioid dependent in the past on methadone maintenance without current physiologic dependence, if return to opioid dependence is a threat.

Previously treated patients. For a two-year period following an episode of methadone maintenance, patients may be readmitted without evidence of current physiologic dependence if the physician documents that return to opioid dependence is imminent.

Persons under 18 years of age. Persons under 18 must have two documented attempts at drug detoxification or drug free treatment with a one-week period between treatment episodes, and they must show evidence of current physiologic dependence on opioids to be eligible for methadone maintenance. A parent, legal guardian, or responsible adult designated by state authority must also complete and sign an official FDA consent form (obtainable from the SSA) to complete the eligibility criteria.

These criteria may vary in that a state can elect to be more stringent; for example, states can require two years of physiologic dependence before methadone maintenance is legal, or they may make the rules for take-home methadone more stringent. FDA regulations permit programs to dispense one or two take-home doses of methadone after a three- to six-month period of good performance in treatment. Some states require longer periods of good performance, and some may not permit take-home doses at all.

If a patient has current physiologic dependence on opioids but does not meet these criteria, methadone can be used for detoxification for up to a 90-day period. This use is defined by FDA regulations as methadone detoxification.

METHADONE MAINTENANCE PROGRAMS

The usual methadone maintenance program offers one-to-one counseling, frequently with an ex-addict counselor, along with a variety of group experiences such as AA or NA, different support groups for women's issues and men's issues, withdrawal groups, educational or vocational training groups, HIV risk-prevention education groups, and minority issues sensitivity groups. The group part of the program tends to differ widely among methadone programs, and some programs involve relatively little group work. In addition to one-to-one counseling and groups, the patient gives urine samples on a more or less regular schedule. Some of these are tested and some are not, but the patient never knows which. Urine results and general program performance determine the take-home dose schedule, which in most clinics is used to reinforce abstinence-promoting behavior.

Since travel to most clinics in early months of treatment is daily, or near daily, many patients find this onerous, and the issue of "take homes" is a sensitive one. With good performance, patients can win take-home privileges after a few weeks or months. Most clinics have some capacity for psychiatric consultation, although such resources are in short supply in most communities.

The physician's role is to make decisions about dose changes in consultation with the patient and, in some clinics, the patient and counselor. The physician also signs off on treatment plans and their usual 90-day updates. The clinic physician is also busy assessing patients' needs for a variety of medical and surgical services. With the advent of HIV, an important task for the clinic physician is monitoring for drug interactions and providing support for dying patients. Physicians differ in their interest in and ability to become involved with many of the activities of a clinic. The Center for Substance Abuse Treatment (CSAT) and the American Society of Addiction Medicine have a very rich assortment of publications for the physician wanting to learn about addiction medicine in depth (see additional resources at the end of this chapter). CSAT also has excellent manuals for learning about minority and ethnic group issues.

As part of a general stigmatization of drug abuse and of those who try to treat it, the physician working in a drug treatment program soon comes to appreciate that drug treatment programs are isolated from primary care and from mental health service systems. The physician frequently has to make repeated inquiries about possible referrals, and this can be time-consuming.

Dose. Dosing decisions are medical matters. Counselors, nurses, and program administrators can and should be part of the information gathering carried out by the physician who is making dose decisions. But ultimately, the physician must decide. If the program has "low dose" policies, the physician should try to educate the program by presenting the data referred to in this text. The physician cannot, on ethical grounds, be part of administrative decisions about methadone that are punitive. This is discussed further in the Administrative Detoxification section. Many hospitals do not carry methadone because they want to avoid the administrative hassles. When methadone maintenance patients need hospitalization, this can be a problem. The program physician should confer with the admitting physician; the usual compromise is that the program delivers the maintenance methadone to the hospital for delivery to the patient. The program physician frequently has to remind the admitting physician or hospital administrator that detoxification is a major stress that could have very serious medical and perhaps legal consequences if combined with other stresses.

Patients' beliefs about methadone. Street lore has is that methadone "gets in your bones," with the result that bones are weakened. Other street beliefs are that methadone rots teeth and damages sexual organs. None of these beliefs has any basis whatsoever in medical evidence, and patients need to know this. I suspect the notion of bone weakening has a basis in experience that the minimally dependent patient has when receiving a higher dose of methadone relative to that of heroin "on the street."[10] Such a patient has heard about bone pain in withdrawal but has never had a strong enough dependence to experience it directly. With chronic, daily administration of methadone, the patient in withdrawal may experience bone pain for the first time and, quite understandably, may attribute this to some direct effect of methadone on the bones.

For females on maintenance, frequently there is a return of menstrual cycles and fertility that street life had diminished or abolished. So the street notion that there is damage to sexual organs is in error.

Patients vary considerably in the degree to which they want to participate in dosing decisions.[11, 12] Some do not want to know their dose and are content to let the clinic physician determine it. Others want to be actively involved, and if they want this, they should have it. The patient should be a full partner in dosing decisions, or at least should be told that he or she can be if desired. If the patient prefers to let the physician handle these decisions, then it is an effective way to do things. Research carried out in two different centers indicates that it does not make any difference who controls dose decisions.[11, 12]

A few patients have phobic concerns and may insist on seeing their dose prepared, as they fear that staff is stealing or somehow mishandling the medicine. There have been instances of staff stealing medicine, and all possibilities must be considered. If the possibility of staff stealing seems remote, the patient should be told that he or she has a phobia about the medicine and that it is not possible, on a routine basis, for the patient to see the dose prepared. Most medication is prepackaged in a quiet atmosphere to minimize the mistakes that can occur if a nurse or pharmacist is busy responding to hurried patients. Increasingly, doses are prepacked by automated procedures; I expect that in the not-too-distant future, computer-driven pumps will create almost all doses.

Consonant with modern understanding that patients are competent adults with a right to know what is being done for them and to them, patients should be full partners in dose changes. A patient who is a full partner in such decisions feels respected and communicated with. A paradigm like this produces a patient who is going to do better, in all spheres, than was the case with the more authoritarian arrangements in many of the early programs.

Blind dose changes. Since trust is so important an issue in a disorder such as heroin dependence, changing a patient's dose without obtaining an explicit agreement with the patient that this might occur is not acceptable practice. Patients need to feel that they are secure against such manipulation. Moreover, in the current environment of possible lawsuits, the doctor breaking this rule could be in serious trouble.

Initial dose. FDA regulations limit the initial dose to 40 mg. Additional doses may be administered on the first day, but there must be documentation in the chart that the dose of 40 mg did not suppress withdrawal satisfactorily. In most U.S. venues, the initial dose should not be greater than 10 to 20 mg, perhaps 30 mg, as the history of recent drug use may be in error, and overdose is thus a risk. Thirty mg of methadone given to a naive subject can be expected to produce considerable sedation. If the patient is using other drugs, as is often the case, or may use them after leaving the clinic, there is risk of potentiation of sedative effects with consequent overdose. In the late 1960s and early 1970s, the starting dose was often 40 mg, and there were no problems. But over the years, the dose of street heroin has gone down, and in the modern setting extra caution is advisable.

If addicts view the treatment center with trust, as they usually do in established programs, their histories are as valid as histories in any other branch of medicine and can be used to judge the amount of the initial dose. One should obtain a quantity-and-frequency history for the preceding three weeks, together with a judgment by the addict of the potency of the heroin he or she has been using. If the addict has been using once or twice a day and rates the potency as low, one would prescribe a 10 mg dose. If the addict has been injecting four or five times a day and rates the potency as high, a dose of 20 mg would be indicated. The optimal procedure is to observe the effects of the dose with respect to both the amelioration of signs and symptoms of opioid withdrawal and the induction of euphoria or sedation. One should explain to the patient that the object is to find a dose that is sufficient to suppress withdrawal without inducing intoxication.

Stabilization/maintenance dose. There is current and important literature critical of agencies or clinics whose policies limit duration of treatment for methadone maintenance and/or place arbitrary, nonclinical limits on the dose that can be prescribed for methadone maintenance.[13-15]

This literature is of major importance on the policy level, as it calls attention to the destructive aspects of policies whose net effects are to send addicts back to the streets in the age of HIV; but on the clinical level it is, in some cases, problematic because it has been taken by some to mean that every patient needs a dose of 60 mg per day or higher. This implies a degree of homogeneity in dose requirements that is at variance with ordinary clinical experience. Although the preponderance of evidence indicates, from a statistical perspective, that patients do better at doses above 60 mg/day, common clinical experience indicates that, to do well, not every methadone maintenance patient needs 60 mg or more of methadone per day. There is a substantial minority who can do well at every dose range, and there is no compelling rationale for trying to raise a patient to higher levels of methadone as long as he or she continues to do well.

There is a compelling rationale for adjusting the dose to the "enough" level. Most patients feel, and I agree with them, that withdrawal is more difficult and prolonged the higher the dose. The clinical implication of this is that one wants to obtain desirable effects from the methadone at the lowest possible dose. The clinician should appreciate that, in general, there is a nonlinear correspondence between dose level and degree of severity of withdrawal during detoxification. Patients taking 10 mg per day will have less pronounced and shorter withdrawal periods than patients taking 100 mg per day, but there may be little difference between those taking 40 mg per day and those taking 60 mg per day.

Methadone maintenance is demanding of patients, and they almost always have hope that someday they will be free of street heroin and of methadone treatment. It is this hope that creates understandable resistance to high doses in many patients.

Some patients report feeling like a "zombie" at doses of 40 to 50 mg/day and do not want or accept continuation of such doses. There are clinically significant differences in dose based on idiosyncratic biological and psychological factors. For example, expectations and beliefs about methadone can influence how high or low a dose can be; individuals differ, from time to time, in the dose required for stabilization depending on stress levels, abuse of alcohol or other drugs, additional necessary medications, and chronic fatigue in response to the burdens of treatment (e.g., regular travel to and from the clinic, waiting in lines for counseling and medication). Finally, some patients differ sharply from others in that they are rapid metabolizers, presenting still another clinically important source of variation.

Clinical experience teaches that methadone maintenance patients distribute themselves along a broad spectrum. At one end there are patients who view everything that happens to them as a function of an inadequate dose. Some of these are probably trying to get a high enough dose to cover their habit while having some left over to sell on the street or perhaps to give to a heroin-addicted spouse/friend who is not in treatment. The other end of the spectrum is represented by addicts who are primarily concerned with minimizing the strength of their methadone habit. Patients in the middle of the spectrum tend to want enough to suppress withdrawal while not acquiring too strong a habit. The best basis for decision making is to observe the effects of doses on the patient for a few hours. In some European countries, regulations permit dosing of methadone without limits, and some clinics dispense doses of 200 to 300 mg/day and even higher.

At this writing there is some activity at the federal level to change the way in which methadone is regulated, but there is nothing concrete. If there are changes, I will write a summary of them and send it to readers free of charge. My address is: 17 East Road, Chesterton, IN 46304.

"High dose" versus "low dose" programs.[16, 17] While statistics suggest that programs with high-dose policies (i.e., an average of 60 mg per day or greater) have more successful patient populations, some of the success of such clinics may be attributable to differences in patient populations being served, size of the clinic, stability of staff, some modicum of community acceptance, adequate funding, and other factors.

Low-dose programs that limit doses to the 40 to 60 mg/day range err in not being flexible enough to recognize that some patients need higher doses to achieve good outcomes. The clinical rule is that one size does not fit all. In a research clinic I was associated with, consisting of long-term, highly successful methadone maintenance patients, the range in doses was from 8 mg/day to 100 mg/day. Patients knew they could get whatever dose they felt they needed. All that was required for an increase was a statement from the patient that he or she had considered the consequences carefully. In such a setting, the average dose for males was 53 mg and for females 43 mg, with patients scattered throughout the dose range at every level.

Even after a patient is stable, the dose that yields the most desirable results may go up or down over the years. We have no good explanation for this variability, but it appears to exist in many cases. Some maintain success with the same dose over decades.

Some patients continually try to raise their dose. Clinical decisions in such cases should be based on observation of the addict at the end of a 24-hour period following the last dose. If there are such signs as elevated pulse, sweating, piloerection, or pupillary dilation, more methadone is indicated. If there are no signs, one should tell the patient that with time, a few weeks perhaps, the body pool of methadone will slowly rise, and craving and mild withdrawal will disappear. Methadone is saleable on the street, and there are a variety of incentives to "hustle" the doctor for more methadone. But this observation must be balanced by the experience that there are many patients who give up "hustling" and do not want, do not seek, and will not accept high doses of methadone.

WITHDRAWAL IN METHADONE MAINTAINED PATIENTS

During a withdrawal attempt, the physician should consider doing it "blind," making an agreement with the patient that the physician will maintain or adjust the dose in response to what the patient is reporting, but without informing the patient. Many addicts like this arrangement, as they recognize the "head trip" aspect of withdrawal symptoms. If addicts want to control their own detoxification, however, they should be permitted to do so in consultation with the program physician.

When patients want to withdraw, they should be counseled to go slowly—on an outpatient basis, the dose should be reduced by about 3 percent per week, with even slower rates as the dose gets below 25 mg per day. It is these lower doses that are the most difficult to withdraw from, and the patient needs extra support and contact during this time. I tell successful methadone maintenance patients who seek my advice on the likelihood of successful withdrawal that there is a 50 percent chance that they will fail in their withdrawal attempt and go back on methadone maintenance. They will usually return to maintenance because they see that they will otherwise lose their job, spouse, or health. One in four patients withdraws successfully and does not need maintenance again, while one in four goes back to the street lifestyle and winds up in jail or perhaps dead.

Withdrawal from methadone maintenance should not be done quickly or without careful planning with the patient and, if relevant, the family. Spouses sometimes put pressure on patients to withdraw when they are not ready for such an attempt. In these cases, the physician should educate the spouse about the probabilities of success of withdrawal attempts and try to understand the source of the pressure for withdrawal.

The need for slow withdrawal, with probable need for pauses, should be stressed. Frequently, patients do not recognize the amount of stress related to withdrawal and have understandable but unrealistic notions about it ("My wife's birthday is next month, and I want to surprise her and be clean by then"; "I'm going to move to a place in the country next month and want to be clean when I move").

THE FAILING PATIENT

While some in treatment make a complete break with the drug culture and adopt a middle-class lifestyle, a substantial fraction do not change from a lifestyle centered on intoxication. These patients often reduce their use of heroin, but they begin to use other intoxicants such as alcohol, marijuana, cocaine, and a variety of sedative/hypnotics, either for their primary effects or to create a state of intoxication from the medically administered methadone. This is described as "boosting" the effects of the methadone.

Many programs are structured so that a patient is given a six- to twelve month period to change lifestyles (sometimes this period is shorter and sometimes longer). I believe one year is the minimum necessary to determine whether patients can begin to make headway with their problems. If they continue to use heroin and/or other drugs, a decision has to be made concerning continued maintenance. Almost every clinic has a waiting list, and the needs of the people on it have to be weighed in making decisions about failing patients. It is worth considering a substantial rise in a failing patient's methadone dose to see if he or she is a rapid metabolizer whose good motivation is being weakened by severe withdrawal, or perhaps is a normal metabolizer who is just underdosed. One might raise the dose by 30 to 80 mg/day before giving up on such a patient. It is best to work in increments of 5 or 10 mg increases every few days, or perhaps each week to 10 days. If a patient is in clear withdrawal 24 hours after taking a known dose, then a 10 mg increment should be tried and the patient observed on the next day. If there is some lessening of the severity of the withdrawal, another 5 mg can be added to the total daily dose. If there is no impact, then another 10 mg should be added, with the observation process continued the next day and the cycle repeated until there is resolution.

If dose manipulation does not change the situation and it appears that the patient is not reducing criminal behavior, is not reducing needle sharing or using, and is using the methadone for no purpose other than to save the money required to buy heroin, the patient should be placed on administrative detoxification. The treatment slot can then be opened to a patient who may use it for positive results. It is destructive to the clinic to have too large a fraction of patients who are not moving out of the drug culture. They form negative cliques and essentially destroy the culture of recovery. Every attempt should be made to move the failing patient to a different level of care, such as a therapeutic community or day care, or perhaps to another clinic or another city.

The failing case is almost always enmeshed in a family and neighborhood that are not friendly to people trying to get clean. I had a patient whose family and extended family were involved in lucrative heroin dealing. The patient wanted to try to overcome her dependence on heroin and had a real desire to do so, as evidenced by her active, honest participation in the treatment program. She attended every group and every one-to-one counseling session, but after a period of six months she was still using. She had relatives in another city who were "straight," and treatment in my clinic concluded with her recognition that she had to move if she were to have any chance to get out of the drug culture. The enmeshment problem has to be identified and responded to by working with the patient on these issues.

THE MYTH OF "21-DAY DETOX"

There is no such thing and never was any such thing, from a clinical point of view, as a 21-day detoxification. This length of time for detoxification of an addict who did not meet the criteria for maintenance was an administrative decision made without reference to clinical realities. The rules have been changed so that any heroin dependent person not meeting criteria for maintenance can be withdrawn in 90 days. When an addict is, or even has been, eligible for methadone maintenance, one can take whatever time one wants for a detoxification attempt. For anyone physically dependent on heroin, a 21-day attempt to withdraw is a recipe for rapid return to street opiates. It is too fast for the patient with any substantial degree of physical dependence.

METHADONE DIVERSION

The FDA regulates methadone for a number of reasons, perhaps the most important of which is methadone diversion. When practitioners were unregulated, a few dispensed methadone freely and created a diversion problem, methadone "fountains" or "filling stations." The problem of diversion must be weighed against the benefits of methadone maintenance programs. Most communities conclude that diversion at low levels appears to be an unavoidable consequence of methadone programs. The clinical expression of this problem comes from patients "working" the doctor for doses higher than are needed for valid clinical purposes so that they can sell the methadone on the street. The best safeguard for the physician is to make judgments about dose based on observations of the patient's clinical status.

If diversion is suspected, one can institute procedures such as observed ingestion of one or more doses every week, limits on take-homes, and the like. Studies of diversion indicate that the diverted methadone is used by some for intoxication, but that others use it to attempt to withdraw from heroin dependence. Many people on the street using heroin state that the rules of methadone programs are onerous, and they prefer to continue using heroin to meeting treatment requirements. They form the primary market for diverted methadone.

If a patient has admitted to or been detected selling his or her methadone, a thorough clinical review is indicated. Frequently, small groups of patients are involved. Program limits need to be instituted for these individuals, or perhaps they should be transferred to another clinic or to a more intensive level of care, such as an intensive day program or therapeutic community. Diversion should be the focus of proactive efforts in discussion with patients about the extremely negative effects on the clinic of diversion. Patient education and periodic reinforcement of the diversion message with notations of such discussions in the charts should be routine for all staff, the physician included.

ADMINISTRATIVE DETOXIFICATION

Most methadone clinics have what are called "cardinal rules," which place strict limits on certain behaviors—for example, threats of violence, selling of drugs or any goods in the clinic, the use of gang-related signals or colors, carrying weapons, or other behaviors that convert what should be a climate of hope and recovery in the clinic to a street-level climate in which recovery is impossible. The clinic then becomes an extension of the drugs-and-crime culture of the streets and loses its reason for being. Clinics must limit these behaviors if they are to survive. In private clinics dependent on fees, consistent nonpayment of fees must also elicit an administrative response. When the breach of rules is flagrant—such as threatening someone with a weapon—the offender has to be excluded from the clinic, and this usually means an administrative detoxification. If there are extenuating circumstances and a remorseful patient, transfer to another clinic may be an option. But the waiting lists of recent years make this less and less an option. The question arises of how the administrative detoxification should be carried out. Administrative detoxification can be offered either just before opening the nurses' station for dosing in the morning, or at the end of the day, to minimize contact of the patient being detoxified with other patients.

I feel strongly that the use of methadone must always be humane and therefore reject "cold turkey" or 21-day detoxification and the like. The detoxification should be carried out according to clinically indicated guidelines, which means that the detoxification should take whatever time is consistent with tolerable levels of withdrawal. With dose levels in the range of 60 mg/day and above, this usually means weeks if not months.

DRUG INTERACTIONS WITH METHADONE

Methadone interacts with a number of other drugs in clinically important ways. Most drugs that interact with methadone have an effect like stress, in that the metabolism of methadone is increased and the dose does not hold the patient for a full 24-hour dosing period.

Rifampin, a drug used to treat tuberculosis, may speed the metabolism of methadone and result in severe withdrawal. Increases in methadone dose of 50 percent or more may be necessary. A patient on methadone who has to take rifampin should be assured that if the rifampin causes withdrawal, the dose will be increased to the point of comfort. This may require a call to the state authority to get approval of a dose over 120 mg/day. When the rifampin is stopped after six to twelve months, adjustments of the dose may be required to avoid sedative effects. Patients taking these two drugs should be monitored carefully to see if dose increases are needed.

Zidovudine (AZT; Retrovir), a drug used in the treatment of HIV-related conditions, may also have the effect of speeding the metabolism of methadone and causing withdrawal. Methadone, in some patients, may interfere with the metabolism of zidovudine and result in zidovudine toxicity. Careful medical monitoring is important in HIV-positive patients taking methadone. With regular monitoring, the two drugs usually cause no problems; there are many methadone patients today taking both drugs without interactive effects.

A methadone maintained patient who is epileptic also requires regular monitoring, because phenytoin (Dilantin) and drugs from the barbiturate class, important in controlling epileptic symptoms, can speed the metabolism of methadone so that the patient may need dose increases. Again, these are possibilities that often do not materialize.

Cimetidine (Tagamet) interacts with methadone in an opposite direction from the drugs discussed above; it slows the metabolism of methadone and may result in sleepiness or other symptoms of methadone toxicity. With monitoring, the two drugs can be used together without incident.

Desipramine, a drug used to treat depression, may interact with methadone to cause sedation, but often it does not have this effect; usually the drugs can be used simultaneously without problems.

Carbamazepine is being explored as a withdrawal treatment for alcohol- and benzodiazepine dependent patients. It can speed the metabolism of methadone and needs to be monitored when used concurrently with methadone.

Drugs with sedative effects can have synergistic effects with methadone. Antidepressant drugs with sedative effects are sometimes used by patients to cause or "boost" the sedative/intoxicating effects of methadone.

Methadone does not interact significantly with most drugs used in psychiatry, such as lithium, phenothiazines, and nonsedating anxiolytics. Methadone can be used safely, with regular monitoring, with disulfiram (Antabuse).

With the rapid growth of knowledge, it is impossible for the clinician to remember all the drug interaction possibilities. I recommend subscribing to a computer program such as the Drug Interaction Program (DIP) produced by the *Medical Letter.*[18] With this program, one can print out or store to disk the interactions and the references on which they are based. In the chapter on dual diagnosis, the value of the DIP is demonstrated by showing what a clinician can get from such a program.

POTENTIAL PROBLEMS FOR THE PHYSICIAN

One common problem for methadone maintenance physicians is a patient who attempts to use one staff member against another or against the program administration. The doctor is not immune to these attempts. In general, the physician should reflect such attempts back by asking the question, "Isn't that something you are bringing to your counselor?" or, "Why are you bringing this to me?" It is best that the program be explicit with the patient that staff members communicate about patients and do not keep secrets from one another. All methadone patients are given a written description of their rights, and one of these rights is the right to appeal to the single state agency, if they feel the program is mistreating them. Of course, the patient may have a legitimate problem. In this event, a case conference among all parties should be held. It is good practice for the physician to confine activities to the medical arena and reflect counseling concerns by telling the patient to take nonmedical issues to the counseling staff.

Patients sometimes ask the doctor's view of whether they should advise a potential employer that they are on methadone. This is a sensitive issue best referred by the physician to counseling. There is no good answer, and the patient is best served by a careful review of the pros and cons. Patients should be assisted in the exploration but should make the decision themselves. Similar questions are sometimes raised about spouses or significant others in the patient's life who are not aware that the patient is taking methadone, or that the patient had a dependence in the past.

A clinical cue that a patient is trying to work the physician to get higher doses than needed is when the physician observes that the patient is studying the physician rather than the reverse. Addict patients who obtain money by "conning" are sometimes very adroit at reading people and attempt this on everybody in the program, physicians included. Sedative/hypnotics are sometimes the goal of such attempts. If sedative/hypnotics are to be used, there should be an explicit written goal (i.e., dealing with a target symptom or symptoms within a specific time frame). Methadone maintenance patients have all the problems other people have, including stress reactions. When the patient is withdrawing or in the stabilization phase, sleep may be a problem; it is legitimate to give sedatives, but in small amounts and for brief periods. I usually advise patients not to take sedative/hypnotics every night. Every other night, or every third night, helps, while minimizing the potential for creating another dependency. Needless to say, such use should be carefully monitored and use of any of these drugs on a chronic basis avoided.

OTHER DRUGS FOR LEGAL OPIOID SUBSTITUTION TREATMENT

L–ALPHA–ACETYL–METHADOL

L-alpha-acetyl-methadol (LAAM) is a congener of methadone and is now approved for use in the treatment of opiate dependence in the United States. A number of studies have established that LAAM and methadone are equivalent in producing success, but it appears that each affects a slightly different subset of patients. FDA regulations limit the use of LAAM by forbidding take-home doses and requiring females to have monthly pregnancy tests, which, if positive, require the patient to shift to methadone. The safety of LAAM in pregnancy has not been established. LAAM has a long duration of action, 48 to 72 hours. This means that dosing can take place every two days or the more usual Monday, Wednesday, and Friday, which contrasts with the daily dosing necessary with methadone.

Pharmacology. LAAM itself is active, but most of its effects are attributable to its two metabolites, nor-LAAM and dinor-LAAM. These metabolites are formed slowly, so the onset of action is delayed relative to methadone. The time to reach steady state with LAAM is roughly twice that of methadone: 8 to 20 days for LAAM and 5 to 8 days for methadone. The stabilization period is therefore longer with LAAM in the modal patient. The slow onset of action carries the danger that users of LAAM who are taking it to become intoxicated may think they have taken a low dose and take more, with the consequence that they may overdose. This possibility probably underlies the FDA's prohibition on take-home LAAM. The equipotent dose between LAAM and methadone is calculated by multiplying the methadone dose by 1.2 or 1.3. It is sometimes necessary to give LAAM patients supplemental methadone in the induction phase, when emergencies arise, and when patients must travel. Once again, there are no circumstances in which take-home LAAM is permitted. When dosing schedules are three times per week, the Friday dose of LAAM is usually 20 to 40 percent higher than the Monday/Wednesday dose.

Side effects of LAAM are constipation (as would be expected with an opioid), nervousness, insomnia, sweating, tearing, and a variety of gastrointestinal and joint pains, which are probably related to withdrawal states. Hypertension and electrocardiographic changes have been reported, but there is no known relationship with LAAM for these findings. The clinical response is the same as that described for methadone. Many patients who have taken both methadone and LAAM report that LAAM is "lighter" than methadone. It is difficult for them to be more precise, but it appears that they experience methadone as a stronger drug. Many do not like this effect and therefore prefer LAAM.

In general, LAAM, as a mu agonist, has the same kinds of interactions with other drugs as methadone. The same cautions are in order for the use of sedative/hypnotics or other drugs used for dual diagnosis patients.

Eligibility. Both methadone and LAAM are subsumed in the FDA regulations, and the same eligibility criteria apply to both, with the exception of persons under 18 and females. Persons under 18 are not eligible for LAAM while they are eligible for methadone, if they have failed in other therapy. If a patient wants LAAM in preference to methadone, then the patient's choice should be respected.

The failing patient on methadone may be a candidate for LAAM to see whether pharmacologic change can improve performance. We do not know if rapid metabolizers of methadone are also rapid metabolizers of LAAM. In a rapid metabolizer, changing to LAAM is an option to explore with the patient. There are some juris-dictions that prohibit take-home methadone. In these areas, LAAM is an attractive alternative.

Induction phase. If a patient has been taking street heroin, the usual first dose of LAAM is calculated by taking a history of recent frequency of use and judging the strength of the heroin, exactly as described for methadone. One would then give a dose between 20 and 40 mg/day, once again erring on the low side to avoid over-dosing. Many patients have good relief from withdrawal relatively rapidly, but many others need dose adjustments upward in the induction period. Some will not be held for the full 48-hour interval, and they may be prescribed supplemental doses of methadone in the 10- to 20-mg range, depending on the severity of the symptoms. As always, observation of the patient after two days have elapsed or for a few hours after dosing provides clinical information that supplements the patient's history.

If a patient is switching from methadone maintenance to LAAM, the conversion is made with the dose-equivalence ratios described above. With close monitoring, the switches either way are usually not problematic.

The commonest problem is Sunday of the three-day weekend period when the Monday/Wednesday/Friday dosing schedule is used. The first remedy is to increase the Friday dose by 10 to 20 mg; the next is to add a supplemental dose of methadone for Sunday. It is important to educate the patient about these matters so that he or she is encouraged by the prospect of reaching stabilization. Prompt response to painful withdrawal is an important part of the always important matter of building a therapeutic alliance with the patient. Some clinicians use an every-two-days dosing schedule, but I have never had to do this. Raising the weekday doses by 10 to 20 mg and the Friday dose by 30 to 50 mg, with an occasional Sunday dose of supplemen-tal methadone, has always been effective for my patients.

Maintenance phase. As with methadone, the optimal dose of LAAM for most pa-tients is enough to achieve the goals of relief of withdrawal and the suppression of craving without sedation or euphoria.

FDA regulations limit the total daily dose of LAAM to 140 mg, but exceptions can be obtained from the single state agency with good justification. Patients distrib-ute themselves throughout the dose range, in parallel with methadone. The modal LAAM dose is 60 mg on Monday and Wednesday and 80 to 90 mg on Friday.

Studies indicate that females and males have about the same success rates on LAAM, but when females take LAAM, they have the burden of monthly pregnancy tests. If they become pregnant, they must be switched to methadone. The reverse change is made by giving a dose of methadone that is roughly 80 percent of the LAAM dose.

If patients need analgesia when on LAAM, their needs are exactly like the needs of methadone maintained patients; they require usual analgesics at usual doses and frequencies. Management of LAAM-maintained patients in the general hospital is as described for methadone.

Missed doses. If patients miss a week and do not use opioids in this time, their tol-erance will probably have been diminished. If they are not in withdrawal, the induction process should be started over from the 40 mg baseline. If patients have missed one dose and are in mild withdrawal, the clinician can give a small supplemental dose of methadone (10 to 20 mg, depending on the severity of the withdrawal) and resume the regular schedule. Observation of the patient and the history and urine screen results determine the correct dosing level and schedule. For vacations, when patients must be switched to methadone, if 80 percent of the LAAM dose is more than 100 mg, the single state agency should be petitioned for an exception. This takes planning and thorough justification to the agency.

Overdose with LAAM has the same concerns as overdose with methadone: naloxone lasts two hours, whereas methadone and LAAM last much longer. There is need for extended observation with both drugs and probable need for multiple naloxone administrations.

Withdrawal from LAAM can be accomplished with gradual dose reductions over an extended period, as is the case with methadone. The clinical path is determined by observation of the effects of dose reductions. Theoretically, LAAM should have a less severe withdrawal than methadone, but that is not my experience. The two drugs do not appear to be different in this regard. One can change back to methadone for the detoxification, but this is a matter of choice by the patient.

The range of clinical problems with LAAM does not differ from those of methadone, as covered above.

BUPRENORPHINE

Buprenorphine[19] is another product of the scientific search to find a pain reliever like morphine without morphine's potential for abuse and dependence.

Pharmacology. Buprenorphine is a partial agonist–antagonist. A partial agonist has effects like morphine, but they are limited to a lower dose range (0.3 mg of buprenorphine is equal to 10 mg of morphine for pain relief, but 0.6 mg does not have much more effect, and neither does 0.9). If a person is dependent on opiates, buprenorphine functions as an antagonist and precipitates withdrawal, with severity depending on the degree of physical dependence. Like methadone, buprenorphine suppresses withdrawal for 24 to 36 hours. It is not effective when swallowed, so its oral use is confined to sublingual administration; absorption through the membranes of the mouth takes a few minutes to occur. Buprenorphine has appeared on the drug scene in Europe. Its abuse/dependence liability in the U.S. is not yet fully determined.

Buprenorphine's slow release from receptor sites appears to ameliorate withdrawal in a highly desirable manner with mild, tolerable degrees of opiate withdrawal. It may turn out to be the standard way to detoxify opiate dependent people.

Clinical use. Buprenorphine is approved for use as a pain reliever but not for use in the treatment of opiate dependence.

Indications. Buprenorphine is approved for analgesia and is being explored in a number of research centers as a drug for maintenance and withdrawal treatment for opiate dependence. There was some evidence that buprenorphine not only had desirable effects on opioid seeking behavior but also appeared to influence cocaine use in opioid dependent populations in desirable directions. Other studies did not confirm these effects.

Dose. In maintenance treatment for opiate dependence, it is not yet determined whether 8, 16, or 64 mg sublingually per day is optimal.

Pregnancy. Buprenorphine is contraindicated in pregnancy because its safety has not been established.

Safety. Respiratory depression may occur in the therapeutic dose range, and naloxone may not reverse the depression. Buprenorphine is synergistic with many other drug classes with sedative properties, and the clinician must monitor for excessive sedation when it is used with these drugs.

Efficacy. In early studies, buprenorphine appears to be as effective as methadone for maintenance treatment of opioid dependence.

Drug interactions. Buprenorphine is contraindicated with CNS depressants. When used concurrently with diazepam, there is a risk of cardiovascular collapse. Buprenorphine's concurrent use with alcohol and monoamine oxidase inhibitors can lead to severe reactions. How these kinds of interactions will play out in treatment populations is not yet clear.

Pain relief in the buprenorphine-maintained patient may be problematic because of its antagonist actions.

This drug should be used only in research settings; if it is approved for use in maintenance, the physician prescribing the drug should receive some training in its use. Given the potentials for drug interactions described above, buprenorphine's role in either maintenance or withdrawal treatment is not yet determined.

THERAPEUTIC COMMUNITIES

A general introduction to therapeutic communities was given in chapter 4. What follows is a detailed description of a composite of a number of currently functioning therapeutic communities for adolescents operated by Interventions, a large Chicago-based treatment provider. It presents the basic concepts and procedures of a modern therapeutic community for a clinician either working in a therapeutic community or with need to know in detail how such communities function on a day-to-day-basis. The general role of the physician in a therapeutic community is that of a triage officer handling a range of common medical problems together with assessment and referral for psychiatric consultation. Depression and suicide are relatively frequent situations presenting for assessment. These and other common problems are discussed briefly following the presentation of the structure and function of a composite therapeutic community.

INCLUSION CRITERIA

1. The patient meets DSM-4 criteria for substance abuse or dependence.

2. A lower intensity of care, such as intensive outpatient, has not been effective or is judged to be inappropriate based on ASAM criteria (i.e., meets criteria dimension 3, "Moderate severity needing a 24-hour structured setting").
3. Suitability: the patient has sufficient communication skills and is organized enough to meet the demands of a therapeutic community.
4. Sex: male for male programs and female for female programs (programs with mixed male and female adolescents have been problematic for the organization).
5. Age: between 13 and 18.

EXCLUSION CRITERIA

1. Acute psychosis
2. History of arson
3. Acute risk of suicide
4. Acute medical needs
5. History of committing a sexual assault
6. Developmental disorder severe enough to preclude participation in community activities
   Potential candidates for admission come from a variety of sources—school systems, criminal-justice agencies, social and mental health agencies of all kinds, and so forth. They are then screened and processed.

PRE–ADMISSION SCREENING

The initial contact is by phone, usually with the intake counselor. An Interventions inquiry sheet is filled out for each phone contact. This form registers caller data, client data, insurance or HMO data, source of support, problem data, and disposition data. The initial contact may result in referral of the client to another service or program according to the judgment of the intake counselor. If the intake counselor decides that the candidate appears to be a potential admission, an appointment is made for a face-to-face interview.

COMPREHENSIVE CLINICAL ASSESSMENT AND TREATMENT PLANNING

Admission process. During the face-to-face interview, the intake counselor fills out a preliminary assessment. This form captures data on demographics, appearance, reasons for seeking help, presenting problem, drug and alcohol usage, medical status, psychological status, employment status, educational status, and legal status; it ends with a written summary of the foregoing and the disposition. If the client is admitted, this constitutes the preliminary treatment plan. The intake counselor determines that the client meets inclusion criteria and does not meet exclusion criteria. While the intake counselor carries out a clinical assessment, a clinic administrator carries out a financial assessment.

If the client has a parent, the intake counselor obtains data from the parent(s) concerning the behavior of the client in a number of domains. This information is recorded on the parent initial questionnaire. If the client does not have a parent, similar data is obtained and recorded on the collateral questionnaire from the legal guardian or state agency. The decision to admit or not to admit a client is based on the intake counselor's integration of the data from all the domains described above. If the decision is to admit, the intake counselor begins to develop a diagnostic summary and a master problem and goal list. These are completed by the client's primary counselor within the first 10 days of treatment and signed by the patient, the client's primary counselor, the family, and a senior-level counselor.

During the pre-admission screening, the new client is made aware of the client's rights, the need for the client and the client's family to agree to admission, the possible need for emergency medical services, and the need to agree to the educational program. These domains have corresponding forms that are signed: admission consent form, client's rights form, leave of medical absence form, emergency medical consent form, school consent form, and a preliminary aftercare plan. In addition, the client is given a written and verbal explanation of the HIV and smoking policy. If the client is a ward of the state, a special agreement form is filled out, permitting information about the client to go to the agency of guardianship.

Formal admission. Interventions staff completes, within 10 days of admission, the Interventions clinical assessment form, which covers the following domains:

- Patient demographics
- Patient appearance
- History and pattern of drug and alcohol usage
- Symptoms of drug and alcohol abuse/dependence
- Withdrawal symptoms
- Alcohol/drug treatment history
- Family alcohol and drug use
- Patient self-assessment
- Legal history and status
- Psychological assessment
- Mini-mental status examination
- Degree of dangerousness to self and others
- Social support network assessment
- Spirituality
- Sexuality
- Educational background
- Vocational history
- Leisure time
- Nutritional background
- Rating of patient functioning
- Global assessment functioning scale (DSM-4)

Planning for aftercare is started in the admission and assessment period and is periodically updated throughout the treatment episode.

The reader should note the comprehensiveness of the workup. On clinical grounds, it provides a good basis for treatment planning; on administrative grounds, it satisfies JCAHO and ASAM dimensions and licensing requirements of the locale in which the programs are situated.

Medical and nursing assessment. Each client is seen by a nurse within 24 hours of admission. The nurse takes vital signs, determines medication needs, evaluates for potential emergency conditions, communicates with the admitting physician, and then records the admission order. The nurse also administers a skin test for tuberculosis. Interventions medical personnel at the Interventions central intake facility carry out a comprehensive medical assessment of each admission within a few days of admission. If medical assessments have been made recently, perhaps by a referring hospital, then the Interventions medical assessment may be waived after the unit physician has reviewed the external records.

Now we turn to the structure of the program, starting with a presentation of the goals of the treatment program.

THERAPEUTIC COMMUNITY GOALS

1. to assist the individual in establishing an effective recovery program; effectiveness requires elimination of drug/alcohol use
2. to increase self-esteem, self-respect, and respect and concern for others
3. to replace dysfunctional cognitions with adaptive thoughts and beliefs
4. to improve control over impulses
5. to strengthen adaptive behaviors in social and recreational areas
6. to remediate vocational and educational deficits
7. to strengthen family and social bonds with significant people in the resident's life
8. to learn about chemical dependency and the concepts and practices of AA

These goals are the only goals of the organization. There are no others. To reach these goals, the program has several interacting structures.

THERAPEUTIC COMMUNITY ORGANIZATIONAL STRUCTURES

STAFF AUTHORITY HIERARCHY

- The basic structure of a therapeutic community is a hierarchical social system with clearly established lines of authority; all share in the community effort to achieve the goals articulated above.
- Authority is rational, not charismatic, and does not require an individual to overvalue the leader or attribute special powers to him/her.
- Authority does not require unthinking, automatic obedience; thinking independently before acting or feeling is encouraged and affirmed by the culture of recovery.
- Authority has a strong horizontal as well as vertical dimension, in that residents are expected to be involved actively in monitoring and assessing one another's

behavior. The culture of recovery attempts to teach that caring enough about others to be involved is a part of recovery for one's self.

- Participation in the community does not require individuals to demean themselves or anyone else.
- The community does not create fatigue or use other procedures for inducing dissociative states to promote group unity or obedience.
- Although there may be outside forces, such as legal or family, pressuring the individual to remain in the community, there are no community constraints, other than rational persuasion by peers and staff, preventing the individual from leaving the community at any time.
- Staff are role models, and residents are expected to be role models for one another.
- Work, assigned in the departments of the community, is a part of treatment; work outside the community for the financial gain of the community is not accepted practice.
- Relationships between staff and residents are professional, never social, personal, religious, or intimate.

The goals and structures of the therapeutic community as defined above clearly distinguish the program from cults. Perhaps the hallmark of the difference is the rational view of leadership versus the charismatic nature of leadership in a cult.

CLIENT STATUS HIERARCHY AND BEHAVIOR CONTROL

When a client enters the program, he or she is given the most menial community tasks, such as cleaning floors and bathrooms or kitchen duties. As a client demonstrates adherence to the program, as judged by staff and peers, he or she is rewarded with an increase in status. Every two weeks, residents are assessed in staff meetings, and new job assignments are made according to the residents' behavior with respect both to work and to progress in the overall program. When the resident conforms, he or she receives "push-ups," recognition and affirmation for the positive behavior, from both peers and staff. For residents making good progress, these assignments bring considerable responsibility as well as status. As described below, "D-heads" and "ramrods" have power and status, because the jobs they perform are critical to the life of the community.

The increase in status is also accompanied by an increase in privileges. Having visitors, telephone privileges, and a variety of passes (from 4 to 33 hours) to leave the facility must be earned by good behavior. Staff evaluates residents weekly to determine status with respect to privileges.

Failure to conform to the house rules is responded to incrementally, with the general rule that the response should be educational. Profanity, running in the house, or sitting improperly in a chair during a group meeting, for example, may be responded to by a peer or staff person with a "pull up." This is a verbal communication that the individual has broken house rules. This is the first level of response, that of awareness. If the individual acknowledges breaking the rules and agrees to correct the behavior, the matter ends there.

If the individual denies the infraction or repeats it, he or she may continue to be confronted by staff and/or peers who will "write up" or "book" the incident, writing a brief description of the problem together with the names of and brief statements from residents who were witnesses to the episode, if any. A write-up automatically refers the problem to the house issues and peer committee meeting. This creates sustained pressure on the individual to acknowledge and change the behavior.

The staff person facilitating the house issues and peer committee considers how to respond to the problem described in the booking. Frequently, this group leader decides to utilize the next level of response, that of education. He or she may prescribe learning experiences (LEs). These involve exercises such as requiring the resident to write an essay on the behavior in question and possible solutions to it. If the incident involves aggression between two residents, the house issues and peer committee breaks up into smaller conflict-resolution groups to process such problems. In the smaller groups, the parties are brought together to attempt a resolution. This often leads to acknowledgment by the parties of their respective roles in the conflict and a promise to make amends. One of the parties may be asked to perform favors for the other; for example, party A is said to owe party B five "good deeds" (getting B soda, putting up B's chair after a meeting, doing some chore for B) as amends for acknowledged guilt.

The staff facilitator of the house issues and peer committee meeting may elect, in some circumstances, to put an individual on "ban" from another resident or from an activity as a way of assisting the individual to work out a problem with the counselor and the peer committee without having to confront the situation every day.

If these measures do not change the behavior, the senior staff (the unit director and the deputy unit director)—and only the senior staff—may prescribe a third level of response, that of discipline or "stips," short for stipulations. Sometimes these are verbal agreements with the resident to avoid certain individuals or activities as a means of controlling the situation so that the individual does not have to be excluded from the community while continuing to work on the problem behavior. In addition to the stipulations, the staff also works with collateral such as state agencies and parole and probation officers to help the resident see what the consequences will be if the resident does not complete the program as prescribed.

If the foregoing fails, senior staff may decide to place the individual on a behavior contract with "points." The client agrees in writing that he or she is in jeopardy of being excluded from the program if there is no change in behavior. The client agrees to a contract that requires him or her to have the staff persons conducting the day's activities sign the points sheet to the effect that the client has conducted himself or herself well in the activity. A behavior contract usually extends for a few weeks. Then senior staff, in consultation with other relevant staff such as the resident's counselor and the recreation therapist, reviews performance and decides whether further contracts are necessary, or if the individual can resume regular participation in the program.

At all levels of response, the behavior in question is reviewed by the individual counselor with the resident. The pressure from the milieu combined with individual counseling creates a strong therapeutic force for positive change.

If the foregoing measures do not resolve the problem, senior staff may decide to invoke loss of privileges (LOPs) in parallel with these measures. Privileges such as passes, telephone access, visiting, and participation in games may be withheld in an attempt to teach the individual that behavior has consequences.

If the behavioral problem is severe and does not yield to the various levels of response, the resident may be placed on probationary status. This is an agreement with the individual that any future problem of any kind will result in exclusion, perhaps immediate, from the program. The resident and family or collateral both receive verbal notification of the change to probationary status, and a formal note is placed in the resident's chart. Any breach of the behavior code of the program while on probationary status results in exclusion from the unit. Probationary status lasts five days, and senior staff in consultation with other relevant staff decide then, on the basis of the resident's performance, what the resident's further program will be.

It is unusual for an individual to have to be excluded from the program; the multilevel response system works most of the time. Every effort is made to refer the individual who has to be excluded to a more appropriate treatment program.

Some common clinical problems are as follows:

- Not following staff directions.
- Not engaging with the program: "hanging tough," or "gang reps" only engaging with one other resident or a clique of residents, "jailing" or going through the motions but not engaging genuinely with the program, making a joke out of everything, withdrawing, and so forth.
- Disrespect of peers and/or staff
- Enabling; for example, a resident knows of another resident's possession of drugs in the facility but does not confront the resident and does not report the problem to the peer committee or the staff
- Threatening peers and/or staff
- Returning late from pass
- Use/possession of intoxicants in the facility
- Returning from pass under the influence
- "Lunacy" or rowdy behavior
- Holiday depression/acting out (holidays remind the resident of what he or she does not have)
- Anniversary reactions (anniversary of the loss of a parent, sibling, or some significant other person)

The house issues and peer committee meeting is described in detail below. It is important to point out that violations of cardinal rules (in general, these are the same as described for methadone clinics—no violence or threats of violence, and so forth) are investigated by staff immediately, and the actions taken are announced in the house issues and peer committee meeting.

DEPARTMENTS

The community is divided into departments to carry out basic community functions. The kitchen, maintenance, and communications departments are operated
solely by the residents. Each department has its own substructure according to its
mission.

Kitchen. The department head or D-head is an advanced client in the therapeutic community. The D-head works with the food-services manager to implement
the menu, which is generated by the dietitian and the food-services manager. The D-
head supervises clients in the chores necessary to the function of the kitchen. The D-
head is assisted in this by the "ramrod," who is also a client. These two supervise the
work of five crews of clients in various stages in the program: the wash crew, responsible for operating the dishwashers; the pots and pans crew, responsible for the manual cleaning of pots and pans; the utilities crew, responsible for the storage of all uten-
sils and for the setup of the kitchen before meals; the dining crew, responsible for
serving the food; and the floor crew, responsible for the maintenance of a clean and
attractive environment in which to serve and consume food.

Maintenance. The maintenance crew is also headed by a D-head who is assisted
by a ramrod. Together they supervise the work of three crews of residents: the grounds
crew, which has its own ramrod and is responsible for the upkeep of the exterior of
the residence; the maintenance crew, which has responsibility for the interior of the
residence; and the laundry crew, which also has its own ramrod and is responsible for
the scheduling of the laundry room and for keeping it clean.

Communications. This department is responsible for monitoring the community
and for integrating the functions of the kitchen and maintenance departments.
Communications has a D-head assisted by a ramrod. The community monitoring
function is carried out by scouts. Under the supervision of the communications
ramrod, the scouts make tours of the entire community every 30 minutes and record
their observations after making these "house runs." They are responsible for enforc-
ing house rules, for being role models, and for reaching out to peers who display
poor attitudes. When they observe poor attitudes, they report their observations to
staff. If the scout "pulls up" a resident on a minor rule violation and the resident does
not respond, the scout writes up or books the incident, and the matter is then brought
up in the peer committee meeting. If a peer reports to a scout about the negative behavior, the scout investigates; and if the report is valid, he or she books it. Major rule
violations such as use of drugs, violence, or threats of violence are reported promptly
to staff, who then make an immediate investigation.

The room monitor, a position filled by a resident advanced in the program, has
specific responsibility for monitoring rules pertaining to the sleeping areas of the residential unit. Residents are not permitted in their rooms at any time during the day,
and they are responsible for maintaining their rooms in clean and attractive fashion.
The room monitor monitors these functions and also monitors the schedule of lights-
out, and then is responsible for keeping sleeping areas quiet once lights-out is called.

The phone monitor is responsible for documenting when and whom residents call on the telephone. The phone monitor records all calls to ensure that residents are calling only approved people; the length of calls is monitored so that others have equal time to make their calls. The phone monitor also obtains staff signatures approving all calls made by residents.

The medical liaison function is also part of the communications department. The medical liaison resident records all requests to see the nurse and prepares a list of residents to be seen for the nurse. The medical liaison resident escorts all residents to their medical and nursing appointments, including sick call. This person is also responsible for monitoring all medication received by residents and for accompanying residents when they have medical appointments off site. All nurse visits must go through the medical liaison resident. The medical liaison resident records all his or her actions so there is full documentation of all medical/nursing contacts.

The orientation advisor is a resident who is responsible for monitoring the orientation activities for new residents. The orientation advisor meets weekly with all Big Sisters or Big Brothers. Big Brothers/Sisters are residents advanced in the program who are assigned to new residents to assist them in orientation. The orientation advisor also organizes and assists staff in orientation groups. The orientation advisor administers the orientation test taken by all new residents.

Medical/Nursing. A nurse is on duty during the day on weekdays. The nurse has sick call every day and is assisted by the medical liaison resident. Once a week, the unit is visited by a physician, who assesses medical problems with the nurse. The unit physician signs off on treatment plans and discharge summaries and participates in client care monitoring. Residents who develop medical problems severe enough to warrant referral to a hospital are referred to a hospital with which Interventions has a letter of agreement.

The nurse monitors all medication needed by residents, as residents cannot keep medication of any kind with their personal belongings. Medical department protocol has been developed that describes the procedures and activities, such as infection control, for the unit. The nurse schedules appointments for medical contacts off site and monitors the results of these contacts. The nurse plays an important role in integrating medical care at the unit with the medical care of the resident in the community.

The unit nurse conducts lecture/discussion seminars once a week on a variety of health related issues, including the effects of common intoxicants on health. These seminars are supplemented by and integrated with parallel sessions for families held by counselors and by the family therapist. Education about the health effects of drugs is thereby implemented for both residents and families.

THERAPEUTIC COMMUNITY PROCESS

Orientation phase. The 14-day orientation period acquaints the client with the philosophy and procedures involved in the therapeutic community's life, beginning with an introduction to the house rules and "tools"(recommended interpersonal behaviors). One counselor supervises the orientation period. The new resident meets this counselor immediately. The individual is advised of her or his rights as a patient of Interventions and of client rights as they pertain to the jurisdiction in which the program is operating. The new client meets his or her individual counselor, who will be the individual counselor for the duration of treatment; has a nursing assessment; and is assigned work in a department by the orientation supervisor.

Soon after admission, the new resident is assigned a Big Brother or Big Sister, a resident who has been in the program for over four months. New residents and Big Brothers or Big Sisters sometimes room together. The older residents are available to explain the program to the new resident and are directed to answer any questions the newcomer might have. Each Big Brother and Big Sister has a written list of the points to be communicated in the orientation period. The new resident participates actively in treatment planning as the treatment plan develops: for example, each resident is assessed for level of educational achievement and recreational patterns, as described above.

Four days per week, new residents attend orientation groups led by the orientation supervisor, who is assisted by an advanced resident called the orientation advisor. In the groups, the orientation supervisor stresses the core concepts of attitude change, behavior change, emotional change, and character change as the focal points of the treatment experience. The average orientation session lasts one hour. The initial workup is completed by the day 10 of the resident's stay, and the information is integrated into the formal treatment plan, which is developed by the counselors and residents and then signed by the client, the counselor, the clinical coordinator (deputy unit director), and the unit physician. This treatment plan attempts to respond to the unique set of problems presented by each individual entering the program.

In the orientation groups, the orientation supervisor assigns the new residents writing exercises focusing on self-observation in relation to drug dependence and its consequences for the resident and for those close to the resident. This material is contained in the autobiography each resident is required to write and is important in the development of the treatment plan. New residents are introduced to the philosophy and methods of Twelve step groups and begin attending AA meetings. The newcomer is given additional written homework on the concepts and rules and tools of the "family" (as all the people in the unit, both staff and clients, are referred to). He or she learns the hierarchy of privileges, the "trust ladder," and other elements of the orientation program. The newcomer is tested in all these domains both verbally by the orientation supervisor and the Big Brother or Big Sister and with written tests. The orientation process is written, and the new resident receives a booklet containing all the information he or she is expected to master in the orientation period.

The new resident has both the orientation advisor and a Big Brother or Big Sister to turn to for help with the tasks described above. Everyone in the program is busy most of the time, so this dual system ensures that the new resident gets help in timely fashion.

The resident's family also receives an orientation concerning the program and what their role in the recovery can be. The family therapist carries out this work in parallel with the orientation of the new resident.

Some orientation groups emphasize support and understanding and attempt to teach the resident how to relate in and what to expect from various groups in the therapeutic community, the house rules and tools. Other orientation groups expand on the work started in the first meetings between the resident and the therapeutic as well as community staff. In these early meetings, the resident is asked to examine the sequence of events that resulted in referral to the therapeutic community. The purpose of this examination is to assist the resident in assuming responsibility for being there; staff does not accept the answer, "I'm here because my parents/parole officer/the court sent me here." The resident is reminded by staff and by peers that his or her behavior and choices have led to the referral. In addition to accepting responsibility for being in treatment, each resident is asked to make a commitment to change.

Community monitoring. The function of monitoring the community is continuous. The monitoring function must be active at all times; for example, staff cannot monitor a recreation area and also make counseling notes or engage in other activities that keep them from attending actively and fully to the interaction in the part of the community they are monitoring. Residents are explicitly told that they should also monitor the community for negative behavior. Several times a day, the facility director and various staff members make house runs, inspections of the entire facility with respect to physical and psychological dimensions. Every aspect of the unit receives this inspection frequently. The director of a facility must participate and must ensure that all staff are trained and active in this critically important function. In one sense, this is the heart of maintaining the integrity of the mission of the community. Monitoring takes discipline on the part of the facility director and staff and communicates that the leadership is involved in and cares about the welfare of the individuals in the community. When carried out correctly, monitoring creates a feeling of safety in the residents, which is needed if they are to attempt to trust staff and one another.

Peers are also involved in the process of community monitoring. Every 30 minutes, peers on the communication crew make a house run and observe the status of the family and the house. In addition, they make a count of the number of residents both on and off site and create a written record of their counts. When residents change from one program element to another, they are required to sign out of the old element and sign in to the new element (when on recreation, for example, they will be signed in on the recreation board; when in school, they are signed in on the schoolroom board). The scouts can account for the whereabouts of the population by examining the sign-in sheets and seeing if all the residents signed in are actually in the room they are supposed to be in. Failure to sign in and sign out can lead to a booking. If the counts do not show the expected number of residents, staff are alerted immediately, and the situation is explored promptly. Since the unit director or the deputy unit director is always in the communication line, there is never a situation in which there is not a senior-level counselor involved in any problem occurring in the facility. Sensitive and constant monitoring by experienced senior staff is the heart of the executive function in the therapeutic community.

When monitoring staff or peers observe an infraction of house rules, such as profanity, they notify the resident; depending on the response of the resident, they may ask the resident to give an account of himself or herself. If the resident does not admit to the behavior, then he or she may be booked or written up. If the infraction is a violation of the cardinal rules of the house, such as a threat of violence, observed by a peer scout, the peer scout reports this to a staff member for staff intervention. Peers are held accountable for ignoring infractions of house rules and may be booked for enabling.

Community meetings. Community meetings (variously called morning meetings, seminars, or house meetings) include all residents and staff on duty at the time, and, in all their forms, serve the general purpose of creating group unity and consensus on the culture of recovery. Problem areas or problem individuals may be the focus of attention, but these meetings may also serve to reward conforming behavior, by staff and/or peer affirmation. The morning meeting is conducted by the night monitor. It is usually short and consists of reciting the Serenity Prayer in addition to announcements of changes in expected schedule and review of any problems that occurred during the night.

The house rules and peer committee meeting each afternoon is the most important meeting of the day; it is a community meeting involving all staff on duty and all the residents. It starts with all staff and residents in a large room seated in one large circle, except for the staff member facilitating the meeting, who stands. The house rules and peer committee assistant, a resident advanced in the program, keeps the minutes of this group. He or she begins the meeting by giving an account of the status of the learning experiences (or other exercises, such as cleaning an area of the house or special writing assignments) mandated the previous day.

The group facilitator then begins to read the new bookings. The individual or individuals involved in the booking stand with their hands behind their backs while the booking is being read. When the reading is finished, the resident says "Valid" or "Invalid" and is not permitted to say anything further. If the resident says valid, a learning experience is assigned. If the resident says invalid, peer and staff witnesses report their observations. If they confirm that there was a violation, the group facilitator assigns a learning experience. If the resident still maintains that the charge is invalid, he or she can take the matter up with staff in a separate meeting before a final decision is made. Then the next booking is read. The peer committee assistant is responsible for following up on the performance of the learning experience and for reporting progress back to the group.

When all the bookings have been read and responded to, the peer committee meeting may be used to welcome new admissions. The newcomer stands, and one by one other residents rise from their seats, approach the newcomer, and shake hands while they give their name, age, drugs of abuse, and length of time they have been in the program. If time permits, this meeting may also be used to bring up reports from various residents concerning achievements, change in probation status, change in health status, or any of a number of areas about which they want to report. Usually, this large community group breaks into smaller conflict-resolution groups to process the events of the peer committee meeting and/or to take up specific conflicts between residents or perhaps between groups of residents. New admissions may be welcomed in other later groups during the day, depending on time of admission.

Late-afternoon meetings tend to have more of a teaching focus and are often called seminars, as they attempt to balance cognitive and emotional forces in residents. Evening meetings have the same general purposes as the others but naturally serve as vehicles for summarizing lessons of the day and providing a concluding and supportive experience for the usually long and intense day. Occasionally, a general meeting is called, usually when there has been some egregious infraction of house rules. All residents and all staff, including those not on duty at the time, are assembled. The incident or problem is reviewed, and remedial actions are taken and explained to the community.

The schedule for any given day of the week consists of a selection from the different types of groups, time in a classroom devoted to accredited regular school subjects, recreation, and work in the various departments.

Conflict-resolution groups. A community meeting can have the same purposes as a conflict-resolution group with the same therapeutic outcome, but the term *conflict-resolution group* usually implies a smaller number of participants than a community meeting. The daily afternoon house issues and peer committee meeting usually has two parts. The first, referred to as the peer committee, reviews bookings and announcements by staff of other educational or disciplinary actions taken; as described above, the afternoon peer committee meeting then breaks up into smaller conflict-resolution groups to "process" or explore the feelings associated with the events in the peer committee, or, in the vernacular of the community, "house issues." Formerly called encounter groups, conflict-resolution groups attempt to identify behaviors, attitudes, or emotions that need to be modified. Staff and/or peers may be involved in describing the behavior, the rule or rules it has violated, and, after giving the miscreant(s) a chance to explain the situation from his or her perspective, some negative sanction may be applied. The negative sanction may range from a loss of telephone time to exclusion from the community. Sometimes these groups prescribe learning experiences. Regardless of the title given to these groups, staff and peers alike attempt to reject the behavior while preserving full respect for the worth of the individual or individuals involved. In this respect, they differ from the classical encounter groups, which were not always careful to distinguish the behavior in question from the issue of personal value.

Conflict-resolution groups usually involve 10 to 20 residents and are at the heart of the therapeutic process, as they focus on the here-and-now behavior of the resident and exert group pressure for recognition and change. They usually last one and a half hours but may be somewhat longer or shorter. The values of honesty in communication and concern for self and others are stressed in these groups.

Those who speak in these groups, including those being confronted, are allowed sufficient time to express their thoughts through what is called the proper respect for the person speaking, or PROPS, value. The profanity of the original therapeutic communities is not permitted, nor are there physical consequences, such as shaving heads bald or wearing signs that identify problem behavior. Basic respect for the personhood of the individual is maintained at all times. In this way, the community lives the values it preaches. By repeated demonstrations of concern accompanied by instructions for behavioral change, the community creates a powerful therapeutic force.

Team building, games, and videos. The purpose of team-building, game, and video groups is to create or to enhance group unity. They attempt to make treatment enjoyable by capitalizing on the adolescent's need to learn by having fun and by interacting with others, in contrast to the purely cognitive tasks of the educational and didactic groups.

Tutorials, seminars, lectures, and videos. Sessions variously labeled tutorials, seminars, lectures, or videos are cognitively oriented and attempt to teach concepts such as the house tools and/or the twelve step program or some aspect of personal growth, such as the need for self-respect and self-esteem. They may be oriented toward house needs and teach about how to run a certain department. They may be used to teach scientific aspects of substance abuse, such as the data that indicate alcoholism has a genetic component, or the chemical elements in nicotine and marijuana smoke.

Self-help AA and NA groups. Self-help groups consist of classical AA or NA techniques. They are an important component of the program and are the centerpiece of the aftercare program of the resident. All residents must attend these groups, and their behaviors are monitored for compliance as in all other elements of the program.

Residents attend AA meetings, read the *Big Book,* and engage in self-help exercises as described in the appendix, which documents the contents of the therapeutic program.

Issues groups. Issues groups have a stable membership formed as successive waves of admissions enter the program. The usual number is six or seven. The group meets once a week, and different staff lead these groups. The purpose is to conduct group therapy on the issues being brought up by the residents or by the therapeutic process to foster positive emotional and cognitive change in members of the group. Issues include gender, minority status, problems with drug using family or friends, and the like.

Caseload outings. Usually once a month, the counselor takes the residents on her or his caseload for a community outing. This may involve a movie, sports, or any of a wide range of activities. Counselors find this a positive addition to the overall program goals of balancing learning with enjoyment.

Individual counseling. Once a week for 30 to 50 minutes, a resident meets with an individual counselor. The purpose is supportive, but this purpose does not exclude frank and open discussion of a wide range of problem areas. Each week the treatment plan is reviewed and updated. The focus of this therapy is on the here-and-now problems of the individual as captured in the treatment plan and as reflected by the behavior of the individual. The active participation of the resident in the creation of the treatment plan forms a solid basis for the individual counseling relationship, as the counselor can measure the behavior of the resident against the agreed-on goals of the treatment plan and can assist the resident in achieving these goals.

Family program. Each Interventions residential unit has a full-time family therapist to engage families in the process of recovery. Each family is oriented to the program for their adolescent and given written copies of the rules on visiting. They are also apprised of the expectations of the community concerning the behavior of the resident when on pass. Multifamily groups are usually held one evening per week and on either Saturday or Sunday for another two-hour period. The purpose of these groups alternates between education/therapy and family recreation. Some of the didactic seminars occur over two sessions. Every other family meeting is usually devoted to family recreation.

The family education groups cover a number of topics, among others:

- Chemical dependency progression
- The disease concept
- Gateway drugs
- Cocaine
- Denial
- Family roles
- Signs of a healthy relationship in family life
- Tough love—setting limits, privileges, and responsibilities
- Positive parenting
- Communications
- Going home
- When your son or daughter comes home
- Suicide
- When your teen is in treatment
- Driving under intoxication
- PAW (post acute withdrawal): What is it?
- What is recovery?
- Family recovery
- What is relapse? Signs and symptoms
- Spirituality
- Working Twelve step programs
- Speakers from AA, NA
- Understanding depression/addiction
- LSD
- AIDS
- Heroin and other drugs
- Inhalants
- Anger
- What is normal?
- Stress

At some point in the client's stay (which can vary from three to six months), the family therapist conducts Family Day. This is an experience modeled on a typical day in treatment for a resident. It demonstrates to family members what the residents' treatment experience is like. Family members may be written up and confronted when they break rules, or they may be affirmed for behavior that promotes program goals. For some components of this day, residents may be called in and may share experiences with family members. Family retreats also occur once in the treatment cycle. These retreats last an entire day, and they give family members an opportunity to discuss common problems and to assimilate all the experiences above.

Since there is a constant flow of new families, the membership of the family program groups is constantly changing. The family therapist is experienced with this aspect of these groups.

PROGRESSIVE ENGAGEMENT

As the client learns the rules and tools of the house, he or she begins to conform to the norms of behavior and speech of the family. As the resident exhibits conforming behavior, he or she earns privileges and rises to higher-status work roles.

Experience over a number of years with program phasing has led Interventions staff to abandon specific program phases. They observed that younger members of the family had different strengths and needs from older members. This made the treatment course different for these different-age populations. In addition, there is considerable variation in the arc of in-treatment development in those of the same age. There is wide variation of degree of strength of support systems, with some individuals enmeshed in currently severely dysfunctional family systems while others have relatively healthy families; there is also a significant number with no family at all. Variations in IQ, self-confidence, and social skills also contribute to lack of uniformity in progress. With different individuals and age groups progressing differently, the uniform application of specific program phases impressed staff as artificial. Progress in the program was, therefore, individualized, and graduation now means that an individual has progressed considerably from where he or she started. There is no implied comparison with a general abstract norm.

Progress in the program is measured by staff according to the general principle of engagement with the individualized treatment plan. The individual participates in the creation of the treatment plan and knows what he or she has to do and how he or she is going to be evaluated. Most residents make developmental strides that they can measure and that lead to genuine increments in self-esteem as the individual perceives that he or she is accomplishing treatment goals.

The issue of "jailing," or appearing to go along with the program but not really engaging with it, frequently arises. Staff may deal with this problem by telling the resident to act "as if" he or she were really engaged, based on the historical experience in therapeutic communities that the desired behavior can be adopted by the resident and will replace the "jailing" behavior. Or staff may try to understand the resistance to engagement and deal with this in counseling. Or they may do both. The issue of motivation for a therapeutic community experience has been classically, and remains, that jailing is a treatable problem. The wisdom of the therapeutic community adage "Give us the body, the mind will follow" continues to be supported by modern experience. Lack of motivation for treatment does not preclude therapeutic effects from treatment, but it is not clinically irrelevant either. It is one of a number of potential problem areas to be solved by the client and the program working together.

Clinical staff judge the resident's progress each week; after a few months in the program, the staff can usually identify that some positive change is occurring for the resident in problem areas. During the last month of the treatment cycle, the resident attends a group specifically focused on issues related to his or her upcoming graduation. One of the lessons imparted to all residents is that sustained recovery requires a sustained commitment to the aftercare program. The treatment experience is a good start, but only that.

Extreme behavioral problems such as fighting, drug/alcohol use, or stealing may require exclusion from the therapeutic community, but if staff judges that the individual can control impulses, he or she may be put on probationary status, with the clear understanding that if there are any more problem behaviors, the resident will have to be excluded from the program.

Recreation and leisure time. A trained and certified recreation therapist assesses each individual utilizing the standard Interventions form. Information is gathered in multiple domains on the usual recreational patterns of the resident. Individual, peer, and family domains are explored. Information is also gathered on the goals of the resident in treatment. The recreation therapist, in consultation with the resident, synthesizes the information in the various domains and creates a program for each individual based on in-house and community resources.

Each resident must engage in recreation and leisure activities for one and a half hours per day. The goal is to provide an enjoyable experience for the residents that also teaches that there are many ways to relax and have a good time. For some, this involves physical activities such as swimming, bowling, dancing, basketball, or softball, but for others it involves a wide range of arts and crafts. Many residents elect different activity classes on different days, such as exercise on one day followed by reading or dramatics the next. Therapeutic goals are often a part of the program of activities. Anger management, for example, may be a goal for an intensively competitive individual who cannot enjoy a sport like basketball unless he or she wins. The recreation therapist teaches that the activity itself has value independent of the outcome of the game.

The experience in recreation therapy attempts to teach appropriate social behavior and to increase the social behavioral repertoire of the individual. It also may introduce the resident to activities such as plays, museums, and art institutes that the resident may not have experienced previously.

The activities therapist participates actively during most recreation program activities. Following these activities, the therapist frequently leads a discussion period to process the experience so that individuals can reflect on their behavior, together with the therapist and their peers, and link it with their goals in treatment. The activities therapist meets regularly with counselors and integrates observations from this domain with the therapeutic goals of treatment.

Off-site outings involve usually twice-a-week visits to a gymnasium that has facilities for a wide variety of exercises and sports. Trips to bowling alleys, roller-skating rinks, and other community-based facilities teach that one can have fun without intoxicants. Activities can be on site or in the community. The activities therapist has a set of games and exercises that are applied depending on how many family members are present and the therapist's judgment of what is needed.

Educational program. Careful measurement of educational status is carried out, and an individualized educational plan (IEP) is constructed for each resident. Participation in the educational component of the therapeutic community program is mandatory. On site, teachers in the therapeutic community conduct classes identical to those of junior or senior high schools. When a program resident returns to his or her home school system, he or she gets full credit for participation in the educational program, which occupies four hours every weekday.

Drug and alcohol testing. On return from all passes, residents must submit a urine sample. If a counselor suspects alcohol intake, staff administers a breathlyzer test. Most of the urine samples are not tested, but the residents do not know which will and which will not be tested. If there are clinical indications of drug use, such as intoxication or late return from passes, the sample is referred off site for testing. A positive test leads to staff inquiry in an attempt to understand the dynamics of the episode of use, to attempt to identify the relapse triggers, and to train the subject to avoid them in the future.

Preparation for aftercare. Aftercare planning is part of the admission process, and the aftercare plan is updated every month by the primary counselor in concert with the resident. Many years of experience have taught Interventions the importance of early and sustained planning for aftercare throughout the treatment period. Aftercare planning is broad in scope with attention to every important domain—family relationships, school, self-help groups, recreational needs, counseling if indicated, and so forth.

Each resident must identify the specific resources to be utilized in the aftercare plan, talk to the person or agency involved, and, if at all possible, visit the person or agencies to establish a firm relationship to ensure smooth transitions to the aftercare component of the total program.

Graduation. Graduation ceremonies are held once a month in the evening. The room in which the ceremonies are held is decorated with banners and streamers with the names of the graduates printed prominently on one banner. All residents and all family members participating in the family program are present. When a resident is to receive the graduation certificate for completing the program, he or she goes to the center of the room with family members (or perhaps a representative from a state agency or other legal guardian). Various counselors and the senior counselors, including the unit director, comment on the graduate's success, and one or two peers may also comment. The comments are usually light-hearted, but serious congratulations for engaging with the program are a central part of the comments. Each graduating group selects a graduation song, and the community sings this song before being served dinner.

Aftercare. After graduation, each former resident is contacted at 30, 60, and 90 days by his or her primary counselor. There is a yearly alumni party for graduates of the program.

COMMON CLINICAL PROBLEMS

Routine physician duties. Usually, treatment plans need to be signed off on by the unit physician as well as other staff. These plans are periodically updated, and the physician should also sign off on these updates. In addition, the unit physician must set up periodic times for general medical call. These usually go through the nurse, but occasionally there may be an immediate presentation to the unit physician of an emergency. The range of these problems is wide. Diabetic patients, patients with epilepsy, dual diagnosis patients taking a wide variety of medications, and patients with sexually transmitted diseases may all need to be monitored by the unit physician, frequently in consultation with other physicians or agencies. Decisions for referral for medical problems are straightforward. Other duties in some therapeutic communities might include carrying out detoxification from low levels of dependence or perhaps monitoring a patient on methadone maintenance who is also in the therapeutic community.

Referrals for behavioral problems. The decision to refer for psychiatric consultation should rest on the determination that general functioning, in the therapeutic community setting, has been impaired by whatever psychiatric disorder is suspected, such as depressed mood, impulse control disorder, antisocial personality disorder, eating disorders, or sleep disorders. In drug abusing populations, there is a lot of dysphoria, low self-esteem, fragile sense of self, and sleep problems. These are very important for the patient's quality of life, but they do not meet criteria for any DSM-4 diagnosis. Most of the time, these problems do not impair ability to participate in the program. Because the setting is so important, the physician should work closely with the counseling staff, particularly with the unit director, to reach a decision. There are usually many cases in a therapeutic community that under more ideal conditions should have access to full dual diagnosis programming, but such facilities are often nonexistent, particularly for adolescents. The staff often has an investment in a patient and wants to try to work with the patient in the therapeutic community setting. Obviously, close monitoring is the key to success in such attempts. If the physician determines that the patient cannot function in the therapeutic community setting, a referral must be made, and disappointment among staff should be explored in an attempt to understand the serious personal risks inherit in working with impaired people in a therapeutic community.

Depression and suicide are frequent problems needing assessment in a therapeutic community. The physician without psychiatric training should become familiar with the DSM-4 criteria for various forms of depression to sharpen skills in assessing these problems. As noted, there is a gray area between negative mood states that do not meet criteria for a mood disorder and those that do. Understanding the criteria will make the physician better at deciding who needs referral and who does not. Any patient meeting criteria for a mood disorder needs specific treatment if there is to be any chance of recovery from substance abuse.

The reader will recall that one of the exclusion criteria is acute suicide risk. Here the decision is clear. The ordinary therapeutic community does not have trained staff and cannot manage acute suicidality. The patient must go to a psychiatric facility until the situation is under control. One of the problems in the current criteria-driven environment is that the criteria are often not clearly distinguishable. The acuteness of suicidality may be a gray area, and if there is any doubt, a formal psychiatric consultation should be sought. The referral process will be improved if the therapeutic community physician learns enough about assessing suicide to couch the referral in specific terms.

The psychiatric consultant assesses a number of factors. Ideas about shooting oneself with a gun are more lethal than ideas about taking pills; specific plans are more lethal than vague thoughts about suicide or general wishes to be dead. Reports from the patient that suicidal thoughts are compelling and hard to resist would probably require transfer to a psychiatric facility independent of any other factors. Previous suicide attempts make a future attempt more likely, and past highly lethal attempts would make a given patient unsuitable for a therapeutic community, if there has been any return of suicidal thinking or depressed mood in this setting. Males are more likely than females to use more lethal means. A positive family history for suicide adds to the gravity of the problem. The presence of a major medical (e.g., HIV) or psychiatric illness enhances risk. The absence of a positive support system, family therapist, or agency worker with an investment in the patient enhances risk. The higher the load of these risk factors, the more likely an attempt, and the greater the need for referral to a psychiatric facility.

Assessment of aggression. Therapeutic communities commonly have personality-disordered patients or patients with impulse control disorders that involve aggression. In parallel with suicide, a past history with a high load on inability to control aggressive impulses makes it less likely that a given patient can make it in a therapeutic community. A history should be taken of antisocial and aggressive behavior beginning in childhood, as a basis for decision making about suitability for a therapeutic community. The physician should review the DSM-4 criteria for diagnosis to know what to ask about. As a rule of thumb, if the physician receives reports that staff or clients are afraid of the patient, and especially if, on examination of the case, the physician is afraid of the patient, the patient should not be kept in the therapeutic community. A therapeutic environment has to be safe, physically and psychologically, or it cannot be therapeutic.

There is, of course, a much wider range of possible problems that come to the attention of a physician in a therapeutic community, and they must be resolved by examination and consultation.

REFERENCES

1. Gritz ER, Shiffman SM, Jarvik ME, et al. Physiological and psychological effects of methadone in man. *Arch Gen Psychiatry* 32:237–242, 1975.
2. Maddox JF, Williams TR, Ziegler DA, et al. Driving records before and during methadone maintenance. *Am J Drug Alcohol Abuse* 4:91–100, 1977.
3. Payte T. *ASAM Methadone Treatment Course for Physicians.* Chicago, IL, ASAM, 1995.
4. Borg L, Ho A, Peters JE, et al. Availability of reliable serum methadone determination for management of symptomatic patients. *J Addictive Dis* 14:83–96, 1995.
5. O'Connor LM, Woody G, Yeh H-S, et al. Methadone and edema. *J Substance Abuse Treatment* 8:153–155, 1991; *Am J Psychiatry* 126:33–40, 1970.
6. Barthwell A, Senay E, Marks R, et al. Patients successfully maintained with methadone escaped human immunodeficiency virus infection. *Arch Gen Psychiatry* 46:957, 1989.
7. Ball JC, Lange WR, Myers E, et al. Reducing the risk of AIDS through methadone maintenance treatment. *J Health Soc Behav* 29:214–26, 1988.
8. Karch SB. *The Pathology of Drug Abuse,* ed 2. Boca Raton, FL, CRC Press, 1996.
9. Code of Federal Regulation.
10. Kanof PD, Aronson MJ, Ness R, et al. Levels of opioid physical dependence in heroin addicts. *Drug Alcohol Depend* 27:253–262, 1991.
11. Havassy B, Hargreaves WA. Allowing methadone clients control over dosage: A 48-week controlled trial. *Addict Behav* 6:283–288, 1981.
12. Senay EC, Dorus W, Showalter C. Methadone detoxification: Self versus physician regulation. *Am J Drug Alcohol Abuse* 10:361–374, 1984.
13. Cooper JR. Ineffective use of psychoactive drugs: Methadone treatment is no exception. *JAMA* 267:281–282, 1992.
14. D'Aunno, TD, Vaughn TE. Variations in methadone treatment practices: Results from a national study. *JAMA* 267:253–258, 1992.
15. Methadone Maintenance: Some Programs Are Not Effective, Greater Federal Oversight Needed. Publication no. GAO/HRD-90–104. General Accounting Office, Washington, DC, 1990.
16. Ball J, Ross A. *The Effectiveness of Methadone Maintenance Treatment.* New York, Springer Verlag, 1991.
17. Hargreaves W. Methadone dosage and duration for maintenance treatment, in Cooper J, Altman Brown B, Czechowicz D (eds), *Research on the Treatment of Narcotic Addiction: State of the Art.* NIDA Treatment Research Monograph Series. DHHS Pub No (ADM) 83-1281, 1983.
18. Medical Letter Drug Interaction Program. The Medical Letter Inc. New Rochelle, NY 10801-7537, 1994.

19. O'Brien CP. Opioids: Antagonists and partial agonists, in Galanter M, Kleber HD (eds), *Textbook of Substance Abuse Treatment*. Washington, DC, American Psychiatric Association Press, 1994.

ADDITIONAL READINGS

Lawson GW, Lawson AW. *Adolescent Substance Abuse: Etiology, Treatment and Prevention*. Gaithersburg, MD, Aspen Publishers, 1992.

Lowinson JH, Ruiz P, Millman RB, et al (eds), Special populations, in *Substance Abuse: Clinical Problems and Perspectives*. Baltimore, MD, Williams & Wilkins, 1992, pp 794–908.

6. Sedative/Hypnotics

Anxiety, insomnia, epilepsy, and muscle spasms are very frequent in the general population and seriously impair the quality of life for large numbers of people. In the past 100 years, the science of pharmacology has provided us with a series of sedative/hypnotic drugs that have given us ameliorative power over these problems to a historically unprecedented degree. But this major accomplishment is not generally recognized because the therapeutic effects have been accompanied by problems such as use by suicidal persons, side effects such as cognitive and motoric impairment, and problems of abuse and dependence.

Sedation refers to calming or tranquilizing effects and *hypnosis* refers to sleep induction. The term *hypnotic* in referring to a drug is a misnomer, because the physiological state resulting from hypnotic drugs is different from that observed in hypnosis. In medical use, benzodiazepines have almost completely displaced the barbiturates and other nonbarbiturate sedative/hypnotics to treat these problems, so they are the chief focus of this chapter.

In the latest study of the epidemiology of mental disorders in the United States, anxiety disorders had a lifetime prevalence of over 24 percent. As discussed by DuPont and Saylor,[1] a significant subset of those afflicted by an anxiety disorder have sustained, relatively trouble-free relief from well-monitored, prescribed use of benzodiazepines. The improvement in the quality of life for these people is enormous. Benzodiazepines are used extensively in anesthesiology and have a variety of other uses, such as in tetanus, but the medical uses are not discussed in this text. While primary use of benzodiazepines for intoxication occurs, unprescribed use of benzodiazepines to enhance effects of other intoxicants or to treat unwanted effects from other drugs (the hyperstimulation from cocaine is a good example) is much more frequently encountered.

Problems of abuse and dependence occur in two quite different populations,[2] those who are prescribed benzodiazepines for one of the four indications described above, and those in the drug culture who purchase benzodiazepine through illicit channels. In the current U. S. drug culture, flunitrazepam (Rohypnol), a benzodiazepine not marketed in the United States but widely available in other parts of the world, is being used to obtain cheap intoxication by taking it concurrently with alcohol. It is a drug combination used mainly by adolescents throughout the country. (Some use the combination for so-called date rape. Flunitrazepam is put in the drink of a female; almost anesthetized, she may not remember the incident because of the anterograde amnesia from the flunitrazepam.) The current patterns in this country have also occurred as fads in other parts of the world in the past, but these patterns have now faded. It is likely that the current U.S. fad will also run its course in time.

The anxious patient who is also a drug abuser is discussed in the chapter on dual diagnosis.

PHARMACOLOGY

Benzodiazepines, alcohol, barbiturates, and other sedative/hypnotics act at the gamma amino butyric acid GABA receptor, which explains their cross-tolerance. All sedative/hypnotics act at the GABA receptor, causing the chloride channel to open and allowing chloride ions to enter it, with the net result that neuronal activity is suppressed. The fact that benzodiazepines do not depress respiration results, however, from their purely potentiating action at the GABA receptor. Benzodiazepines do not cause direct suppression of the receptor, as do all the other sedative/hypnotics. Potentiation versus suppression makes it next to impossible to use benzodiazepines alone to commit suicide, so they have a degree of safety not shared by other sedative/hypnotics. Differences in the area of the GABA receptor occupied by different benzodiazepines partially account for clinically significant differences in anxiolysis, effect on seizures, reduction of muscle spasms, and relief from insomnia.

PHYSICAL DEPENDENCE AND ABUSE LIABILITY

In sufficient dose, all the benzodiazepines cause dependence leading to clinically significant withdrawal, but there is not consensus that all benzodiazepines have an equal abuse liability. Most clinicians believe there are substantive differences. I have examined this question exhaustively as a paid consultant to Hoffmann La Roche. On the basis of my review, I advised the company that the evidence for significant differences between benzodiazepines with respect to abuse liability does not provide sufficient control for dose. My belief is based also on substantial clinical experience with these drugs.[3] In an extensive review of benzodiazepines, Woods and colleagues also take the position that the evidence for significant differences in abuse liability among benzodiazepines is flawed.[4] But there are many experts in the field, such as those who were involved in the American Psychiatric Association's review of benzodiazepines,[5] who believe that rapid-acting benzodiazepines have a higher abuse potential than benzodiazepines such as oxazepam or halazepam. If you encounter this question on a board exam, answer that there are differences, but in the clinic be aware that they all probably have some abuse liability in sufficient dose. In my opinion, use of benzodiazepines such as oxazepam and halazepam to produce the desired robust clinical effects must be at doses that make them parallel to other benzodiazepines in abuse-liability potential. Any drug that can produce physical dependence with clinically significant withdrawal and sedation should be monitored carefully, and oxazepam and halazepam both have these properties.

Benzodiazepines differ in lipophilicity, half-life, and metabolic pathway. These differences explain various clinically important phenomena.

The marked differences in degree of lipophilicity among benzodiazepines determine the rapidity of onset of effects. The route of biotransformation (e.g., liver oxidation versus conjugation) determines other clinically significant effects. Lorazepam and oxazepam, for example, are conjugated rather than oxidized by the liver. They may be preferred over benzodiazepines oxidized in the liver (diazepam and most other benzodiazepines) in cases of liver disease. Most benzodiazepines are more effective orally than by injection. Lorazepam is an exception, and this determines its usefulness in the management of severe delirium tremens, in which oral administration is not possible. Diazepam and chlordiazepoxide are both poorly absorbed parenterally. When oral administration is not possible, lorazepam is the drug of choice.

The half-life of benzodiazepines determines the period between stopping chronic administration and the onset of withdrawal. Onset of withdrawal from chronic benzodiazepine administration can range from a few hours after sudden cessation (such as with alprazolam) to 7 to 10 days (for diazepam and chlordiazepoxide). A classic case is the patient admitted to the hospital who is taking benzodiazepines, usually diazepam, as prescribed and forgets to tell the surgeon (and is not asked). On the fifth to the seventh hospital day, there is a seizure. As noted in chapter 1, all histories in all branches of medicine should contain a detailed section on current (past three weeks) and lifetime drug use.

Concurrent versus sequential use of sedative/hypnotics can produce quite different effects. A person a with heavy intake of alcohol, barbiturates, or benzodiazepines shows tolerance to the effects of each of the other classes. But the phenomenon of tolerance is evident when the drugs are being taken sequentially. When sedative/hypnotics are competing with one another for the same oxidative pathway, as in the case when the drugs are taken concurrently, the biotransformation of both may be slowed, resulting in increases in blood levels relative to what they would be if only one drug were involved.[6] This is important clinically, as it accounts for the fact that benzodiazepines are so often implicated in suicides, although taken alone they are free of this risk. In addition, this explains why patients on methadone sometimes take benzodiazepines to boost the effect of the methadone. By so doing, they slow the biotransformation of the methadone, changing a therapeutic dose (one that suppresses withdrawal and craving without psychoactive effects) into a dose that causes intoxication. The use of concurrent benzodiazepines also prolongs the effects of the methadone dose. The concurrent use of flunitrazepam and alcohol, as discussed above, is another example of this phenomenon. As noted, lorazepam is conjugated and is therefore preferable for use in methadone maintenance populations requiring benzodiazepine treatment.

AGONISTS, ANTAGONISTS, AND INVERSE AGONISTS

Benzodiazepines that reverse the suppressing effects of usual benzodiazepines at the GABA receptor have been discovered. Flumazenil is one such benzodiazepine antagonist, and it has medical use in reversing the benzodiazepine component in some mixed overdoses; it also reverses surgically induced anesthesia with benzodiazepines.[7]

Antagonists occupy the GABA receptor binding site and block regular agonists. Antagonists also block the actions of another class of drugs called inverse agonists, such as betacarboline. Inverse agonists produce effects that are the opposite of agonists (e.g., they increase rather than decrease anxiety). In medical use of flumazenil, one has to be careful not to give too high a dose when reversing benzodiazepine induced coma to avoid seizures.

BENZODIAZEPINES IN THE ELDERLY

Benzodiazepines have much stronger and more prolonged effects in the elderly. With advancing age, blood flow to the liver is decreased, with the consequence that benzodiazepines are biotransformed much more slowly than they are in the young. For whatever indication, one should monitor carefully and begin with half the dose one would use in a healthy young person. I have seen many elderly people almost anesthetized by doses appropriate only for younger patients. With marked reductions in dose, therapeutic effects can occur without the sedation or intoxication. Differences in biotransformation with aging probably also account for falls in the elderly taking benzodiazepines.[8]

THERAPEUTIC VERSUS SIDE EFFECTS

As noted, benzodiazepines have pronounced effects on anxiety; in sufficient dose, they induce sleep. They have marked effects in reducing muscle spasms, and they are effective anticonvulsants. But these positive effects are sometimes accompanied by side effects such as impairment of sleep architecture, ataxia, dysarthria, amnesia, impairment in motor functions accompanied by lack of recognition of the degree of impairment, cognitive impairment, daytime sleepiness, and disinhibition reactions in which individuals exhibit uncharacteristic behavior (e.g., bizarre behavior, rage, hostility). In addition, there is a range of other rare effects such as allergies and hematologic abnormalities. Many of the negative effects can be minimized by decreasing the dose.

Some of these problems are probably rooted in the fact that in premarketing clinical trials, for many indications, only drug experienced individuals can be entered into the testing. These individuals are frequently tolerant to sedative/hypnotics, and, as a result, therapeutic doses are arrived at that are sometimes too high for the nontolerant user. The clinician using benzodiazepines should be aware of this and perhaps start at lower doses than recommended in package inserts, particularly in patients with no previous exposure to drugs or alcohol. If therapeutic effects are not achieved with these lower doses, the dose can always be raised.

A pregnant woman who uses benzodiazepines may deliver an infant with benzodiazepine withdrawal symptoms.[9]

WITHDRAWAL FROM BENZODIAZEPINES

DSM-4 criteria for the diagnosis of Sedative, Hypnotic, or Anxiolytic Withdrawal

A. Cessation of (or reduction in) sedative, hypnotic, or anxiolytic use that has been heavy and prolonged

B. Two (or more) of the following, developing within several hours to a few days after criterion A:
   1) autonomic hyperactivity (e.g., sweating or pulse rate greater than 100)
   2) increased hand tremor
   3) insomnia
   4) nausea or vomiting
   5) transient visual, tactile, or auditory hallucinations or illusions
   6) psychomotor agitation
   7) anxiety
   8) grand mal seizures

C. The symptoms in criterion B cause clinically significant distress or impairment in social, occupational, or other important areas of functioning.

D. The symptoms are not due to a general medical condition and are not better accounted for by another mental disorder.

Specify if:
With perceptual disturbances: This specifier may be noted when hallucinations with intact reality testing or auditory, visual, or tactile illusions occur in the absence of a delirium. Intact reality testing means that the person knows that the hallucinations are induced by the substance and do not represent external reality. When hallucinations occur in the absence of intact reality testing, a diagnosis of Substance Induced Psychotic Disorder, with Hallucinations, should be considered.

In general, the severity of withdrawal is greater with longer term use and higher doses. It can include delirium and, in individuals with a complicating condition such as cardiovascular disease, death, so dependence on these drugs is a serious clinical problem.[10-12] The clinician should review the general principles of management of withdrawal presented in chapter 1. Dependence on benzodiazepines can occur at therapeutic levels of use. Withdrawal from such doses, while usually manageable with slow reduction, is occasionally accompanied by severe symptoms. Slow outpatient withdrawal can be defined as a reduction of 5 to 10 percent per week when starting the withdrawal, to 2 to 3 percent per week for the lower-dose segment of the regimen. If severe symptoms such as hallucinations, severe cramping, fear of going insane, or the like occur, one should entertain hospitalization and/or referral to an addiction medicine unit. In these difficult cases, the quality of the total withdrawal program, and especially the quality of the therapeutic relationship, can be critical to success.

As with most other drugs of dependence, it is ideal to gain control over all withdrawal symptoms for one to two days as a stabilization period before beginning the detoxification. In this time one can build a relationship and describe roles and the program elements, as detailed in chapter 1.

In drug abusing populations, very high doses of benzodiazepines (e.g., 5 to 20 times higher than the therapeutic level) are sometimes encountered. It is probably best to hospitalize these cases because of the danger of a fatal withdrawal delirium. The likelihood of multiple simultaneous dependencies should be entertained in these instances and toxicology screens taken on admission with this possibility in mind. If alprazolam, a triazolo benzodiazepine, is the drug of dependence, then other benzodiazepines cannot substitute for it. One can substitute phenobarbital at a dose of 30 mg of phenobarbital for each 1 mg of alprazolam,[13] or one can use alprazolam itself if the phenobarbital substitution is problematic.

Smith and Wesson have a list of phenobarbital equivalents that is useful for the clinician wanting to use the phenobarbital substitution method for benzodiazepine withdrawal.[14] For multiple simultaneous dependencies (e.g., alcohol, benzodiazepines, and some other sedative/hypnotic drugs), phenobarbital substitution offers a single drug method of accomplishing withdrawal. As discussed in chapter 1, the clinician may have to give a dose and observe the effects, building the withdrawal regimen based on clinical response.

Sedative/Hypnotics and Their Phenobarbital Withdrawal Equivalents

Generic name	Trade name	Common Therapeutic Indications	Therapeutic Dose Range (mg/day)	Dose Equivalent to 30 mg Phenobarbital for Withdrawal (mg)
Barbiturates				
Amobarbital	Amytal	Sedative	50–150	100
Butabarbital	Butisol	Sedative	45–120	100
Butalbital	Fiorinal	Sedative/analgesic	100–300	100
Pentobarbital	Nembutal	Hypnotic	50–100[b]	100
Secobarbital	Seconal	Hypnotic	50–100[b]	100
Other sedative/hypnotics				
Buspirone	BuSpar	Sedative	15–60	NC
Chloral hydrate	Noctec, Somnos	Hypnotic	250–1000	500
Ethchlorvynol	Placidyl	Hypnotic	500–1000	500
Glutethimide	Doriden	Hypnotic	250–500	250
Meprobamate	Miltown, Equanil, Equagesic	Sedative	1200–1600	400
Methyprylon	Noludar	Hypnotic	200–400	200

Note: NC = not cross-tolerant with barbiturates

A phenobarbital withdrawal conversion equivalence is not the same as therapeutic dose equivalency. Withdrawal equivalence is the amount of the drug that 30 mg of phenobarbital will substitute for, and for which it will prevent serious high-dose withdrawal signs and symptoms. Butalbital is usually available in combination with opiate or nonopiate analgesics.

RETURN AND REBOUND OF SYMPTOMS

Return of symptoms refers to the reappearance of the symptoms for which the benzodiazepines were prescribed after withdrawal has been completed; symptom rebound means that the symptoms return but in more severe form. In rebound, the implication is that withdrawal may be complicating the picture, and this should be considered. One might reinstitute slow withdrawal to escape the rebound phenomenon, but in perhaps one third of cases, withdrawal from benzodiazepines is difficult and can be protracted for many weeks or months. The quality of the recovery program can be very important in managing these symptoms; it helps patients get through the difficult withdrawal and become comfortable again.

INTOXICATION WITH BENZODIAZEPINES: DIAGNOSTIC CRITERIA

DSM-4 criteria for benzodiazepine intoxication are as follows:

DSM-4 Diagnosis Criteria for 292.89 Sedative, Hypnotic, or Anxiolytic Intoxication

A. Recent use of a sedative, hypnotic, or anxiolytic

B. Clinically significant maladaptive behavioral or psychological changes (e.g., inappropriate sexual or aggressive behavior, mood lability, impaired judgment, impaired social or occupational functioning) that developed during, or shortly after, sedative, hypnotic, or anxiolytic use

C. One (or more) of the following signs, developing during, or shortly after, sedative, hypnotic, or anxiolytic use
    1) slurred speech
    2) incoordination
    3) unsteady gait
    4) nystagmus
    5) impairment in attention or memory
    6) stupor or coma

D. The symptoms are not due to a general medical condition and are not better accounted for by another mental disorder.

Management of these states has been described in chapter 1.

The reader will note that criterion B raises a host of clinical and medicolegal questions. On a clinical level, what kind of pathology does someone with these behaviors have? My experience strongly suggests that the benzodiazepines release feelings and wishes that are current and strongly conflictual for the patient. In other words, the drugs do not generate a behavior; they can only release what is already there. Benzodiazepines can influence the neuronal assemblies that underlie judgment, and in this sense they are causative; but the person is responsible for the released behaviors if he or she has taken the drug to produce intoxication.

In the legal arena, the question is similar. Can benzodiazepines create aggression, or do they release aggression that is already there? If someone takes benzodiazepines to get intoxicated and then becomes assaultive, is it the benzodiazepines that are responsible, or is the person responsible? Is the manufacturer liable? Given the fact that benzodiazepines are among the most frequently used drugs, with literally billions of doses used every year, the number of times these questions arise is so small that, in my mind, the notion that benzodiazepines cause aggression or ruin people's lives is without any logical basis.

Response to benzodiazepines is dependent partially on prior use of alcohol and other drugs.[15-17] A number of studies indicate that normals do not like the effects of benzodiazepines, and that under double-blind conditions, they select placebo in preference to benzodiazepines (and other sedatives). When subjects with a history of drug dependence are studied under double-blind conditions, they prefer benzodiazepines and other sedatives to placebo.

These findings from the research laboratory confirm the clinical experience that people who abuse benzodiazepines frequently have had previous heavy intake of alcohol and/or other drugs. The clinician using benzodiazepines to treat indicated conditions for these drugs needs to have a careful history confirmed by a third party, if possible, to avoid abuse or dependence on benzodiazepines as a complication of therapeutic use.

OTHER SEDATIVE/HYPNOTICS

Barbiturates and nonbarbiturate sedative/hypnotics are increasingly not used in mainstream medicine, with the exception of some barbiturates for epilepsy, but they are found frequently enough in the drug culture to be represented in emergency-room mentions. Drugs such as ethchlorvynol (Placidyl) and glutethimide (Doriden) are occasionally used by street addicts, usually in combination with codeine-containing cough syrup (e.g., "syrup and beans" for codeine-containing cough syrup taken with ethchlorvinyl, and "doors and fours" for Doriden taken with codeine-containing cough syrup). Other drugs of this class used on the street are methaqualone (Quaalude), methyprylon (Noludar), and meprobamate (Milltown). All these non-benzodiazepines have the potential for use in suicide and for overdose. In addition, they have narrow margins between toxic and therapeutic effects, and they have negative effects on sleep architecture. If current trends continue, they may soon be of historical interest only.

REFERENCES

1. DuPont RL, Saylor KE. Sedative/hypnotics and benzodiazepines, in Frances RS, Miller SI (eds), *Clinical Textbook of Addictive Disorders*. New York, Guilford Press, 1991.
2. Miller NS, Gold MS. Abuse, addiction, tolerance, and dependence to benzodiazepines in medical and nonmedical populations. *Am J Drug Alcohol Abuse* 17:27–37, 1991.

3. Senay EC. Addictive behaviors and benzodiazepines: Are there differences between benzodiazepines in potential for physical dependence and abuse liability? *Adv Alcohol Substance Abuse* 9:53–64, 1990.

4. Woods JH, Katz JL, Winger G. Abuse liability of benzodiazepines. *Pharm Rev* 39:254–390, 1987.

5. American Psychiatric Association Task Force on Benzodiazepine Dependency. *Benzodiazepine Dependence, Toxicity, and Abuse.* American Psychiatric Association, Washington, DC, 1990.

6. Schuckit M. *Drug and Alcohol Abuse*, ed 4. New York, Plenum, 1995, p 29.

7. Hubbs WR, Rall TW, Verdoorn TA. Hypnotics and sedatives: Ethanol, in Hardman JG, Limbird LE (eds), *Goodman & Gilman's The Pharmacologic Basis of Therapeutics*, ed 9. New York, McGraw Hill, 1996, pp 364–365.

8. Ray WA, Griffin MR, Downey W. Benzodiazepines of long and short elimination half-life and the risk of hip fracture. *JAMA* 262:3303–3307, 1989.

9. Bergman U, Rosa FW, Baum C, et al. Effects of exposure to benzodiazepine during fetal life. *Lancet* 340:694–696, 1992.

10. Rickels K, Case WG, Schweizer EE, et al. Low-dose dependence in chronic benzodiazepine users: A preliminary report on 119 patients. *Psychopharmacology* 22:407–415, 1986.

11. Busto U, Sellers EM, Naranjo CA, et al. Withdrawal reaction after long-term therapeutic use of benzodiazepines. *N Engl J Med* 315:854–859, 1986.

12. Smith DE, Wesson DR. Benzodiazepine dependency syndromes. *J Psychoactive Drugs* 15:85–95, 1983.

13. Ravi NV, Maany I, Burke WM, et al. Detoxification with phenobarbital of alprazolam dependent poly-substance abusers. *J Substance Abuse Treatment* 7:55–58, 1990.

14. Smith DE, Wesson DR. Benzodiazepines and other sedative hypnotics, in Galanter M, Kleber H (eds), *Textbook of Substance Abuse Treatment.* Washington, DC, American Psychiatric Press, 1994, p 188.

15. Johanson CE, Uhlenhuth EH. Drug preference and mood in humans: Diazepam. *Psychopharmacology* 71:269–273, 1980.

16. DeWit H, Johanson CE, Uhlenhuth EH. Reinforcing properties of lorazepam in normal volunteer subjects. *Drug Alcohol Dependence* 13:31–41, 1984.

17. DeWit H, Uhlenhuth EH, Johanson CE. Lack of preference for flurazepam in normal volunteers. *Pharmacol Biochem Behav* 21:865–869, 1984.

7. Tobacco Products

Tobacco products kill 440,000 people a year in the United States, more people than are killed by all other legal and illegal intoxicants taken together. It is the number-one cause of preventable death and our most destructive public health problem by a great margin. No form of drug dependence illustrates the many contradictory faces of the dependence problem better than nicotine. There are a few people who "chip," in the language of the drug world; that is, they use nicotine cigarettes only occasionally, and then just one or a few at a time. They can take it or leave it, and they never develop problems of any kind from this drug. For most people, however, once use starts, sooner or later it escalates to the pack-a-day level or higher, and the habit is ultimately lethal for a great many users. For many, nicotine cigarettes rank with the most severe of intoxicants with respect to rapidity of onset of dependence, relapse potential, and frequent and serious health problems.[1]

Many studies show that smokers are aware of the risks, and most attempt to quit because of this awareness. Attempts to quit are usually not successful,[2] but after many serious attempts to quit, about 50 percent finally succeed. Most of those who do quit do so without treatment. It is estimated that with treatment, about 25 percent are abstinent at one year. In my experience, abstinence of this duration usually means that abstinence will be sustained. As is the case with most other drugs of dependence, relapse rates are highest in the time immediately after stopping. In general, after three months of abstinence, the likelihood of eventual complete abstinence increases steadily with the passage of time, if abstinence is maintained.

A large number of studies indicate that smokers want health care professionals to detect and treat their nicotine habit. But most health care professionals are not trained to diagnose or treat any behavioral problem and often have defeatist attitudes. These attitudes reinforce the negative pole of the ambivalence of the drug dependent person, and they become part of the problem. At a minimum, health care professionals should take histories and offer advice and self-help materials to all smokers in their practice. Glyn and Manley have summarized large-scale studies showing that these efforts help many people who otherwise would not change their habits.[3] The April 24, 1996, issue of the *Journal of the American Medical Association* also contains excellent material on smoking cessation for the interested physician or health professional.[4] The American Psychiatric Association has developed a practice guideline for the treatment of patients with nicotine dependence that is focused on the psychiatric aspects of the problem.[5]

When a problem such as nicotine smoking is so pervasive, costly, and long established, there is a tendency both personally and socially to believe that there is not much anyone can do, and that we just have to put up with it as best we can. But we have not always had such widespread smoking of tobacco products. In the 1920s, alcohol and nicotine-cigarette smoking increased markedly in the United States. The chief vehicle for these increases was the commercialization of their use by the alcohol and nicotine industries through the entertainment/information community. (Almost certainly, the same degree of spread can be anticipated by the same mechanism if the marijuana lobby succeeds in its efforts to legalize marijuana.)

PHARMACOLOGY

Nicotine is a base. In acid media, it is ionized and therefore is not absorbed across membranes. In alkaline media, it is not ionized and is absorbed across membranes. Nicotine gum is, therefore, alkaline to support the buccal absorption of nicotine. Nicotine is rapidly metabolized in the liver, and it has a half-life of approximately 120 minutes. Its major metabolite, cotinine, has a much longer half-life, thus making it useful for monitoring tobacco use in treatment or in epidemiologic studies. Nicotine has complex effects on a large number of biologic systems, including release of ACTH, B-endorphin, B-lipotropin, growth hormone, and vasopressin. It also stimulates release of epinephrine and norepinephrine from the adrenal gland. Recent research has found that nicotine lowers monamine oxidase B in the brain, thus extending the stimulating activity of dopamine in synaptic clefts, an effect long thought to be related to pleasure.[6]

Nicotine increases heart rate and blood pressure and causes peripheral vasoconstriction; through acetylcholine release, it increases gastrointestinal tone and motor activity of the bowel.

Inhaled sidestream smoke or environmental tobacco smoke has been studied extensively and has proven to be toxic, with many of the same consequences as smoking nicotine cigarettes directly. The pulmonary membrane is much more efficient in absorbing particulate matter than the membrane of the gastrointestinal tract. Repace notes, "In a healthy adult, 5 percent of a gram of (orally) ingested lead will be absorbed while 95 percent of the same amount of lead inhaled as a fume from automobile exhaust will be absorbed."[7] Repace also points out the weakness of our response to the tobacco problem, which reflects the political power of tobacco money. In 1988, Chilean grapes were banned in the United States because they had cyanide levels a few percent of those delivered by smoking one cigarette.

NICOTINE WITHDRAWAL

Nicotine has a distinct withdrawal syndrome. The DSM-4 criteria are as follows:

DSM-4 Diagnosis Criteria for Nicotine Withdrawal

A.   Daily use of nicotine for at least several weeks

B. Abrupt cessation of nicotine use, or reduction in the amount of nicotine used, followed
    within 24 hours by four (or more) of the following signs:
    1) dysphoric or depressed mood
    2) insomnia
    3) irritability, frustration, or anger
    4) anxiety
    5) difficulty concentrating
    6) restlessness
    7) decreased heart rate
    8) increased appetite or weight gain

C. The symptoms in criterion B cause clinically significant distress or impairment in social,
    occupational, or other important areas of functioning.

D. The symptoms are not due to a general medical condition and are not better accounted for
    by another mental disorder.

In addition to these signs and symptoms, nicotine withdrawal involves a number of other cognitive disturbances, such as impaired arithmetic ability and impaired logical reasoning. These impairments are rapidly reversed by nicotine self-administration.

Tolerance occurs with repeated use of nicotine. When the dependent person lowers the amount of intake, craving for the drug increases. For most users, craving, in combination with the factors reviewed above, exerts powerful control over behavior and accounts for the large numbers of people who have great difficulty stopping this behavioral pattern. Most physicians have seen patients with severe chronic pulmonary disease who have literally smoked themselves to death, completely unable to stop smoking even with good treatment.

DIAGNOSIS AND TREATMENT OF NICOTINE DEPENDENCE

Diagnosis is based on the criteria reviewed in chapter 1 for dependence. Nicotine abuse is not a DSM-4 diagnosis. In addition to establishing a diagnosis, the physician should also administer the Fagerstrom test for nicotine dependence. Scores range from 0 to 10, with increasing scores indicating more severe dependence and an increasing likelihood that nicotine substitution will increase the chance of a good treatment outcome.

In the managed care environment, scales like this will probably become the standard for clinical practice. On a clinical level, prior to the development of such scoring systems, I approximated them by asking two questions: How many cigarettes a day do you smoke? and Do you smoke first thing in the morning? More than 15 cigarettes a day and/or yes to the second question marked those for whom I would recommend nicotine substitution as one element in a cessation program.

Items and Scoring for Fagerstrom Test for Nicotine Dependence
Adapted from Fagerstrom KO, Heatherton TF. Kozlowski LT. Nicotine addiction and its assessment. *Ear Nose Throat J* 69:763–767, 1992.

Questions	Answers	Points
1. How soon after you wake up do you smoke your first cigarette?	Within 5 minutes	3
	6–30 minutes	2
	31–60 minutes	1
	After 60 minutes	0
2. Do you find it difficult to refrain from smoking in places where it is forbidden, e.g., in church, at the library, in a cinema?	Yes	1
	No	0
3. Which cigarette would you hate most to give up?	The first one in the morning	1
	All others	0
4. How many cigarettes/day do you smoke?	10 or less	0
	11–20	1
	21–30	2
	31 or more	3
5. Do you smoke more frequently during the first hours after waking than during the rest of the day?	Yes	1
	No	0
6. Do you smoke if you are so ill that you are in bed most of the day?	Yes	1
	No	0
Proposed scoring cut-offs	0–2	Very Low
	3–4	Low
	5	Medium
	6–7	High (heavy)
	8–10	Very High

Ideally, all physicians would implement the following for nicotine diagnosis and treatment.

- Take a history of nicotine use from every patient as part of a more general substance abuse history. Note the results in the chart. If the history is positive, continue to monitor the natural course of the problem and the results of any interventions you may make, and note changes in the chart.
- Use the "Here's the problem—here's the solution" approach described in chapter 1 for all who are dependent. Assess reasons for wanting to quit and barriers to quitting. Common reasons for wanting to quit are health concerns, resentment about not having control, and hygiene, while fear of not being able to quit and

weight gain for both males and females are common barriers. These reasons should be reviewed; such a review usually reveals a relatively distinctive profile of pros and cons for quitting for each individual. It is important to use this profile in affirming and supporting the individual during the attempt to quit.

The fear of gaining weight should be dealt with by education. The usual number of pounds gained in the successful attempt to stop smoking is 4 to 10 pounds. In addition, the patient should be reassured that a 10-pound weight gain is far less harmful than continuing to smoke. Patients should be advised to eat lower-calorie foods and to adopt some form of increased exercise while attempting to quit. Dieting is not recommended during a quit attempt, but a gradual shift to healthier foods and an exercise program are advisable. There are excellent self-help manuals available from the sources cited at the end of this chapter.

- Either provide some minimal counseling and nicotine substitution treatment in the office or refer the patient to a smoking-cessation program, if one exists in the community. The best treatment results can be obtained from referral to a behavioral medicine clinic, where behavior therapies such as skills training, relapse prevention, stimulus control, cue exposure, and others (which are reviewed well in the APA guideline[5]) are combined with nicotine substitution. As is the case in treating any abuse or dependence, treatment failures should receive a more intensive level of treatment with higher doses of substituted nicotine, more counseling, and the like. Alternative therapies such as acupuncture and hypnosis can be tried. I believe any kind of treatment attempt is better than none. I have used inpatient hospitalization for treatment of refractory cases with end-stage medical problems and intractable smoking.
- Maintain an interest in the problem even if you refer patients to specialists. The more people who are interested and supportive, the better the chance of success in treatment.
- The goal of treatment is total abstinence. There is a consensus that sudden stopping is the preferred method because of extensive clinical experience that slow withdrawal or lowered levels of intake cannot be sustained by most nicotine dependent people. Patients should be told respectfully that these approaches will probably fail and will only waste time, but if a patient is adamant and wants to try tapering, work with the patient to try to make this successful.
- The environment is critical for sustained abstinence. If the nicotine dependent person is married to or in a close relationship with another nicotine dependent person, the couple should be treated. For any recovering user, socializing with users is a recipe for relapse.
- If the physician does the counseling for the person trying to quit, there are some general principles to follow. Set a quit date, and prior to this date have the patient inform friends, family, and co-workers of the attempt to quit. The patient should be instructed to remove all tobacco and tobacco paraphernalia from every environment the patient is in, as these can serve as cues or triggers for relapse. Alcohol intake should be moderated or avoided completely, as intoxication may

lead to reinstatement of the nicotine dependence. Take a careful history of previous attempts to quit and use the lessons to create a better plan for this attempt.

Educate the patient to the fact that with continued abstinence, urges and craving diminish in frequency and intensity until they disappear or diminish to the point of not driving behavior. The patient's job is to hold out. When temptation becomes overwhelming, the patient should call the therapist or other support person including the physician, change environments, or do whatever is necessary so as not to give in to the craving. Materials on smoking can be obtained from the sources identified at the end of this chapter. They can be tailored to the age, culture, race, and educational level of the patient.

- Groups can be as effective as individual sessions for smoking cessation for most patients. There are some patients who cannot be comfortable in a group, and they need and should get one-to-one counseling. These patients are usually quite forthright and explicit about their inability to get anything out of groups.
- Careful review of relapse experiences should be projected as a standard part of treatment. A relapse should not be viewed as failure; rather, it should be viewed as additional information on what has to change for eventual success. If a behavioral therapist is part of the treatment, the chances of success are increased. A complete mapping of the triggers for relapse should be carried out, and the patient should review how to cope with these triggers.
- Nicotine dependence has the same underlying continuum of stages of change as any other form of dependence. A few patients are ready for change and will have completed a lot of preparation at the time of workup. Simple advice and support may be all they need to be successful in stopping. But these patients do not define the population of nicotine dependent people any more than those who are totally refractory to any form of therapy. As noted above, this end of the continuum is marked by smoking that literally causes death or the kind of extreme disability seen in emphysema. Most patients are in the middle of the continuum. It is important to place them correctly, as this will lead to the best treatment plan.
- Co-morbid disorders, especially anxiety and depression, often prevent success in stopping smoking. This appears to be especially true in females, who more often use nicotine for mood control than is the case in males. Referral to a psychiatrist for recommendations on treatment of the depression may be necessary for success in stopping smoking.

PHARMACOTHERAPY OF NICOTINE DEPENDENCE[5]

NICOTINE GUM

Nicotine gum in 2 mg and 4 mg doses is a common method of providing nicotine substitution treatment. The 2 mg gum is used for patients with lesser degrees of dependence, as measured on the Fagerstrom scale, whereas for patients scoring 7 or above, the 4 mg gum would be indicated. The APA guidelines recommend 1 piece of gum per hour rather than the older approach of using gum only when the patient experiences craving. Problems with the gum include jaw soreness, dyspepsia, and hiccups. Patients should not drink coffee, juice, or soda when using the gum, as this acidifies the mouth and prevents buccal absorption of the nicotine.

The Smoking Cessation Clinical Practice Guideline[4] recommends an eight-week period for nicotine substitution therapy, with the first four weeks at a high stable dose and the next two to four weeks at lowered doses (e.g., for Nicoderm and Habitrol, 21 mg per day for the first four weeks, then 14 mg per day for two weeks, and 7 mg per day for the final two weeks). Patients should be advised not to use more than 30 pieces of the 2 mg gum or 20 pieces of the 4 mg gum in any 24-hour period, as such use may lead to nicotine toxicity (nausea, vomiting, abdominal pain, labile blood pressure, and, in the extreme, death from circulatory collapse or apnea).

Some patients are successful in stopping nicotine smoking but become dependent on the gum. Unless there is a complicating medical condition, this is a more benign dependence than cigarette smoking, and the clinician should help the patient maintain abstinence from nicotine cigarettes while slowly working on the gum dependence problem. As discussed in chapter 1, failure of treatment at any given intensity requires a more intensive program, and this should be implemented. Referral to an ASAM-certified physician or behavioral medicine practitioner should be considered, or the possibility of group or individual sessions should be entertained. The history should indicate what is needed.

Nicotine substitution creates blood levels of nicotine that are 5 to 10 times lower than levels associated with regular smoking. If the disparity between the levels achieved with the gum and the patient's usual levels is large, the patient may not get much help from the gum even with the 4 mg dose. If this is the case, the gum can be combined with nicotine patches.

NICOTINE PATCHES

Nicotine is readily absorbed through the skin, and patches capitalize on this. Patches are available that deliver either 24-hour-a-day or 16-hour-a-day dosing. One of the side effects of the patches is insomnia and vivid dreams. In these cases, one would switch to the 16-hour-a-day dosing regimen to see if this helps. Patches provide a blood level that is about half what is achieved through regular smoking. The dose per patch at the start of treatment is 21 to 22 mg for the 24-hour patch and 15 to 16 mg per patch for the 16-hour patch. After four to six weeks, the dose is reduced to 14 mg for the 24-hour patch and to 10 mg for the 16-hour patch; after 2 to 4 weeks, to 7 mg for the 24-hour patch and 5 mg for the 16-hour patch. The usual duration of treatment with the patch is between 6 and 12 weeks.

Skin reactions are common and are dealt with by rotating the site of the patches or applying cortisone creams if a site is severely irritated.

NICOTINE NASAL SPRAY

Nicotine nasal spray comes in a bottle, from which it can be delivered to the nasal mucosa in a spray. This product has just come on the market, and it provides a rise in nicotine blood levels that is faster and higher than levels associated with nicotine gum. Patients are advised to use the spray up to 30 times a day for 12 weeks, with a tapering period determined by clinical response. Side effects are common and include irritation of the nasal mucosa and throat, watery eyes, sneezing, and coughing. The APA guidelines suggest that the nasal spray be used after gum and patches have been tried. In practice, one should discuss all the above possibilities together with their side effects, and patient choice should ultimately determine what is tried first.

Nicotine abstinence is mandatory while using nicotine substitution therapy to avoid nicotine poisoning, and patients should be so advised.

RELATIVE CONTRAINDICATIONS FOR NICOTINE SUBSTITUTION THERAPY

Pregnancy is a relative contraindication for nicotine substitution therapy because the vasoconstricting effects of the nicotine lower blood delivery to the fetus. Benowitz, however, in a review of the problem, concludes that the benefits of substitution therapy outweigh the risks for pregnant women who are heavy smokers and who are not responsive to psychosocial treatment.[8] Lactating women should not receive nicotine substitution treatment without careful weighing of the risk/benefit ratio. Cardiovascular problems such as arrhythmias or angina are relative contraindications for nicotine substitution. If clinical circumstance dictates that nicotine substitution should be tried (e.g., a patient has had prior success; the consequences of continuing smoking, such as severe cough, carry risk in themselves), then, with formal medical consultation, the gum, patch, or spray can be used. Monitoring should be frequent, and if negative consequences occur, the attempt should be aborted.

OTHER PHARMACOLOGIC TREATMENTS FOR NICOTINE DEPENDENCE

CLONIDINE

For treatment of refractory patients, clonidine should be considered. Clonidine can be given either orally or by transdermal patch in doses of 0.1 to 0.4 mg per day for two to six days. It must then be tapered off in the second week, as use of clonidine for more than two weeks may be associated with a withdrawal syndrome from the clonidine. If possible, clonidine should be given in conjunction with behavioral therapy. The side effects of clonidine as used for smoking cessation are dry mouth, sedation, and constipation. With this drug, hypotension, rebound hypertension on cessation of intake, and depression are infrequent but must be weighed carefully before committing to this therapy.

BUSPIRONE

Buspirone is a serotonergic agonist with minimal side effects. It has been used for smokers with high anxiety levels and may have some utility for others. In treatment of refractory patients, it may be considered.

ANTIDEPRESSANTS

For smokers with a history of major depression or dysphoria, a trial of antidepressants may be considered. The drug should be started well in advance of the quit date so that its effects are active at the time of cessation.

A complete listing of the health consequences of tobacco use is beyond the scope of this book, but the following table, reprinted from Shopland and Burns,[9] is a good summary of the major consequences. These should be known by every physician and carefully reviewed with every patient.

The Health Consequences of Smoking and the Benefits of Quitting at a Glance

Health Consequences	Benefits of Quitting
Overall mortality risk is 2 times higher in cigarette smokers compared to nonsmokers.	Stopping smoking reduces the risk of premature death, with 50 percent of the risk eliminated within 5 years of quitting. After 15 years off cigarettes, a former smoker's risk is nearly identical to that of life-long nonsmoker.
Lung cancer risk in smokers is more than 20 times higher in men and 12 times higher in women.	After 10 years of abstinence, the risk of lung cancer is reduced by 30 to 50 percent. The longer the period of cessation, the greater the reduction in risk.
The risk of cancer of the oral cavity in men is more than 20 times higher in smokers. The risk in women smokers is between 5 and 10 times greater.	Quitting halves the risk compared to continued smoking as soon as 5 years after cessation. Further risk reduction occurs over a longer period of abstinence.
The risk of cancer of the esophagus among smokers is between 5 and 10 times higher.	Quitting significantly reduces risk; 5 years following cessation, the risk is reduced by 50 percent.
Pancreatic cancer risks in smokers are 2 to 3 times higher.	Cessation reduces risk, although it may only be measurable after 10 years of abstinence.
Bladder cancer risks in smokers are between 2 and 4 times greater among both men and women.	Cessation reduces risk by about 50 percent after only a few years.
Cervical cancer risk among women who smoke is approximately 2 to 3 times higher.	The risk in women who have stopped smoking is substantially lower even in the first few years after cessation.

Coronary heart disease (CHD) risks due to smoking are higher at younger than older age groups. For both men and women under age 65 years, CHD risks in smokers are 3 times higher than for nonsmokers.	The risk is reduced among men and women of all ages. Excess risk of CHD caused by smoking is reduced by about half after 1 year of abstinence. After 15 years of abstinence, the risk of CHD is similar to that of persons who have never smoked.
Individuals with diagnosed CHD	The risk of recurrent infarction or premature death is reduced by 50 percent or more.
Peripheral artery occlusive disease	Cessation substantially reduces risk.
Ischemic stroke and subarachnoid hemorrhage are between 2 and 5 times more common in smokers.	After cessation, risk is reduced to the level of never-smokers after approximately 10 years of abstinence.
Respiratory symptoms such as cough, sputum production, and wheezing	The rates are reduced compared to continued smoking; often symptoms disappear within 6 months following cessation.
Persons without overt chronic obstructive pulmonary disease (COPD)	Pulmonary function can improve slightly (about 5 percent) within a few months after cessation.
Accelerates the age-related decline in lung function	With sustained abstinence from smoking, the rate of decline in the pulmonary function of former smokers returns to that of never-smokers.
COPD mortality rates among smokers are 10 times higher than in nonsmokers.	Sustained abstinence reduces COPD mortality rates in comparison with continuing smokers.
Low-birth-weight babies	Women who stop smoking before pregnancy have infants of the same birth weight as those born to never-smokers.
Smoking cessation any time up to the 30th week of gestation results in infants with higher birth weight than if smoking continues throughout pregnancy.	Quitting before the start of the second trimester results in infants with birth weight similar to those born to never-smoking women.
Onset of menopause	Smoking causes women to have natural menopause 1 to 2 years early. Former smokers have an age at natural menopause similar to that of never-smokers.
Duodenal and gastric ulcers	The increased risk is reduced by smoking cessation. Smoking cessation is often medically necessary to promote healing.

Nicotine is discussed further in the chapter on dual diagnosis.

REFERENCES

1. Henningfield JE, Cohen C, Slade JD. Is nicotine more addictive than cocaine? *Br J Addict* 86:565–569, 1991.
2. US Department of Health and Human Services. *Preventing Tobacco Use Among Young People: A Report of the Surgeon General.* Washington, DC, US Government Printing Office, 1994.
3. Glyn TJ, Manley MW. *How to Help Your Patients Stop Smoking: A National Cancer Institute Manual for Physicians.* US Department of Health and Human Services, NIH Publication No 89-3064, 1989.
4. *JAMA* 275:1215–1290, 1996.
5. *Practice Guideline for the Treatment of Patients With Nicotine Dependence.* Washington, DC, American Psychiatric Press, 1995.
6. Clues found to tobacco addiction. *JAMA* 275:1217–1218, 1996.
7. Repace JL. Tobacco smoke pollution, in Orleans CT, Slade J (eds), *Nicotine Addiction: Principles and Management.* Oxford, England, Oxford University Press, 1993.
8. Benowitz NL. Nicotine replacement therapy during pregnancy. *JAMA* 266:3174–3177, 1991.
9. Shopland DR, Burns DM. Medical and public health implications of tobacco addiction, in Orleans CT, Slade J (eds), *Nicotine Addiction.* Oxford, England, Oxford University Press, 1991.

RESOURCES

American Cancer Society
1599 Clifton Road NE
Atlanta, GA 30329
404-320-3333

American Heart Association
7272 Greenville Avenue
Dallas, TX 75231
214-373-6300
1-800-242-8721

American Lung Association
1740 Broadway, 14th Floor
New York, NY 10019
212-315-8700
1-800-586-4872

Hazelden Educational Materials
15245 Pleasant Valley Road
Center City, MN 55012-0176
1-800-328-9000

National Cancer Institute
Publications Ordering Service
P.O. Box 24128
Baltimore Highlands, MD 21227
1-800-422-6237

Terry A. Rustin, M.D.
Behavioral Medicine
9731 Greenwillow
Houston, TX 77096
713-728-4473

8. Stimulants

Goodman and Gilman's textbook does not define formally the term *stimulant* and does not discuss stimulants under one heading. Cocaine is presented under local anesthetics, amphetamine, miscellaneous adrenergic agonists and caffeine, and drugs useful in asthma; all are discussed in the chapter on drug addiction and drug abuse, where they are grouped under the heading CNS Sympathomimetics.[1] The term *stimulants* lacks a precise scientific definition and refers, loosely, to a set of drugs that share, to varying degrees, a complex of subjective and physiological effects including euphoria; increases in energy, alertness, and self-confidence; elevations of blood pressure and respiratory rate; suppression of appetite; reduced fatigue; and reduced fatigue induced decrements in performance. Stimulants decrease REM sleep as an acute effect, with increases in REM sleep in withdrawal.

Withdrawal from stimulants is characterized by dysphoria, irritability, depression, insomnia, and, with some members of this class, periods of intense craving. Results of studies of stimulant self-administration in animals range from self-administration to the exclusion of all other activities until death for cocaine, to weak or absent self-administration for caffeine, to no self-administration with phenylpropanolamine. In human populations, with respect to abuse liability and dependence potential, this class includes one of the most malignant drugs, cocaine, as well as one of the most benign, caffeine.

Stimulants and hallucinogens are closely related and cannot be separated with scientific rigor. Before its perceptual changes occur, LSD, for example, has stimulant effects indistinguishable from the effects of amphetamine or cocaine. Many users of stimulants, especially in high doses, experience perceptual changes as well as stimulation. At sufficient dose, most stimulants and hallucinogens are psychotogenic (i.e., they induce delusions and/or hallucinations with loss of judgment).

This chapter presents in some detail three members of the stimulant class; cocaine, amphetamine, and caffeine. Two other members are discussed in passing, as well as methamphetamine or "ice" and methcathinone or "khat."

COCAINE

Cocaine, derived from chewing the coca leaf, has been used in religious rites, as a currency, and as an antidote to fatigue and hunger by indigenous peoples of South America for over a thousand years. Pharmaceutic cocaine was first produced around 1860; in subsequent years, its anesthetic and euphorigenic properties were discovered by Freud, William Halstead, and many others. They praised its effects, at least initially.

Freud thought it might be the antidepressant that he had predicted would be found, and others initially believed it was a "gift of the gods."

Vin Mariani, a combination of cocaine and wine, was popular in Europe and in America in the latter part of the 19th century. Cocaine's dependence-producing potential was only gradually appreciated by Freud as he slowly began to realize that he was "hooked." Its negative effects were not widely appreciated, however, and, at the turn of the century, cocaine was an ingredient of Coca-Cola. Cocaine was eventually excluded from Coca-Cola when it was included in a federal effort to combat problems arising from use of narcotics and stimulants in medicines and "tonics" freely available to the public.

In the early 20th century, cocaine became associated with racial stereotypes; in the legal arena, it came to be classified as a narcotic. The legal description of cocaine as a narcotic persists, in many state laws, to this day. Pharmacologically, of course, cocaine is not a narcotic, but the legal definition, in essence, means a drug that causes trouble and is used by people we fear or don't like.

As noted above, cocaine's potential with respect to drug dependence came to be appreciated by Freud and many others, but it appears that each generation has to learn about this problem for itself. Grinspoon and Bakalar, in the 1980 edition of Kaplan and Saddock's *Comprehensive Textbook of Psychiatry*, wrote: "Used no more than two or three times a week, cocaine creates no serious problem. In daily and fairly large amounts, it can produce minor psychological disturbances. Chronic cocaine abuse usually does not appear as a medical problem."[2] In the last decade, the national experience indicates that alkaloidal cocaine (that is, "base" or "crack") appears to be the most powerful dependence-producing drug ever encountered. The full array of its negative effects may not yet have been realized, because we do not have a scientific study of these effects over a lifespan. Its effects on the fetus and on growth and development are under study, and early indications are not encouraging.

Girl, lady, blow, snow, flake, base, and *crack* are a few of the many slang terms for cocaine. Heroin is usually masculine in street culture, while cocaine is feminine. Thus a *speed ball*, a street name for a combination of heroin and cocaine, is sometimes called *boy and girl*.

PHARMACOLOGY

Cocaine is rapidly metabolized by serum esterases and by the liver to benzoylecognine. The duration of its stimulant effects is correspondingly short, varying from 3 to 45 minutes, depending on dose and route of administration. The initial phase of stimulation is often followed by a depressive phase characterized by dysphoria and craving. In high-dose use, the dysphoria may be accompanied by hyperstimulation, which causes the subject to use depressants such as alcohol, benzodiazepines, marijuana, and heroin for relief. Multiple drug dependence may result, and the clinician must have a high index of suspicion of multiple simultaneous dependencies when any cocaine dependent patient is examined.

Cocaine blocks reuptake of dopamine, and its intense euphorigenic effects are thought to be mediated by persisting dopaminergic effects at synapses in the midbrain pleasure centers. Cocaine also blocks reuptake of norepinephrine and serotonin. Cocaine may be insufflated ("snorted"), injected intravenously, or, in its "base" form, smoked. Oral cocaine is not very effective, and cocaine is sometimes used vaginally or rectally. Onset of action is fastest for smoking (8 to 10 seconds) versus intravenous use (30 to 45 seconds), while onset of action for insufflation is 3 to 10 minutes. Blood levels following intravenous use and smoking are much higher than those following insufflation, with an attendant telescoping of addictive behaviors; that is, the time to develop dependence following first-ever injection or smoking is in terms of weeks to months, in contrast with the months to years to develop dependence for most other common intoxicants.

Prior to the early 1980s, cocaine, in the so-called developed world, was always used as its hydrochloride salt. Attempts to smoke cocaine hydrochloride were infrequent because effects could not be obtained with this form of utilization. Cocaine hydrochloride does not volatilize until temperatures are reached approximating those of burning nicotine cigarettes, 900 F. or thereabouts. At such high temperatures, most or all of the cocaine is destroyed, so there is not much point in smoking the salt form. As described by Inciardi,[3] if users treat the salt form with a base such as baking soda or ammonia, the cocaine is freed from its bond with the hydrochloride, thus creating the free radical. This radical has a very much lower volatility point than the salt, 90 F. versus 1,000 F. At 1,000 F., all the cocaine is destroyed, but at the lower temperature, the cocaine is not destroyed but converted to a vapor. This creates a technology for delivery of very large amounts of cocaine to the brain in a shorter time than was ever previously possible.

In street parlance, the process of converting the salt form to the base is called "free-basing" or just "basing." Until recently, basing was the preferred method of use in Chicago. Users in Chicago, for no apparent reason, preferred to buy the salt and do their own chemistry. This contrasted with the New York scene, in which users preferred to have the dealer do the chemistry and to buy the free radical in crystalline form, so-called crack. It should be noted that it is the same drug in roughly the same doses with the same consequences. Media stories sometimes incorrectly report that crack cocaine is fundamentally different from free-base cocaine.

Tolerance, especially for base or crack, develops rapidly in some individuals and leads to an escalation of daily dosage from the milligram range (e.g., 400 to 500 mg/day) to the gram range (4 to 5 grams/day). In other individuals, loss of control appears to take more time. Some patients report that they could control use for many months or years, but then suddenly, without apparent reason, experienced rapid loss of control with dose escalation. The development of tolerance to cocaine's effects depends on the pattern of administration. Tolerance develops when cocaine is used at intervals of minutes or hours.

There is abundant animal evidence that when the interval of administration is a day or more, there is reverse tolerance, at least for cocaine's propensity to produce seizures. Post, in a classic study, administered cocaine to rats and noted that repeated daily administration of single, nonconvulsant doses eventually produced seizures.[4] He postulated "kindling" in the amygdala as a mechanism. It is possible that kindling may underlie the appearance of panic attacks[5] in some cocaine users, and that it may be involved in the power of cocaine to lead to the strong conditioned responses that drive behavior for many cocaine dependent persons.

Cocaine can combine with alcohol to form cocaethylene. Cocaethylene is active at the dopamine receptor as if it were cocaine alone. Cocaethylene, however, is much longer lasting than cocaine, and this may explain some of the pathology of cocaine combined with alcohol, such as death at low doses.

Fischman and co-workers conducted studies indicating that drug experienced subjects cannot distinguish the effects of cocaine from the effects of amphetamine, at least for the first half hour after administration.[6] Subjects knew that amphetamine lasted longer and could discriminate between the two drugs, but only on the duration-of-action dimension. Acutely, the drugs appear to have identical effects.

The general clinical experience that cocaine is the most addicting drug ever encountered is also apparent in a study from behavioral pharmacology.[7] Laboratory rats were given unlimited access to intravenous cocaine hydrochloride or heroin hydrochloride. Rats self-administering cocaine quickly developed a pattern of episodic drug intake, with periods of excessive cocaine self-administration alternating with brief periods of abstinence. Rats allowed continuous access to intravenous heroin showed stable drug self-administration, with a gradual increase over the first two weeks of testing. The general health of the animals became markedly different: those self-administering heroin maintained grooming behavior, pretesting body weight, and a good state of general health; rats self-administering cocaine tended to cease grooming behavior, to lose up to 47 percent of their pretesting body weight, and to show a pronounced deterioration in general health. The mortality rate for 30 days of continuous testing was 36 percent for animals self-administering heroin and 90 percent for those self-administering cocaine.

MEDICAL COMPLICATIONS OF COCAINE USE

Cardiovascular. Tachycardias regularly follow cocaine use. Karch notes that cocaine concentrates in heart muscle for a short period after acute administration, and it would appear logical that tachycardias could develop into arrhythmias, sometimes lethal.[8] Blood-pressure rises accompanying acute cocaine use may cause strokes, and neonates of cocaine using mothers have been born with hemiplegias. Cocaine use can aggravate every form of cardiovascular disease and, in the extreme, can lead to death from myocardial infarction or from dissection of the aorta.

Respiratory. Cocaine use may lead to a variety of pathologies in the lungs, including pneumomediastinum, aggravation of asthma, and pulmonary barotrauma. A relatively new condition is that of "crack lung," in which there is fever, dyspnea, and severe chest pain not associated with radiologic abnormalities and not responsive to antibiotics. Crack lung may be fatal. Most texts cite nasal hyperemia and perforations of the nasal septum as frequent in cocaine snorters. My clinical experience has been that nasal perforation occurs but is rare in users of any drug, including cocaine.

Central nervous system. Cocaine, even in low doses, may cause seizures, hyperpyrexia, and death. In "body packers" or "mules," persons who have swallowed balloons or condoms filled with cocaine for smuggling purposes, a sudden very large bolus of cocaine is delivered if the container ruptures, causing death unless the resulting seizures, hyperpyrexia, hypertension, and arrthymias are treated promptly. Benzodiazepines (i.e., diazepam 5 to 10 mg IV, no more than 5 mg per minute) are recommended for seizures, with resuscitation equipment available to treat possible respiratory depression from the benzodiazepines. If seizures are multiple, intubation is recommended over further IV diazepam because of the possibility of apnea or laryngospasm. For body temperatures over 102 F., ice packs and hypothermic blankets are indicated. If blood pressure rises, the administration of diazepam may have positive effects, but if not, phentolamine 2 to 10 mg over a 10-minute period is indicated. In extreme cases, sodium nitroprusside 0.5 to 10 mcg/kg/minute may be called for. The use of beta blockers such as propanolol was once recommended by many authors, but clinical experience and animal model data indicate that they exacerbate cocaine toxicity.

Hypervigilance, tics, ataxia, stereotypies, and perseveration may be associated with chronic cocaine use. Cocaine, in both acute and chronic use, may lead to the development of a psychosis indistinguishable from paranoid schizophrenia. The hypervigilant, suspicious cocaine user develops delusions of persecution and hallucinations, sometimes accompanied by formication or "coke bugs." If possible, such a patient should be managed by lowering the level of stimulation and attempting to form a positive relationship while monitoring for violence and being careful to explain any necessary procedures. If neuroleptics are necessary, haldol, because of its low degree of anticholinergic activity, is preferred over other possible drugs such as chlorpromazine to avoid anticholinergic or hypotensive episodes. Haldol must be used with caution because it lowers the seizure threshold. Physical restraints should be avoided, if at all possible, to minimize risks of hyperthermia or rhabdomyolysis with associated renal failure.

As is the case with other classes of drug abusers, cocaine users have higher rates of depression than the general population. However, there appears to be more bipolar affective disorder in cocaine users than in other classes of drug users. Data from the National Institute of Mental Health epidemiology study of the incidence of mental illness in the United States, in the early 1980s, showed that cocaine use increased the odds of suicide 62 times over persons not using cocaine.[9] The extreme behavioral toxicity of cocaine is highlighted by comparing its suicidal risk with other conditions: the odds were 41 times greater than for major depression, 18 times greater than for alcoholism, and 11 times greater following separation or divorce than was observed in persons without these risk factors. People with eating disorders may be more prone to use cocaine. Cocaine may precipitate or aggravate panic disorders.

Endocrine. An occasional subject using cocaine may develop gynecomastia because of disruption of dopamine inhibition of prolactin secretion. Many high-dose users report loss of interest in sex and a variety of sexual-performance problems.

Reproductive. Cocaine, because of its intense vasoconstriction, reduces blood flow to the uterus and fetus, with a range of resulting pathologies. These include placental abruption, spontaneous abortion, preterm labor, fetal cerebral infarction, low birth weight and head circumference, fetal malformations, and behavioral and neurologic problems including "jittery baby," failure to thrive, and vulnerability to sudden infant death syndrome, among others. Cocaine can be passed through breast milk in sufficient concentration to cause hypertension, tachycardia, and apnea. There are some reports of severe, sometimes lethal, neurologic syndromes in infants subjected to ambient air cocaine from parental use of crack.[8] Females may become dysmenorrheic when using cocaine frequently.

EPIDEMIOLOGY[10]

A number of studies indicate that there has been a reduction of cocaine use in the general population, but there has probably not been a parallel reduction in populations not in school, the homeless, or those in the prison system. Among the "haves," rates of use of cocaine appear to be related to perceptions of the risk of using cocaine. The data on the "have nots" indicates that there has been little change in cocaine related problems in these populations.

MEDICAL USE

Cocaine remains an excellent topical anesthetic. Its use for topical anesthesia can result in urine levels above NIDA cut-off levels, and thus urine tests may be reported as positive. Medical review officers need to have a specific history of this possibility. Cocaine has no other medical use.

TOXICOLOGY

Benzoylecognine is the major metabolite of cocaine; it is detectable for two to four days after use, depending on dose.

DIAGNOSIS OF COCAINE WITHDRAWAL (292.0)

DSM-4 Diagnosis Criteria for Cocaine Withdrawal

A.   Cessation of (or reduction in) cocaine use that has been heavy and prolonged

B.   Dysphoric mood and two (or more) of the following physiological changes, developing within a few hours to several days after criterion A:
1) fatigue
2) vivid, unpleasant dreams

3) insomnia or hypersomnia
4) increased appetite
5) psychomotor retardation or agitation

C. The symptoms in criterion B cause clinically significant distress or impairment in social, occupational, or other important areas of functioning.

D. The symptoms are not due to a general medical condition and are not better accounted for by another mental disorder.

Cocaine withdrawal is not life-threatening but can be severe in terms of depression, dysphoria, restlessness, insomnia, and periods of intense craving. Some observers believe there are distinct phases of withdrawal (the "crash," "withdrawal" followed by "extinction"), but others have not confirmed these observations.[11] In my experience, cocaine withdrawal effects are quite variable when they occur. Some believe that if a patient meets criteria for major depression, pharmacological treatment should be initiated immediately, but others believe that one should give the cocaine withdrawal a two- to four-week period to resolve itself and then initiate treatment if criteria for depression persist. I believe in the early treatment of depression. If mood normalizes rapidly, then the antidepressant can be discontinued.

Gawin and colleagues published a study of desipramine, lithium, and placebo in subjects withdrawing from cocaine.[12] The desipramine group had a substantial reduction in craving and better treatment outcome than the lithium or placebo groups. Several attempts to replicate these findings have not succeeded.[13] A range of drugs—bromocriptine, amantadine, carbamazepine, flupenthixol, buprenorphine, sertraline, and nifedipine—have all been tried, but early encouraging results from open trials either have not been not confirmed in double-blind placebo–controlled studies or such studies are lacking.[13] The use of antipsychotic drugs, many of which are dopamine antagonists, is problematic because these drugs appear to increase cocaine craving.

Buprenorphine appeared to be of great interest because animal data and some studies in humans suggested that it could reduce both opiate and cocaine use, but this has not been confirmed in subsequent studies.[13] The use of tricyclic antidepressants in cocaine dependent people must be monitored closely. If patients taking tricyclics take cocaine concurrently, it can lead to the tricyclic jittery syndrome, which is characterized by anxiety, a feeling of being speeded up or "raciness," insomnia, and intense cocaine craving leading to relapse.

The use of all the above-mentioned agents should be confined to research studies, because they all carry risk of significant side effects. With lack of clear evidence of effectiveness, the clinician using them is on shaky medicolegal ground.

TREATMENT OF COCAINE DEPENDENCE AND ABUSE

At this writing, we have no specific pharmacologic or psychologic treatment of cocaine dependence and abuse. Treatment proceeds according to the general guidelines presented in chapter 1. Behavioral treatments are showing much promise but are not widespread "on-line" procedures. The average treatment clinic does not have the specialized staff to carry out behavior-modification protocols nor the resources to pay patients for clean urines and the like. Studies carried out by Rawson and co-authors at UCLA[14] and by Higgins and colleagues at Vermont[15] indicate that cocaine use can be reduced and patients maintained in treatment by employing intensive outpatient treatment based partly on behavior modification protocols, including positive reinforcement for positive performance (for example, a negative urine for cocaine in the program proposed by Higgins and colleagues earns the client money, which a counselor monitors to purchase something useful for the patient in recovery).

In controlled studies, these approaches are superior to standard counseling and 12-step programs, but the numbers of people studied are relatively small, and some of the subjects in these studies were recruited through newspaper ads. These factors could account for results that appear astonishing to those working with street populations seeking treatment for cocaine dependence and abuse. Community-based programs could not afford the $10-per-client-per-day positive reinforcement for clean urines because most cannot afford the underlying cost of doing four or more urines per client per week.

For middle-class cocaine users, intensive evening programs appear to be useful. These programs provide counseling, groups, twelve step elements, and education, often combined with family support. The programs have not received the research or evaluation they deserve, for on a clinical level they appear to positively influence the course of cocaine dependence. Cocaine dependence, in my experience, has been a frustrating condition to try to treat. Drop-out rates are high, and the intense disruption of both physiological and psychological domains secondary to acute high-dose cocaine use make the creation of any kind of therapeutic contract problematic, particularly for multiproblem inner-city populations.

Therapeutic communities can be effective for these patients. As noted, the patients need placement along the patient placement continuum according to need at various stages of the development of the problems and then at various stages of progression in recovery.

AMPHETAMINE

Ma-huang, a Chinese medicine, has a history dating over 5,000 years. In the middle of the 19th century, ephedrine was isolated from ma-huang, but it took many decades before medicinal chemists realized that ephedrine had many of the same effects as epinephrine but was, in contrast with epinephrine, effective orally and for longer periods, and had more dependable central effects and fewer side effects. As these effects became known, they increased interest in the stimulant class. In 1887, Edelano had produced phenylisopropylamine. After the turn of the century, its physiology was investigated, and it was termed, along with many other compounds, a sympathomimetic amine. In the late 1920s, a conscious search for an improved ephedrine or an attempt to synthesize ephedrine, depending on which historian one reads, was started with an exploration of the pharmacology of racemic phenylisopropylamine. In Japan, a parallel search produced methamphetamine.

In 1932, a benzedrine inhaler was marketed that was effective for its intended purpose of relieving nasal congestion. Street users soon discovered its euphorigenic properties, and a decades-long problem of public health proportions was born. Amphetamines were used by both sides in World War II to combat fatigue, and this military use probably fueled the problem. Japan had a major epidemic of amphetamine abuse following World War II, which they solved by prohibition. In the 1950s, Lasagna and co-workers published a study in which drug naive medical student volunteers were given, in rotating fashion under blind conditions, amphetamines, barbiturates, morphine, or heroin.[16] They were then asked to rate these drugs for preference. Most of the subjects chose amphetamine over the other classes. Lasagna and co-authors wrote: "Although amphetamine is generally acknowledged to be capable of inducing euphoria, we were surprised at the intensity of this response to the drug. The descriptions of our normal subjects after receiving amphetamine were closer to the usual textbook and literary descriptions of the euphoric effects of opiates than were the reactions to morphine or heroin."

This was one of the first experimental clues to the powerful abuse liability of some stimulant drugs. There had been a long medical literature on the occasional pathologic effects of stimulants, but there was always the implication that these cases were not usual, not frequent, not something for the ordinary person to worry about. Here there was evidence that stimulants were more immediately attractive than barbiturates, morphine, or heroin to most normal volunteers.

"Ice" or "crystal meth"—crystalline methamphetamine—has been associated with minor epidemics but has never become as popular as cocaine or amphetamine. Some writers feel that the methamphetamine high is not quite as intense and its duration of action much longer in comparison with cocaine, and that this explains why cocaine has a much wider consumption than ice. The extended duration of action of methamphetamine makes it too difficult to focus on work or family or anything else, including criminal behavior, and this appears to be a factor limiting sustained use. Amphetamine and cocaine use/abuse can be more easily balanced with maintenance of other activities.

Common street names for amphetamines include *speed, uppers, bennies, dexies,* and *black beauties.*

PHARMACOLOGY

Amphetamine is biotransformed in the liver by N-demethylation, P-hydroxylation, deamination, and conjugation, but most of the drug is excreted unchanged in urine at a rate determined by blood pH. At acidic levels, amphetamine is 80 percent excreted in urine; at alkaline levels, 8 percent is excreted in urine. Thus acidification of urine is logical in amphetamine poisoning. Methamphetamine, at 12 hours, has a much longer half-life than amphetamine. Some of it is demethylated to amphetamine and to ephedrine, both of which are psychoactive. In parallel with amphetamine, urinary excretion of methamphetamine is a major means of disposition, and it too is hastened in acid urine.

TOXICOLOGY

Amphetamine is detected for 24 to 48 hours after use in urine with current detection technology. For methamphetamine to be declared positive, there must be 200 ng of amphetamine also detected. Amphetamine is a major metabolic breakdown product for methamphetamine, as methamphetamine is demethylated to amphetamine.

TOLERANCE AND DEPENDENCE

Tolerance to amphetamine can be very great. In the heyday of Haight Ashbury, many "speed freaks" reported shooting 5 grams per day. At these levels of intake, emaciation, stereotypies, and psychotic behavior were frequent.

Dependence and abuse are diagnosed according to the general criteria of DSM-4, as presented earlier in this text.

TOXICITY

Cardiovascular. Karch writes that the cardiovascular effects of amphetamines are similar to those of cocaine, and both are related to catecholamine increases: "High circulating catecholamine increases are cardiotoxic no matter what the cause."[8] Because there are some differences between cocaine and amphetamine, he feels that infarction is more frequent with cocaine, and cardiomyopathy with amphetamines. Both cause arrhythmia, and these can be lethal in non-dose-related fashion. Necrotizing vasculitis has been reported after intravenous use of amphetamines, and there appears to be an association between amphetamine use, stroke, and hyperpyrexia, sometimes lethal.

Pulmonary toxicity. Talc granulomas can cause serious pulmonary pathology when users crush and then inject tablets with fillers such as microcellulose, cornstarch, or cotton fibers. Pulmonary hypertension can appear in therapeutic dose ranges of some amphetamine analogs such as fenfluramine, propylhexedrine, and phenmetrazine. One amphetamine analog, aminorex, was taken off the European market following a series of cases of associated pulmonary hypertension.

Behavioral. After high doses or after sustained periods of use, amphetamine users may become agitated, hypervigilant, and suspicious. These symptoms may progress to auditory, visual, or tactile hallucinations and to frank psychoses with delusions of persecution. There is no way of knowing from acute symptoms and signs whether one is dealing with an amphetamine induced psychosis or naturally occurring schizophrenia, even if there are positive urines for amphetamines. People with schizophrenia abuse drugs with higher frequencies than other populations, and they do not exclude stimulants. Clinical observation indicates that stimulants make psychoses worse, although users may get some short-term euphoria or relief from depressant effects of other drugs.

Renal. There are a few cases of reversible renal failure that appear to be related to use of amphetamines. Karch believes there may be some relationship between rhabdomyolysis and the renal syndrome.[8]

Hepatic. Hepatic damage as a result of therapeutic use of methylphenidale (Ritalin) has been reported, although it is rare.[8]

Medical Use. Amphetamines have a long history of use for the treatment of obesity, but large-scale reviews of the data indicate that short-term gains from anorexiants are soon lost. Use of amphetamines carries risk of development of abuse and dependence. The current posture of most of the medical community is that the risk of developing abusive patterns is not justified by any substantial and sustained benefit. Use of stimulants for obesity has been declining for many years. The recent FDA revocation of approval of fenfluramine as an anorexiant will strengthen this trend.

Amphetamines continue to be used for narcolepsy and for hyperactivity associated with attention deficit disorder. They also continue to be useful as decongestants and antidotes to hypotension, and they are tried occasionally in the treatment of refractory depression. Most texts mention the use of stimulants in Parkinson's disease.

TREATMENT

Psychological and social treatment measures for dependence on amphetamine and related drugs is generic.

CAFFEINE[17, 18]

Some writers ascribe the origins of caffeine to the experimentation of Kaldi, an Arab goatherd, who noticed that when his goats ate a certain plant, they were energized. Legend has it that he brewed a concoction from this plant, which he found to be stimulating and pleasant. He thus became the first coffee brewer. When first introduced to the Muslim world, there was debate about its status, for if defined as an intoxicant, it would have been prohibited by the Koran. Muslim authorities concluded that it was not an intoxicant, and so its use became widespread in the Muslim world.

When caffeine was first used by large numbers of people in Europe and America, there was some fear that it would lead to severe mental and emotional deterioration, but these fears proved baseless. When first introduced in England, its use in coffee houses was associated with political opposition to the king. Attempts at prohibiting caffeine (and opposition to the king), of course, failed, and caffeine use became widespread in all classes of English society.

Ambivalence about this drug continues to the present. There was considerable debate among DSM-4 preparers concerning what, if anything, to say about its abuse liability and dependence potential.

Caffeine has some street use in so-called lookalikes but, in view of the fact that caffeine is the most-consumed psychoactive drug in the world, it must be ranked as having an extremely low abuse liability and dependence potential. In addition, relative to its consumption (estimated by Greden and Walters to be in the billions of kilograms per year[17]) its potential for causing social problems is almost negligible.

TOLERANCE AND DEPENDENCE

According to Greden and Walters, perhaps as many as 10 percent of frequent users have identifiable withdrawal symptoms.[17] This figure may be low, according to a recent study by Silverman and colleagues.[19] Sixty users of caffeine, in the 2.5 cups/235 mg per day range, were administered caffeine or placebo under double-blind conditions after cessation of caffeine intake. Significant differences were observed between groups: the placebo group had elevated Beck depression inventory scores and elevated state-trait anxiety scores, and 52 percent more placebo subjects reported moderate or severe headache than active drug groups. A few subjects reported substantial distress in the placebo period, likening the syndrome to the flu. Clinically, caffeine, in some individuals, can have discrete withdrawal symptoms of sufficient severity to drive caffeine-ingesting behavior.

What may be unique about the dependence/withdrawal syndrome related to caffeine is the absence of an effect on important life domains. Caffeine use does not seem to lead the user to focus his or her life on acquiring and using it; its use does not lead to immediate life-compromising health problems; it has no association with crime, family disruption, loss of ability to drive an automobile or operate a machine, or any others of the familiar problems with alcohol, nicotine, marijuana, and other common intoxicants. No one has ever called me and said, "Dr. Senay, I'm desperate, you've got to help me. I've got a jones on coffee, and I'm stealing from my mother to get Maxwell House." In brief, dependence on caffeine does not, at least in enormous numbers of people, lead to short- or long-term social, legal, vocational, or familial toxicity or effects in most other domains. If caffeine dependence were our only drug problem, we would have a much more benign world than we have at present.

Studies indicating that caffeine use is associated with a number of health problems, such as breast cancer or cardiovascular disease, have not been replicated. In the medical arena, patients with an ulcer diathesis are well advised to stay away from caffeine, and in psychiatric populations excess use can aggravate sleep and anxiety disorders, or any severe mental problem, because of the induction of anxiety.

Greden and Walters feel that heavy intake is defined at the 250 mg/day level, and caution that coffee is by no means the sole source of caffeine.[17] In history taking, one must ask about cola drinks, tea, coffee, cough and cold medications, and a variety of analgesics. DSM-4 offers a succinct guide to calculating caffeine intake: coffee contains 100 to 150 mg per cup; tea is about half as strong; a glass of cola is about one third as strong. Most caffeine-containing over-the-counter and prescription medications contain one third to one half as much caffeine as a cup of coffee, with the exceptions that migraine and some over-the-counter medications contain 100 mg of caffeine. If anxiety symptoms or sleep problems are present, abstinence from caffeine is indicated to see if symptoms are lessened or eliminated.

PHARMACOLOGY

Caffeine is well absorbed from the gastrointestinal tract; it is partially bound to plasma albumin and has a half-life of 3 to 5 hours. It is biotransformed in the liver. Concurrent nicotine use appears to speed the biotransformation of caffeine. Almost all caffeine is metabolized, and there is no day-to-day accumulation of this drug. Caffeine has low toxicity; overdose with oral forms is next to impossible. Greden and Walters estimate that an adult male would have to ingest 5 to 10 grams for a fatal oral overdose, which would require 50 to 100 cups of coffee.[17]

Caffeine acts in the central nervous system as a competitive antagonist of adenosine. Adenosine and its agonists have sedative, anxiolytic, anticonvulsant, and vasodilating actions at widespread receptor sites in the CNS. Caffeine preferentially occupies these receptor sites and prevents the actions of adenosine. The vasoconstricting effects probably explain why caffeine is effective in some types of headaches. Caffeine has well-documented stimulating effects on heart rate and force of contraction, but these effects may be canceled out by caffeine's opposite effects centrally. Caffeine delays sleep onset, reduces duration of sleep, and increases REM sleep early in the night, while reducing the overall amount of REM sleep.

Caffeine stimulates gastric secretion, and its diuretic effects are well known. Caffeine's possible relationship with a variety of medical conditions such as cardiovascular disease, fibrocystic disease of the breast, and a variety of cancers is the subject of intense but unresolved debate among experts. It is probably wise to avoid caffeine during pregnancy, as there is some evidence in animals and humans to suggest a link between caffeine and perinatal morbidity and mortality. There is evidence to support the position that anyone with cardiac arrhythmias or panic or anxiety disorders should avoid caffeine. Consumption of doses of caffeine above 200 to 300 mg per day may worsen schizophrenic symptoms.

Caffeine does not cause a surge in catecholamines or in EEG alpha, as do cocaine and amphetamine, and this probably accounts for the fact that caffeine is relatively innocuous compared with these drugs in human populations, and for the striking differences in self-administration, in animal models, where caffeine self-administration is weak or absent.

A recent study by Graham and Spriet presents evidence contradicting the general rule that stimulants only restore fatigue induced decrements of performance while not improving performance when fatigue is not a factor.[20] Elite runners were given 9 mg/kg of caffeine in a controlled study. Caffeine-treated subjects increased the time they could run on a treadmill by 70 percent. There was no evidence of toxicity, and the levels of caffeine produced in blood did not exceed the disqualification levels of the International Olympic Committee.

MEDICAL USE

Caffeine is used as a stimulant for apnea of the newborn. It also is used as an adjunct to a variety of analgesics, based on sound research demonstrating that the addition of caffeine improves analgesia.

DIAGNOSIS AND TREATMENT

The symptoms of caffeine intoxication or "caffeinism" are as follows in DSM-4.

DSM-4 Diagnosis Criteria for Caffeine Intoxication

A. Recent consumption of caffeine, usually in excess of 250 mg

B. At least five of the following signs:
    1) restlessness
    2) nervousness
    3) excitement
    4) insomnia
    5) flushed face
    6) diuresis
    7) gastrointestinal disturbance
    8) muscle twitching
    9) rambling flow of thought or speech
    10) tachycardia or cardiac arrhythmia
    11) periods of inexhaustibility
    12) psychomotor agitation

DSM-4 states that the five or more items from the list above must be associated with social or occupational impairment or "clinically significant distress." I have never seen a case of caffeine intoxication, although I have looked.

What could account for the apparent large difference between ordinary clinical experience and the results of careful research studies indicating widespread withdrawal symptoms? Greden and Walters feel it may involve 10 percent of the population.[17] I believe there are two factors of possible importance. The first is that caffeine dependent people stay caffeine dependent over decades and so rarely have occasion to know that they are dependent. Since caffeine dependence appears to produce little impairment in major life domains, no one complains. A second factor explaining the 90 percent of the using population who do not have withdrawal is related to the pattern of use. Seven intoxicating doses of alcohol, cocaine, or heroin taken in one hour produce effects much different from taking the seven doses in seven hours. Most people sip coffee, and so do not get boluses of caffeine with associated large spikes in the blood level, which probably underlie the development of dependence and withdrawal. Doses of caffeine used in experiments, or when taken on the street as lookalikes, are sometimes given as bolus doses.

DSM-4 does not define a caffeine withdrawal syndrome, but the evidence reviewed above indicates that fatigue, dysphoria, depression, anxiety, and headache would be prominent complaints in persons attempting to withdraw from caffeine.

Greden and Walters cite the desirability of demonstrating to a patient that caffeine is responsible for symptoms by using what they describe as the A-B-A approach: have the patient stop for a period, observe that the symptoms of caffeine intoxication abate or disappear, and then begin caffeine ingestion again to once more produce symptoms.[17] These authors also caution that all sources of caffeine must be accounted for in the treatment plan. Family members should be involved, and the final attempt to give up caffeine should be by sudden and complete cessation of intake.

KHAT

Khat, from the bush *Catha edulis*, which grows in the mountains of Yemen, has cathinone as its active ingredient. Cathinone has sympathomimetic effects apparently more toward the amphetamine/cocaine than the caffeine end of the spectrum of stimulants with respect to abuse liability. Prior to the last decade, its use was confined to inhabitants of these rugged mountains. One of the factors limiting use is that two to three days after harvesting, the leaves of this bush lose potency. With the possibilities opened up by improved transportation in Yemen, now the leaves can be picked and delivered by jet to London or other capitals to be used by people in the local drug scene. There are a few cases of clinically significant problems from the abuse of cathinone.

REFERENCES

1. Hardman JG, Limbird LE (eds), *Goodman & Gilman's The Pharmacological Basis of Therapeutics*, ed 9. New York, McGraw Hill, 1996.
2. Grinspoon L, Bakalar JB. Drug dependence: Non-narcotic agents, in Kaplan HI, Freedman AM, Saddock BJ (eds), *Comprehensive Textbook of Psychiatry*, ed 3. Baltimore, MD, Williams & Wilkins, 1980.
3. Inciardi JA. Crack cocaine in Miami, in Schober S, Schade C (eds), *The Epidemiology of Cocaine Use and Abuse*. NIDA Monograph #110, DHHS Pub #(ADM) 91–1787, 1991.
4. Post RM. Progressive changes in behavior and seizures following chronic cocaine administration: Relationship of kindling and psychosis, in Ellinwood EH, Kilbey MM (eds), *Advances in Behavioral Biology*, vol 21, *Cocaine and Other Stimulants*. New York, Plenum, 1976, pp 353–372.
5. Louie AK, Lannon RA, Ketter TA. Treatment of cocaine induced panic disorder. *Am J Psychiatry* 146:1, 1989.

6. Fischman MW, Schuster CR, Resenekov I, et al. Cardiovascular and subjective effects of intravenous cocaine administration in humans. *Arch Gen Psychiatry* 10:535–546, 1976.

7. Bozarth MA, Wise RA. Toxicity associated with long-term intravenous heroin and cocaine self-administration in the rat. *JAMA* 254:81–83, 1985.

8. Karch SB. *The Pathology of Drug Abuse*, ed 2. Boca Raton, FL, CRC Press, 1996.

9. Petronis KR, et al. An epidemiologic investigation of potential risk factors for suicide attempts. *Soc Psychiatry Psychiatric Epidemiol* 25:193–195, 1990.

10. Community Epidemiology Working Group, National Institute on Drug Abuse. *Epidemiologic Trends in Drug Abuse*, vol 1, *Highlights and Executive Summary*. NIH Pub #96-4126(CEWG). Rockville, MD, 1996, p 3.

11. Weddington WW, Brown BS, Haertzen CA, et al. Change in mood, craving and sleep during short-term abstinence reported by male cocaine addicts. *Arch Gen Psychiatry* 47:861–868, 1990.

12. Gawin FH, Kleber HD, Byck R, et al. Desipramine facilitation of initial cocaine abstinence. *Arch Gen Psychiatry* 46:117–121, 1989.

13. American Psychiatric Association guidelines for the treatment of patients with substance use disorders: Alcohol, cocaine, opioids. *Am J Psychiatry* (suppl) 152:36–37, 1995.

14. Rawson RA, Obert JL, McCann MJ, et al. Neurobehavioral treatment of cocaine dependency: A preliminary evaluation, in Tims FM, Leukefeld CG (eds), *Cocaine Treatment: Research and Clinical Objectives*. NIDA Research Monograph 135, NIH Publication #93-3693. Rockville, MD, 1993.

15. Higgins ST, Budney AJ, Bickel WK. Applying behavioral concepts and principles to the treatment of cocaine dependence. *Drug Alcohol Depend* 34:87–97, 1994.

16. Lasagna L, von Felsinger JM, Beecher HK. Drug induced changes in man. *JAMA* 157:1006–1020, 1955.

17. Greden JF, Walters A. Caffeine, in Lowinson JH, Ruiz P, Millman RB, et al (eds), *Substance Abuse: A Comprehensive Textbook*. Baltimore, MD, Williams & Wilkins, 1992.

18. Griffiths RR, Holtzman SG, Daly JW, et al. Caffeine: A model drug of abuse, in NIDA Research Monograph #162, *Problems of Drug Dependence*. Proceedings of the 57th Annual Meeting. NIH Publication #96-4116. Rockville, MD, 1996, pp 73–75.

19. Silverman K, Evans SM, Strain EC, et al. Withdrawal syndrome after double-blind cessation of caffeine consumption. *N Engl J Med* 327:1109–1114, 1992.

20. Graham T, Spriet L. Performance and metabolic responses to a high caffeine dose during exercise. *J Appl Physiol* 71:2292–2298, 1991.

ADDITIONAL READINGS

Earley PH. *The Cocaine Recovery Book* and *The Cocaine Recovery Workbook*. Newbury Park, CA, Sage Publications, 1991.

Erickson PG, Adlaf EM, Smart RG, et al. [R]The Steel Drug: Cocaine and Crack in Perspective[R], ed 2. New York, Lexington Books, 1994.

Platt JJ. *Cocaine Addiction: Theory, Research and Treatment*. Cambridge, MA, Harvard University Press, 1997.

9. Marijuana

This chapter devotes some space to recent research on marijuana that is not of immediate clinical relevance. Physicians need to be educated about the health consequences of marijuana for a number of reasons. Clinically, it is important because education on health effects of common intoxicants should be part of every treatment program. The physician should be knowledgeable about the medical content of these educational components. In addition, there is a well-financed and active marijuana lobby, in exact parallel with the nicotine lobby, which argues that there is no evidence of problems from marijuana, or that the evidence we have is not based on good science. Physicians should be on the front line in this debate, hence the need for careful review of the growing evidence that this drug has the same potential for abuse and dependence as other common intoxicants such as nicotine, heroin, and cocaine, and that it has a range of negative consequences for both body and mind.

For many years marijuana has been described as a "soft" drug, and until recently, from both clinical and scientific perspectives, this seemed to be the case. In practice, in the 1960s and early 1970s, clinicians never saw anyone who complained of dependence on or abuse of marijuana. In this period, I saw two cases with severe, clinically significant cognitive impairment from heavy use, but they had no other marijuana-related problems. As reviewed by Grinspoon and Bakalar, studies in heavily marijuana-using populations in Greece, Jamaica, and Costa Rica found no severe degrees of dependence and little or no pathology.[1] Clinical experience of the rarity of problems from marijuana use was fully supported by NIDA-funded research in a variety of heavily using populations.

By the latter part of the 1970s, I began to see a few people who complained of needing marijuana to function ("I can't concentrate until I smoke a joint in the morning"). One had such a severe cough, presumably from day-in, day-out marijuana and nicotine smoking, that history taking was difficult. There were no complaints of withdrawal, but clearly behavior was, at least partially, controlled by need for the drug. Slowly, during the 1980s, more cases presented themselves, but because they were so infrequent in relation to the large numbers of people using the drug, I still regarded them as aberrations, from a general public health point of view. Some of these people complained of withdrawal, and the withdrawal appeared to lead to use of the drug to relieve withdrawal. I saw one patient in whom two to three days of nausea, insomnia, and marijuana craving appeared to represent classical withdrawal, albeit in mild form.

In the 1990s, however, marijuana no longer appears "soft." Particularly in adolescent populations,[2] dependence and abuse now appear as classical drug problems not different from those of alcohol, cocaine, or heroin. In some adolescent facilities where I am active, marijuana has replaced cocaine and alcohol as the most frequent primary drug of abuse. In adult residential or inpatient facilities, however, it is still unusual for marijuana to be a primary drug of abuse or dependence.

The change from "soft" drug—or "herb," in some '60s propaganda—to "hard" drug has no well-established scientific explanation. As reviewed in this chapter, there was a universal clinical experience bolstered by many scientific studies to support the notion that marijuana was a "soft" drug. In my opinion, the changes we are seeing are attributable mainly to increasing dose. Marijuana users now frequently use "blunts" or hollowed-out cigars filled with marijuana "joints." In this method of use, four or five joints are consumed in one blunt, in contrast to the use of one or two joints in an equivalent period in years past. In addition, the technology of plant growth now produces a plant with much higher concentrations of tetrahydrocannabinol (THC) than was the case in the past. Another possibly relevant factor is an earlier onset of heavy use in adolescent populations with a vulnerability factor such as attention deficit hyperactivity disorder (ADHD) or conduct disorder. Some of these young adolescents are, according to their statements on admission to treatment, powerfully affected by the drug, and the increased doses now appear to drive behavior in a classical manner for abuse/dependence.

The implication for the future is not clear. If marijuana is the primary drug of abuse for adolescents, this pattern may maintain itself over a career, as is the case for nicotine, cocaine, alcohol, and heroin. However, the primary drug of abuse in adolescent populations that now have marijuana as a primary drug may become cocaine or other drugs. While marijuana may be the primary drug of abuse for adolescents and adults, it is rarely the only drug. Alcohol, cocaine, nicotine, and recently heroin, in variable subsets changing with time, are also used in problematic fashion in these in-treatment populations, in addition to problematic use of marijuana.

PHARMACOLOGY

The major, but not sole, active ingredient in marijuana smoke is delta-9-tetrahydrocannabinol or THC. Marijuana is usually smoked but can be consumed as a tea or in combination with different foods. When the leaves, stems, and flowering tops are chopped together, they form the contents of the usual joint or marijuana cigarette. When smoked, a joint delivers a dose of 4 to 10 mg of THC. Hashish is the resin of the plant, and this resin concentrates the THC. When it is smoked, it delivers a dose some three to five times higher than is delivered by a joint.

At low doses, THC usually induces euphoria and changes in perception that the user may find striking or amusing. In higher doses, as with hashish, frank perceptual changes may border on the hallucinatory, with possible loss of reality testing. Chronic use of hashish can result in a syndrome of drug induced cognitive impairment that may last for weeks after the drug is stopped. Not all THC use is euphorigenic. Some users become anxious, sometimes to the point of panic, and/or suspicious, while others experience dysphoria. These experiences do not usually lead to medical contact, and the user recovers spontaneously.

Effects occur within minutes of smoking and usually last about two hours. With oral ingestion, onset of action is slowed; perhaps 30 minutes elapse before the above-described effects occur, and the duration of effects is prolonged two to three times compared with smoking. THC is intensely lipophilic, and this leads to a window of detection in body fluids of weeks.

THC ingestion induces a degree of sedation/relaxation and impairs time perception. In addition, there is some impairment of short-term memory. In sufficient dose, judgment can become impaired and reflexes slowed. Heart rate is increased, and there may be tremors and ataxia. THC may increase the diameter of bronchial tubes, but with continued use this effect reverses itself, so the drug in not useful for asthmatics. Frequently, marijuana smoking causes conjunctival vasodilation.

EPIDEMIOLOGY

The United States Department of Health and Human Services (DHHS), through its institutes, conducts periodic surveys of the drug abuse/alcohol problems in the nation as a whole and in special populations, such as its annual survey of high school seniors. These studies are designed and carried out with scientific procedures that have broad acceptance in the social science community in the United States and throughout the world. During 1994, the National Household Survey on Drug Abuse[3] found that 8.5 percent of the entire United States population (about 17.9 million people) had used marijuana at least once, and that 5.1 million people had used marijuana one or more times per week. The ratio of 17.9 to 5.1 million, roughly 3 to 1, is significant because, as is established below, use of marijuana on a weekly or more frequent basis creates a substantial risk of developing dependence on this drug.

The National Household Survey also found that marijuana use was again on the rise, with an estimated 1.75 million new users each year between 1987 and 1989. The National Survey of High School Seniors, conducted by Johnston and colleagues at the University of Michigan, also found that use was increasing, with one third of high school seniors using marijuana at some time during 1994.[4] Of greatest public health concern was the finding of a doubling of daily use of marijuana by high school seniors, to 3.6 percent in 1994 from 1.5 percent in 1993.

MARIJUANA DEPENDENCE

In the National Comorbidity Study conducted by DHHS in the period from 1990 to 1992, the number of people of all ages who were diagnosable as dependent on marijuana was found to be 4.2 percent[5]; this made marijuana dependence, in the period studied, the most frequent form of illicit drug dependence in the United States. Because this data is at such variance with the popular perception that marijuana is more of an herb than a drug or is a "soft" drug, it must be emphasized that there were more people in the country dependent on marijuana than on heroin or cocaine between 1990 and 1992. More recent studies indicate that, if anything, there is more marijuana dependence now than then.

Data from all the above studies indicate that the rate of dependence among those who have ever tried marijuana is 9.1 percent. This rate is very similar to that observed in an earlier study of 97 marijuana smokers who had smoked the drug over a 10-year period,[6] and it is very similar to the risk of developing dependence from ever using alcohol. It also appears that for those who use marijuana more than a few times—and weekly use is a considerably higher level of use—the risk of developing dependence may be as high as 20 to 30 percent.[7]

ABUSE/DEPENDENCE POTENTIAL OF MARIJUANA

The discovery of a specific marijuana receptor and a specific marijuana receptor antagonist now establishes that dependence on marijuana has receptor-mediated tolerance and withdrawal.[8] This is exactly the same as with heroin and cocaine. Twenty-four years ago, Jones and colleagues demonstrated a definite withdrawal syndrome from marijuana.[9] Many dismissed these findings as interesting but having nothing to do with actual use of marijuana, because the researchers used doses that were out of the usual range of social use.[9] Research in recent years, however, appears to establish that withdrawal is frequent and troublesome, contradicting the myth that marijuana use is easy to control. In my opinion, the doses used in the research by Jones and colleagues are the doses in common use today.

Roffman and Stephens recently reviewed the literature on problems experienced by chronic marijuana smokers and concluded: "A substantial percentage of heavy users express motivation to stop or cut back and many make numerous attempts to quit; heavy users commonly report adverse consequences that include impairment in memory and concentration, reduced energy or motivation, procrastination and health concerns."[10]

Crowley presented a study of patterns of use and consequences in adolescent males and females with legal and substance abuse problems and found that "progression from first to regular cannabis use was as rapid as tobacco progression, and more rapid than that of alcohol, indicating potent reinforcement from marijuana. Most patients described serious problems from cannabis; 78.6% met standard adult criteria for cannabis dependence. Two thirds of cannabis dependent patients reported withdrawal."[2] All the experience we have suggests that 13- to 19-year-olds with these kinds of drug problems are highly likely to have a range of biological, psychological, social, and legal problems of serious public health significance as they mature.

BEHAVIORAL EFFECTS OF MARIJUANA

INTOXICATION

DSM-4 Diagnosis Criteria for Cannabis Intoxication

A. Recent use of cannabis

B. Clinically significant maladaptive behavioral or psychological changes (e.g., impaired motor coordination, euphoria, anxiety, sensation of slowed time, impaired judgment, social withdrawal) that developed during, or shortly after, cannabis use

C. Two or more of the following signs, developing within 2 hours of cannabis use:
    1) conjunctival injection
    2) increased appetite
    3) dry mouth
    4) tachycardia

D. The symptoms are not due to a general medical condition and are not better accounted for by another mental disorder.

    Specify if: with perceptual disturbances

DRIVING IMPAIRMENT

A growing number of studies indicate that marijuana impairs driving performance. For example, in a recent double-blind controlled study, marijuana impaired subjects on two of four standardized field sobriety tests.[11] It is difficult to separate the contribution of marijuana to accident statistics because alcohol and/or other drug use so frequently co-occurs. The preponderance of evidence, however, indicates that marijuana has a dose dependent effect of impairing driving performance. This is at variance with the '60s view that marijuana enhanced driving performance because it made drivers cautious. The studies of Yesavage and co-workers in the laboratory demonstrate that marijuana impairment, in exact parallel with alcohol induced impairment, occurs without awareness on the part of the person impaired.[12]

COGNITIVE IMPAIRMENT

I have mentioned above my clinical observation of severe marijuana induced cognitive impairment in college-age males in otherwise good health. A recent study by Pope and Yurgelun-Todd found that heavy users of marijuana "displayed significantly greater impairment than light users on attentional/executive functions, as evidenced particularly by greater perseverations on card sorting and reduced learning of word lists. These differences remained after controlling for potential confounding variables, such as estimated levels of premorbid cognitive functioning, and for use of alcohol and other substances in the two groups."[13] These authors concluded, "Heavy marijuana use is associated with residual neuropsychological effects even after a day of supervised abstinence from the drug. However, the question remains open as to whether this impairment is due to a residue of drug in the brain, a withdrawal effect from the drug, or a frank neurotoxic effect of the drug."

Criteria for diagnosis of DSM-4 dependence and abuse are general and have been covered in chapter 1.

MEDICAL CONSEQUENCES OF MARIJUANA SMOKING

Pulmonary. Marijuana smoke contains tar with 50 percent more carcinogens than nicotine cigarette smoke. Tashkin's work at UCLA appears to establish that "only 3 to 4 marijuana joints a day have a frequency of chronic respiratory symptoms and tracheobronchial histopathology similar to that of smokers of 20 or more tobacco cigarettes a day."[14] His work also indicates that marijuana smoke affects large airways more than small airways, with the consequence that marijuana smoking may not lead to chronic obstructive pulmonary disease. However, there is the same type of chronic inflammatory disease of the oropharynx and lungs with the same types of loss of cilia, and the production of a variety of precancerous changes including basal cell hyperplasia, stratification, squamous metaplasia, goblet cell hyperplasia, cellular disorganization, nuclear variation, mitotic figures, increased nuclear-to-cytoplasmic ratio, inflammation, and basement membrane thickening from chronic marijuana smoking.

Most people who smoke marijuana also smoke nicotine cigarettes. This gives salience to Tashkin's finding that for "nearly all histologic features examined, abnormalities were noted more frequently in the combined smokers of marijuana and tobacco than in smokers of either substance alone, suggesting additive effects of marijuana and tobacco on bronchial epithelial histopathology." Tashkin concludes, "These findings support the concept that habitual smoking of marijuana may be an important risk factor for the development of respiratory tract malignancy."[14]

Although there are only a few cases, we may be seeing the beginning of the expected harvest of marijuana-caused cancers in a recent report by Taylor of cancers of the tongue, tonsil, lip, larynx, and lung in relatively young (less than 40 years of age) marijuana smokers[15] and in a report by Caplan and Brigham of carcinoma of the tongue in two men who chronically smoked marijuana but had no other risk factors for cancer.[16]

Cardiovascular. Because those smoking marijuana hold the smoke in longer than is the case with inhaled nicotine smoke, there is a correspondingly greater amount of carbon monoxide inhaled. This reduces available oxygen in the face of a THC induced acceleration in heart rate. In individuals with coronary artery disease, this could lead to a critical imbalance, creating a danger from cannabis use for anyone with underlying coronary artery disease.[17]

Immune system. It is now known that there are cannabis (CB1) receptors on macrophages, T lymphocytes, and B lymphocytes. When activated, these receptors act to suppress immune function. In low doses, the signaling system by which CD4 cells orchestrate immune functions is impaired, and in high doses there is an added primary impairment of macrophages. Since macrophage action is the primary line of defense against invasion by a host of organisms, the loss of this part of the immune response opens the way for infections to occur. These primary effects of marijuana almost certainly play a major role in the chronic infection and the many precancerous changes seen in the pulmonary systems of marijuana smokers.[18]

Marijuana and pregnancy. Human studies with statistical control for use of other drugs have found that marijuana use during pregnancy results in a reduction in oxygen delivery to the fetus, preterm deliveries, and low birth weights. In addition, impairments in children's cognitive function after delivery have been attributed to marijuana use by a number of investigators. Tremors, exaggerated startle responses, increased hand-to-mouth behaviors, and disturbed sleep cycling and motility have all been attributed to marijuana use during pregnancy.[19-21] In Fried's review of marijuana and pregnancy, he cites studies that have not confirmed these findings.[22] However, we cannot yet dismiss these findings and must wait for further research. Fried, in long-term studies, has found that marijuana use during pregnancy may have negative effects on cognitive function of offspring at age seven. If confirmed, this would raise a host of legal and ethical questions about marijuana and its use by females of childbearing age.

Hormonal effects of THC. In heavy users, THC impairs sperm production and leads to decrease in the size of testes and the prostate gland in males. In females, THC blocks ovulation and may result in absent menstrual cycles. These changes are reversible with abstinence from THC.[23, 24]

TREATMENT

No marijuana-specific treatment components have been established by clinical experience or research. In parallel with most other classes of intoxicants, treatment is generic and consists of a subset of the elements described in chapter 1. Withdrawal from THC is not life-threatening, and assignment to the ASAM continuum does not need to be above level 2, if marijuana is the sole or major drug of abuse/dependence.

Active research on marijuana-specific treatment is quite promising. Stephens and Roffman have studied marijuana use by recruiting through newspaper ads.[10] Their findings, indicating that marijuana users have chronic and disturbing problems, have been summarized above. They have developed an approach, currently under evaluation, that has a marijuana-specific focus and is time limited. They have developed a manual from which the interested clinician could learn about this approach. Staff with a background in psychology and behavior modification is needed to implement this model, or at least to train anyone wanting to use this model.

The clinical field is split on what to do about tobacco smoking in the marijuana-using adolescent. Many highly experienced, competent clinicians feel that it is asking an adolescent to change too many things to require cessation of nicotine when he or she is trying to become abstinent from marijuana. Other clinicians, just as experienced and competent, do not agree and therefore require adolescents to become abstinent from both at the same time. I am with this group. My experience suggests that if the administration of the program is united on this issue and has a rationale, which it explains to both staff and patients, that all intoxicants need to be eliminated, then it is a nonissue.

REFERENCES

1. Grinspoon L, Bakalar JB. Marijuana, in Lowinson JH, Ruiz P, Millman RB (eds), *Substance Abuse: Clinical Problems and Perspectives*. Baltimore, Williams & Wilkins, 1992.
2. Crowley T. Marijuana Dependence and Adolescent Conduct Disorder. NIDA National Conference on Marijuana Use Prevention, Treatment, and Research. Arlington, VA, 1995.
3. Preliminary Estimates from the 1994 National Household Survey on Drug Abuse. Advance Data Report #10. Substance Abuse and Mental Health Administration Office of Applied Studies. Rockville, MD, 1995.
4. Johnston LD, Bachman JG, O'Malley PM. News and Information Services, University of Michigan, 31 January 1994.
5. Anthony JC, Warner LA, Kessler RC. Comparative epidemiology of tobacco, alcohol, controlled substances, and inhalants: Basic findings from the National Comorbidity Study. *Clin Exp Psychopharmacol,* to be published.
6. Weller RA, Halikas JA. Objective criteria for the diagnosis of marijuana abuse. *J Nerv Ment Dis* 168:98–103, 1980.
7. Hall W, Solowij N, Lemon J. *The Health and Psychological Consequences of Cannabis Use*. Monograph Series #25. Australian Government Publishing Service, Canberra, Australia, 1994.
8. Martin BR. Marijuana: What It Is and What It Does. NIDA National Conference on Marijuana Use, Prevention, Treatment, and Research. Arlington, VA, 1995.
9. Jones RT, Benowitz NL, Herning RI. Clinical relevance of cannabis tolerance and dependence. *J Clin Pharmacol* 21:143S–152S, 1981.
10. Roffman RA, Stephens RS. Assessment and treatment of cannabis dependence, in Dunner DL (ed), *Current Psychiatric Therapy*, vol 11. Philadelphia, PA, WB Saunders, 1996.
11. Taylor RC, Heishman SJ. Marijuana impairs performance on standardized field sobriety tests. Paper presented at the Eastern Psychological Association Meeting, Philadelphia, PA, 1996.
12. Leirer VO, Yesavage JA, Morrow DG. Marijuana carry-over effects on aircraft pilot performance: a preliminary report. *Aviation, Space and Environmental Medicine* 62:221–227, 1991.
13. Pope HG, Yurgelun-Todd D. The residual cognitive effects of heavy marijuana use in college students. *JAMA* 275:521–527, 1996.
14. Tashkin DP. Cannabis effects on the respiratory system: Review of the literature. Los Angeles, CA, UCLA School of Medicine, June 1994.

15. Taylor FM. Marijuana as a potential respiratory tract carcinogen. *South Med J* 81:1213–1216, 1988.
16. Caplan GA, Brigham BA. Marijuana smoking and carcinoma of the tongue: Is there an association? *Cancer* 66:1005–1006, 1990.
17. Gottschalk LA, Aronow WS, Prakash R. Effect of marijuana and placebo-marijuana smoking on psychological state and psychophysiological cardiovascular functioning in anginal patients. *Biol Psychiatry* 12:255–266, 1977.
18. Cabral GA. Effects of marijuana on the immune system. NIDA National Conference on Marijuana Use, Prevention, Treatment, and Research. Arlington, VA, 1995.
19. Zuckerman B, Frank DA, Hingson R, et al. Effects of marijuana and cocaine use on fetal growth. *N Engl J Med* 320:762–768, 1989.
20. Hatch EE, Bracken MB. Effect of marijuana use in pregnancy on fetal growth. *Am J Epidemiol* 124:986–993, 1986.
21. Scher MS, Richardson GA, Coble PA, et al. The effects of prenatal alcohol and marijuana exposure: Disturbances in neonatal sleep cycling and arousal. *Pediatr Res* 24:101–105, 1988.
22. Fried PA. Perinatal and Developmental Effects of Marijuana. NIDA National Conference on Marijuana Use, Prevention, Treatment, and Research. Arlington, VA, 1995.
23. Block RI, Farinpour R, Schlechte JA. Effects of chronic marijuana use on testerone, luteinizing hormone, follicle stimulating hormone, prolactin and cortisol in men and women. *Drug Alcohol Depend* 28:121–128, 1991.
24. Dax EM, Pilotte NS, Adler WH, et al. The effects of 9-one-tetrahydrocannabinol on hormone release and immune function. *J Steroid Biochem* 34:263–270, 1989.

10. Dual Diagnosis Programs

All the components of current dual diagnosis programs were derived from historically diverse treatment elements, each of which was directly, vehemently, and persistently hostile to all the others. The culture of AA and its offspring—the Minnesota model, methadone maintenance, and therapeutic communities—were based on different theories, had unique treatment methods, and addressed different populations whose members used different intoxicants. Each had a distrust of psychiatry, usually for good reason, and psychiatry returned the favor by not wanting to get involved with "those people." Until recently, it was highly improbable that a person with schizophrenia could attend and be accepted at an AA meeting. But the basic AA model proved to be adaptable, and now AA groups for the dually diagnosed are a standard part of dual diagnosis programs in which they are often called "double trouble" meetings.

Mental health programs, both public and private, have usually quite explicitly excluded people with drug or alcohol problems. In Illinois, for many years there were separate subsections in the State Department of Mental Health for alcohol, drugs, mental health, and developmental disabilities, but no section for the modal person using the system who tended to have two or more of these problems. This is changing as programs merge and develop dual diagnosis programming. But the change is difficult and slow, as these various elements have administrative, theoretical, and politically based reasons not to change. On a federal level, for example, we still have the National Institute on Mental Health, the National Institute on Drug Abuse, and the National Institute on Alcoholism and Alcohol Abuse, despite the facts that substance abuse or dependence involving multiple drugs and alcohol has been, by a very large margin, the modal clinical pattern encountered for over two decades; and that a large number of studies demonstrate that drug and alcohol problems are strongly correlated with other mental disorders and are also correlated with a variety of other medical, social, vocational, and legal problems. The institutional response to modern problems lags behind the emergence of these problems by many decades.

HISTORY OF ALCOHOLICS ANONYMOUS

AA was founded in the 1930s by Dr. Bob, a surgeon, and Bill W., a businessman. They were recruits to the drug culture of the 1920s, namely to alcohol and tobacco. Searching for a way out of their alcoholism, they returned to the conservative values under which they had been raised. These values are the inverse of the values of the drug culture. Family, community, spirituality, anonymity, and sobriety are antithetical to the values of the self and intoxication. (It is an interesting sidelight that both men developed severe consequences from their nicotine addiction, and one of them died from nicotine-related disease.) The movement they founded offered hope to hundreds of thousands of people with alcohol problems, and it is an integral element in dual diagnosis programs today. AA was also the source of the Minnesota model for alcoholism. This model married AA to medical treatment for withdrawal.[1] AA is spiritual, not religious, but this distinction is lost on many people and makes AA unacceptable for many for whom this fellowship would be beneficial.

AA gave rise to NA (Narcotics Anonymous) and then to CA (Cocaine Anonymous) as a response to pressure to provide service to people using alcohol and narcotics or alcohol and cocaine. Younger persons in these groups do not adhere to the old AA admission definition of having an alcohol problem, period. AA, NA, and CA all had much difficulty accepting that some people need mood-altering drugs to treat legitimate mental disorders. This acceptance is by no means complete, however, even at present, and represents a barrier for many dual diagnosis patients.

THE THERAPEUTIC COMMUNITY OF CHARLES DIEDERICH[2]

Charles Diederich was a recovering alcoholic who ran AA groups in Santa Monica, California, in the 1950s. Heroin addicts pressured him to let them in the AA groups, and Diederich started to study their problems. He concluded that they needed to be isolated from society and that they needed total socialization or complete resocialization. He began Synanon, a residential treatment unit, to accomplish these goals. Diederich read widely and specifically rejected the psychiatric notion of the unconscious. In his view, addicts used such a theory to "con" people, including themselves. To get into Synanon, one had to be quite verbal and could not be disoriented or psychotic. Total abstinence from all mood-altering drugs, except tobacco, was also required. The therapeutic community created by Diederich differed dramatically from the therapeutic community created in psychiatry by Maxwell Jones, as the following list illustrates:

Diederich	Jones
Rigid hierarchy	Democratic process
Charismatic leader	Leadership not emphasized
Leadership absolute	Leadership in the group
Access very difficult	Access warm, humanistic
Groups harshly confrontational	Groups warm and supportive
Sanctions harsh; peers not involved	Minimal sanctions of any kind; peers involved
Shaved heads, wore signs	No public censure

Isolation from family	Family ties maintained
Isolation from friends	Friendships maintained
Goal: total socialization, lifelong immersion in Synanon	Do away with effects of stigmatization, accept self, return to normal community living

This last item is worth stressing, for it led to a splintering of the Synanon family. Diederich felt strongly that society would be lethal for members of Synanon who attempted to return to community living. Not everyone agreed in Synanon, and a group split from Synanon, starting Daytop Village in New York.[3] Daytop used the same treatment methods developed by Diederich but taught that return to the community was the ultimate goal of treatment. This view certainly has proved valid, as a great many therapeutic community graduates have adopted positive lifestyles and have vastly improved their quality of life. Synanon has built its own society with its own schools, and Synanon remains a lifelong commitment for its members.

There have been dramatic changes to the therapeutic community model that have made it much more effective and relevant in the current environment.[4] Particularly in the criminal justice system, therapeutic communities treat drug/alcohol problems with associated mental illness (MI) problems compounded by criminal behavior.[5] These modern therapeutic communities, because they are demonstrating effectiveness, are slowly changing long-standing, severely critical attitudes in the criminal justice system toward treatment for drug and alcohol problems.

THE METHADONE MAINTENANCE MODEL

The methadone maintenance system of care has functioned in isolation from the other historically important treatment efforts because of the controversy over substitution therapy.

The AA community viewed giving methadone to heroin addicts as something akin to giving alcoholics bourbon. The therapeutic community movement objected on the ideological grounds that giving methadone continued drug dependency. On empirical grounds, many heroin addicts find that methadone does not intoxicate; rather, it normalizes them and frees them from having to steal to get heroin. As reviewed in this text, the evidence is that it is useful for many addicts, and there are now over 115,000 people on methadone. In a dual diagnosis unit, the patient taking methadone should be viewed as equivalent to the patient taking antidepressants or antipsychotics.

NICOTINE IN DUAL DIAGNOSIS PROGRAMS

Most drug and alcohol treatment programs have historically neglected to recognize that nicotine is the most lethal of all drugs of abuse and dependence. Some in the mental health community, and especially some family members, feel strongly that people with schizophrenic disorders cannot tolerate being denied nicotine and that since their lives are so empty of gratification, it is cruel to deny them something they enjoy. A growing number of studies, however, indicate that adding treatment for nicotine to therapeutic communities or dual diagnosis programs is accepted by almost everyone and is a positive element in treatment.[6, 7] I take the position that nicotine may have some short-term benefits for a person with a serious mental disorder but that its overall effects probably worsen psychopathology of all kinds.

PSYCHOSIS VERSUS ADDICTION

There are many parallels between mental and substance related disorders (Tables 1 and 2).[8] The physician and all other staff need to know these parallels because all the staff are the carriers of a treatment culture they must teach the patients. It is critical for the clinician to realize that for successful treatment of dual diagnosis patients, all the elements of the treatment program must be in place for benefits to occur in any sphere. There must be a comprehensive plan that includes elements for the substance related disorder and the mental health disorder together with family, vocational, social, and other components, according to need. The leadership must be comfortable with all the elements of the plan, regardless of which tradition they might have had primary experience and training in.

Table 1: Parallels Between Psychosis (mental illness) and Addiction/Alcoholism

- Biological illness
- Hereditary (in part)
- Chronic
- Incurable
- Leads to lack of control of behavior and emotions
- Affects the whole family
- Symptoms can be controlled with proper treatment
- Disease progresses without treatment
- Disease of denial
- Facing the disease can lead to depression and despair
- Disease is often seen as a moral issue, due to personal weakness rather than biological causes
- Feelings of guilt, failure, shame, and stigma
- Disease has physical, mental, and spiritual components

Table 2 describes the parallels between the treatment necessary in the different domains. Here again, it is necessary for the staff to know and to teach these parallels to the patients.

Table 2: Parallels Between Process of Recovery

Addiction	*Mental illness*
Phase one: Acute Stabilization	
Detoxification	*Stabilize Acute Psychosis*
• Usually inpatient, may be involuntary	• Usually inpatient, may be involuntary
• Usually need medication	• Medication
• 3–5 days (alcohol); 2–3 weeks (downers)	• 2 weeks to 6 months
• Includes assessment for other diagnoses	• Includes assessment for effects of substances and for addiction
• Engagement of the patient in ongoing treatment is crucial for recovery to proceed	• Engagement of the patient in ongoing treatment is crucial for recovery to proceed
Phase Two: Prolonged Stabilization (1 Year)	
Continued Abstinence	*Continued Med Compliance*
• Patient must voluntarily participate in ongoing treatment, but treatment is often coerced and may at times be legally mandated (probation)	• Patient must usually voluntarily participate in ongoing treatment, but treatment is often coerced and may at times be legally mandated (med guardianship)
• May need inpatient or day treatment rehabilitation for 2–4 weeks	• May need extended inpatient stay or day treatment for 3–12 months
• Need education about addiction and how to stay abstinent	• Need education about mental illness and how to prevent relapse
• Need to overcome denial and admit powerlessness over alcohol/drugs	• Need to overcome denial and admit powerlessness over illness
• Need to develop support system to ask for help, usually intensive AA (90 meetings in 90 days)	• Need to develop support system to ask for help, with meds, therapy, day programs
• Must learn to accept the illness and deal with shame, stigma, guilt, and despair	• Must learn to accept the illness and deal with shame, stigma, guilt, and despair
• Family needs to be involved; must learn to detach and set limits	• Family needs to be involved; must learn to detach and set limits
• May need 6–12 months residential placement	• May need residential placement
• Continuing assessment	• Continuing assessment
• Risk of relapse continues	• Risk of relapse continues
Phase Three: Recovery (1–30 Years)	
Continued Sobriety	*Recovery; Continued Stability*
• Voluntary, active involvement in treatment	• Voluntary, active involvement in treatment
• Stability precedes growth; no growth is possible unless sobriety is fairly secure; growth occurs slowly, one day at a time	• Stability precedes growth; no growth is possible unless stabilization of psychosis is solid (may be symptomatic, but stable); growth occurs slowly, one day at a time

Table 2: Parallels Between Process of Recovery (continued)

Addiction	*Mental illness*
• Continued work in the AA program on growing, changing, dealing with feelings (twelve Steps, step meetings)	• Continued medication, but reduced to lowest level needed for maintenance; continued work in treatment program with increasing work on feelings in therapy, processing the impact of illness
• Thinking continues to clear	• Thinking continues to clear
• New skills for dealing with feelings, situations	• New skills for dealing with feelings, situations
• Increasing responsibility for illness, and recovery program brings increasing control of one's life	• Increasing responsibility for illness, and recovery program brings increasing control of one's life
• Increasing capacity to work and to have relationships	• Increasing capacity to work and relate (vocational rehab, clubhouse programs)
• Recovery is never complete, always ongoing	• Recovery is never complete, always ongoing
• Eventual goal is peace of mind and serenity	• Eventual goal is peace of mind and serenity

One element in table 2 that is particularly important to appreciate is the disturbance in thinking that occurs in drug dependence. Traditionally, the alcohol community has identified this defect as "stinking thinking." This is often a subtle defect. The drug dependent person appears to be able to think and speak quite logically, but as one learns about the history in detail, it becomes clear that thinking has been impaired and judgment has not been normal. With dual diagnosis patients, particularly those with cognitive impairments from schizophrenia or bipolar affective disorder, the therapist has to work with the patient to see when judgment is impaired and to involve family members and/or other members of the treatment team to work with the patient to prevent actions based on impaired judgment.

DIAGNOSTIC PROBLEMS IN DUAL DIAGNOSIS PROGRAMS

PCP, SCHIZOPHRENIA, OR BOTH?

Substance related disorders are rule-outs for most major DSM-4 diagnostic categories. When onset of a major psychiatric disorder is followed by the onset of drug abuse, the diagnosis is clear. But there are cases in which decisions about diagnosis are less obvious. For example, a young person takes PCP, confirmed by urine screen, then develops an acute psychosis that never completely resolves and that eventually reaches criteria for schizophrenia. DSM-4 states, in relation to the differential diagnosis of schizophrenia: "The disorder is not due to the direct physiologic effects of a substance (e.g., a drug of abuse/...)." This determines that the chronic condition in the example would be diagnosed as schizophrenia because, after six months of no PCP use, there could be no "direct effects."

I believe most PCP psychoses resolve in a few days and that there are no chronic sequelae from a single episode, but it is conceivable that some individuals may be vulnerable to long-term sequelae from an acute exposure, or more likely from repeated acute exposures, to PCP. Stress sometimes appears to trigger schizophrenia, and there is no reason why the stress from the major disruptive behavioral effects of PCP could not serve as a trigger. In addition, we know that people with schizophrenia take all kinds of drugs, including PCP, at high rates.

The acute diagnosis between a drug related disorder and the onset of schizophrenia cannot be made firmly. When persons with a clear diagnosis of schizophrenia take PCP, it appears to worsen the underlying condition and produce florid pathology. The management of these situations has been covered in previous chapters.

One aspect of the PCP-or-schizophrenia diagnostic debate revolves around the issue of self-medication. It is clear that some of the associated problems with schizophrenia are treatable with any drug with sedative and tranquilizing effects. Sleep, for example, is difficult, especially for someone with repeated, highly dysphoric hallucinations, and cannabis or PCP may help; but the sedative effect is followed by a worsening of other pathology, such as dissociation and inappropriate affect. It is true that the patient is self-medicating, but from another vantage point the patient is making the basic pathology worse. From a clinical perspective, one must teach the patient, if the patient does not already appreciate this, that self-medication causes more problems than it solves.

ANXIETY

Anxiety (and dysphoria) is a common result of high doses of many drug classes and of the withdrawal from almost all drugs of abuse. In dual diagnosis populations, it is frequently encountered[9] and presents the same diagnostic problems as the PCP-or-schizophrenia distinction. Is one dealing with a symptom of an anxiety disorder, or is one dealing with an expression of a drug related diagnosis? There is no simple acute solution. One has to monitor clinically and decide, usually on the basis of sustained manifestations of anxiety, that the anxiety disorder is primary. Onset of an anxiety disorder before the onset of substance abuse would argue for the anxiety disorder diagnosis.[10] The underlying presumption is that withdrawal-related expressions of anxiety are short lived, and that persistence of anxiety symptoms probably means there is an independent anxiety disorder.

If the patient with a clear diagnosis of drug dependence is also to be treated for an anxiety disorder, nondrug treatment such as behavior modification, self-help, psychotherapy, and family education should be tried, but many cases also need drug therapy. Pharmacotherapy with buspirone or antidepressants should be added to the treatment regimen. There are some patients with a history of drug dependence, however, often alcohol and/or benzodiazepine related, with severe panic that responds only to benzodiazepines. When the benzodiazepine therapy is accompanied by a sound general treatment program with good monitoring by the physician and significant others, substantial improvement in the quality of life for the patient can be achieved without a relapse to substance abuse.[11]

DEPRESSION

In exact parallel with anxiety, depression can be a direct effect of intoxicants, or it may be an expression of withdrawal; it presents the same diagnostic problem discussed above.[12] In the withdrawing patient, severity and persistence of depressive symptoms, particularly if combined with a positive family history of depression, dictate starting immediate treatment for depression. If the depression resolves, the antidepressant can be discontinued; but if there is primary depression, there will be a lag time before the drug effects are evident, and the prompt start will have been justified. Acute suicidal thinking, if combined with depressive mood, also argues against waiting to see if the depressive mood is an expression of withdrawal.

On a clinical level, with recovery there is usually an improvement in mood, often striking in quality. The difference in mood between active drug use and sobriety is sometimes so dramatic that it leads me to believe the intoxicant was probably responsible for the depressive symptoms. It would make pharmacological sense, since all the intoxicants are ultimately depressant to CNS cells and neuronal assemblies, although they may have initial stimulant effects.

AXIS 2 DISORDERS

Rates of antisocial personality disorder are elevated in drug abusing populations[13]; and other axis 2 disorders, particularly in the cluster 2 group, also appear to be frequent in drug abusers, regardless of the drug abused. All types of personality disorders appear in drug dependent populations, and the notion of a specific personality structure—the "addictive personality"—predisposing people to become drug dependent has been proven wrong by modern clinical experience and research. What is striking is the variety of co-occurring disorders with primary drug dependence, ranging from schizophrenia and bipolar affective disorder to a subset of drug dependent persons with no other axis 1 or axis 2 disorders. Although research is being carried out on treatments for axis 2 disorders, at present there is no widely accepted, effective treatment.

MIX OF ELEMENTS IN DUAL DIAGNOSIS PROGRAMS

Some programs identify themselves as being for mentally ill substance abusers, whereas others identify themselves as being for the chemically dependent mentally ill. While sharing a core of self-help, psychiatric medication (including agents used in the treatment of substance abuse), one-to-one counseling, therapy groups, educational components, and family education, different programs may have special components to deal with specific population needs. For example, programs serving schizophrenic dual diagnosis patients may have groups focused on developing social skills. For many dual diagnosis populations, there is no need for such a component, as social skills are well developed.

In a similar vein, there may be a need for housing, education, or employment in some populations but not in others. Such needs determine the form, content, site, and fit of the treatment unit into the continuum of care. Although it has not yet been proven by scientific study, clinical experience suggests strongly that the more complete the response to the domains of need in a patient, the better the outcome. For example, in a treatment unit for pregnant heroin dependent females, we improved prenatal care by providing transportation. We had studied why attendance for prenatal care was so poor and found that transportation and care of other children were major problems. When we dedicated a car and a driver and provided on-site child care, attendance approached 100 percent; no other program elements were as important in normalizing birth weights, head circumference, reduction of prematurity, and other desirable outcomes as these two measures. Over a 10-year period, we delivered close to 1,500 babies, so these measures were consequential for many newborns who otherwise might have been severely compromised by lack of adequate prenatal care.

The degree of family involvement also varies according to the population served. Most programs describe family involvement as educational and supportive and avoid any inference that the family is responsible for all or part of the patient's drug problem. One has to start with the notion that the patient is the problem until there is substantial clinical evidence to indicate otherwise. As evidence of enabling behavior (family behavior that worsens pathology) is solidified, one may attempt to work more therapeutically with the family member, but this is in addition to the core of family education. The construction of a sound therapeutic alliance, based on education and support, facilitates the transition to family therapy when it is indicated.

Family involvement may also mean that a counselor meets with the patient and the family after the family group education session to work on issues specific to the family. In Galanter's view, anyone from the patient's social network may be viewed as family for the purpose of enhancing recovery.[14] A friend who wants to help may serve in the place of family members. Family involvement in treatment is very important, but it is disheartening to observe that many family members will not participate.

PSYCHOTHERAPY WITH DRUG DEPENDENT POPULATIONS

Once a patient has a stable program of recovery in operation, psychotherapy may proceed as with any other kind of disorder; but until stability is achieved, the therapist may have to contend with a degree of instability in the transference that is probably traceable to drug effects on mental function. Most significant is the substantial degree of impairment from high doses of drugs such as cocaine or methamphetamine or hashish. I conducted a two-hour examination of a patient who was basing high doses of cocaine with heavy use of other drugs, then reexamined the patient the next day and found that he had only a spotty recall of what he had told me. As discussed in excellent fashion by Kaufman,[15] transference reactions can be unusually volatile with drug toxic patients.

In the early phases of recovery, when patients have not yet regained full ability to relate and to think abstractly, the therapist needs to be supportive and directive to help the patient lock onto the recovery program. The therapist has to be aware that the patient in a dual diagnosis program has relationships with many people, and the patient should be assisted to balance these relationships. Teamwork is essential here so that all the staff are integrating what they are doing without manipulation, or without confusing the patient with different messages about the nature of the problem or what has to be done about it. For the same reason, work with the patient's family also has to be integrated by the treatment team.

Kaufman recommends that the therapist make continuation of psychotherapy contingent on the patient's agreement to adhere to the entire program.[15] He describes the elements of the contract, such as attendance at a specified number of daily AA or NA meetings, number of weekly educational groups, and the number of other components, together with making a commitment to all the elements of the total program. As sobriety lengthens, the therapist can shift to a more traditional focus on recognizing and dealing with dysfunctional defenses such as narcissism, entitlement, and the like.

DRUG INTERACTIONS

As a rule of thumb, drugs used for drug abuse are compatible with drugs used for other psychiatric conditions. Lithium, for example, can be given in normal doses to a person on methadone maintenance. As noted earlier, methadone and zidovudine sometimes interact, with the consequence that methadone is metabolized more rapidly; but this does not always happen. I have had many patients on both for extended periods without this interaction ever appearing. It is reasonable to prescribe drugs with known interactions and observe whether or not they have the interaction in the individual patient. Obviously, one should monitor carefully and document in the chart what is being monitored. The number of drug interactions is so large that one needs to subscribe to a drug interaction program that is computerized and periodically updated. One can use the *Physician's Desk Reference*, but the *Medical Letter's* Drug Interaction Program is much faster, more comprehensive, and easier to use.[16] Each year the number of clinically significant interactions gets larger, and the need for computerized data is greater.

The interactions for disulfiram (Antabuse) from a recent edition of the *Medical Letter* are reproduced below. I have selected three illustrative interactions to demonstrate the importance of having such information. It is highly likely that the drugs involved in these interactions will be needed clinically in at least a few cases. The completeness of the information and the speed with which it is available are remarkable.

Drugs Interacting with Disulfiram

- Alcohol
- Anticoagulants
- Antidepressants, tricyclic
- Benzodiazepines
- Caffeine
- Chloroxazole
- Isoniazid
- Marijuana smoking
- Metronidazole
- Omprazole
- Phenothiazines
- Phenytoin
- Theophyllines

The list of drugs interacting with disulfiram is then made specific:

	Interaction for	Effect	Comment/ recommendation	Reference
1.	Disulfiram Isoniazid	Psychotic episodes, ataxia (altered dopamine metabolism)	Avoid concurrent use	O'Connell DF, Managing the Dually Diagnosed Patient: Current Issues and Clinical Approaches, 1990, The Haworth Press.
2.	Disulfiram Benzodiazepines	Possible benzodiazepine toxicity (decreased metabolism)	Alprazolam and oxazepam do not interact and may be used with disulfiram	Mayfield, DG and Coleman, LL, Alcohol use and affective disorder, 1968, Diseases of the Nervous System, 29:467-474.
3.	Disulfiram Antidepressants, tricyclic	Organic brain syndrome (decreased metabolism)	Monitor mental status	Ciraulo, DA, et al, Pharmacokinetic interaction of disulfiram and antidepressants, 1985, American Journal of Psychiatry, 142:1373.

REFERENCES

1. Geller A. Rehabilitation programs and halfway houses, in Lowinson JH, Ruiz P, Millman RB, et al (eds), *Substance Abuse: A Comprehensive Textbook*. Baltimore, MD, Williams & Wilkins, 1992.
2. Yablonsky W. *Synanon: The Tunnel Back*. New York, Macmillan, 1965.
3. Deitch DA. Personal communication, June 1992.
4. Densen-Gerber J. *We Mainline Dreams: The Odyssey House Story*. Garden City, NY, Doubleday, 1973.
5. Barthwell A, Bokos P, Bailey J, et al, Interventions/Wilmer: A continuum of care for substance abusers in the criminal justice system. *J Psychoactive Drugs* 27(1):39–47, 1995.

6. Haller E, McNiel DE, Binder RL. Impact of a smoking ban on a locked psychiatric unit. *J Clin Psychiatry* 57:8, 1996.
7. Kempf J, Stanley A. Impact of tobacco-free policy on recruitment and retention of adolescents in residential substance abuse treatment. *J Addictive Dis* 15(2):1–11, 1996.
8. Minkoff K. An integrated treatment model for dual diagnosis of psychosis and addiction. *Hosp Community Psychiatry* 40:1030–1036, 1989.
9. Noyes R, Crowe RR, Harris EL. Relationship between panic disorder and agoraphobia. *Arch Gen Psychiatry* 43:227–232, 1986.
10. Schuckit M. *Drug and Alcohol Abuse*, ed 4. New York, Plenum, 1995, pp 299–300.
11. DuPont RL, Saylor KE. Sedative/hypnotics and benzodiazepines, in Frances RS, Miller SI (eds), *Clinical Textbook of Addictive Disorders*. New York, Guilford Press, 1991.
12. Schuckit MA. Alcohol and depression: A clinical perspective. *Acta Psychiatrica Scand* 377:28–32, 1994.
13. Helzer JE, Pryzbeck TR. The co-occurrence of alcoholism with other psychiatric disorders in the general population and its impact on treatment. *J Stud Alcohol* 49:219–224, 1988.
14. Galanter M. Network therapy for the office practitioner, in Lowinson JH, Ruiz P, Millman RB, et al (eds), *Substance Abuse: A Comprehensive Textbook*. Baltimore, MD, Williams & Wilkins, 1992.
15. Kaufman E. The psychotherapy of dually diagnosed patients. *J Subst Abuse Treat* 6:9–18, 1989.
16. Medical Letter Drug Interaction Program. The Medical Letter Inc (1000 Main Street, New Rochelle, NY 10801-7537), yearly update, June 1996.

11. Other Drugs: Arylcyclohexylamines; PCP and Its Congeners; Hallucinogens; Steroids; Inhalants

In the 1950s, medicinal chemists at Parke-Davis designed phencyclidine, or PCP,* to overcome the major problems of brainstem-mediated depression of breathing and blood pressure that were characteristic of the then-current anesthetic agents. They succeeded. PCP, in human trials, did not depress respiration or blood pressure but usually stimulated them, and, in addition to having profound anesthetic effects, PCP had the added benefit of producing analgesia. Use of PCP in humans, however, was rapidly discontinued when it was observed that 20 percent or more of patients woke from anesthesia experiencing a variety of symptoms including confusion, terror, disorientation, and hallucinations.[1] Veterinarians were able to continue use of this agent, and it was from their supplies that "street people" first stole the drug and began experimenting with it. One of the early street names of PCP was "hog" or "elephant tranqs." Veterinarians were barred from using PCP in 1979 by the federal government when epidemiologic studies indicated that about 7 million people in the United States had used PCP and that rates of experimentation with PCP were increasing rapidly.

PHARMACOLOGY

PCP and other arylcyclohexylamines have anesthetic, analgesic, stimulant, convulsant, euphorigenic, depressant, and hallucinogenic potentials.[2] Given this range of possible effects, pharmacological classification is difficult. In early clinical trials, patients were observed to be anesthetized but appeared to be relatively alert compared to the usual degree of profound sedation produced by anesthetics. The term *dissociative anesthetic* was coined to describe this unique form of anesthesia. PCP is intensely lipophilic. It has a half-life of over three days and a window of detection in usual drug screens of two to three weeks and sometimes more. It is biotransformed in the liver by oxidation, hydroxylation, and conjugation with glucoronic acid, with only a small amount of drug excreted in the urine.

The cycling of behaviorally toxic effects with a normal sensorium depends on two characteristics of PCP. PCP is stored in body fat, and its presence in the bloodstream depends on the acidity of the blood. When the pH is acidic, the drug appears

---

* Street names for PCP include *rocket fuel, zoom, angel dust, supercoke, tic-tac, TCH,* and, when mixed with marijuana, *mint leaf, shermans* or *sherms,* and *dream team,* among many others.

in plasma. When the pH is more alkaline, the drug stays in body fat stores and has no psychoactive effects. A second mechanism accounting for clinical cycling of toxic effects occurs in the stomach. The acidity of the stomach pulls the PCP from the blood, which lessens or aborts its psychoactive effects; but then PCP enters the small intestine, where the pH is alkaline, and enterohepatic recirculation may result in the drug's reintroduction into the bloodstream with possible recurrence of symptoms.

At low doses (5 to 10 mg) in nontolerant individuals PCP usually but not always induces euphoria and a feeling of weightlessness ("spacey," "ozoned"). The feeling of weightlessness probably reflects PCP's blocking action on proprioceptive impulses and may reflect the ego experience of being removed from ordinary levels of control of movement, secondary to PCP's anesthetic effect on large cortical motor cells. Nontolerant users of low doses report unpleasant effects such as abdominal pain, nausea, vomiting, depression, paranoia, and hyperacusis about 20 percent of the time. These negative experiences do not appear to be severe enough to influence drug taking, because those reporting such effects usually do not seek help and continue to use PCP. As dose increases, from 10 mg to 30 mg, again in nontolerant individuals, PCP users begin to experience stimulation, illusions (misperceptions of real stimuli), and hallucinogenic effects.[3]

PCP comes in every form—powder, capsule, tablet, liquid, and so on. It can be almost any color, and it can be taken by any route of administration. Commonly, PCP is smoked in a mixture with parsley, mint leaves, or marijuana. Smoking became the preferred route of self-administration because users observed that the dose could be controlled better than was the case with oral or IV use. Control of effects is critical with a drug such as PCP that has the potential for serious and sometimes sustained behaviorally disruptive effects.

Clinically, while PCP can be synthesized by amateur chemists, their efforts frequently produce an array of psychoactive arylcyclohexylamines. If a syndrome appearing to meet criteria for PCP intoxication or psychosis is accompanied by bloody vomiting, it may be that the patient has taken PCC, 1-cyclohexanecyanonitrile. These patients have detectable levels of cyanide in the bloodstream.[4] There appears to be no clinical significance to these cyanide levels. Street users have used PHP, a PCP congener, in an attempt to escape having urines positive for PCP.

PCP has complex effects on multiple important body systems. As reviewed by Schuckit[5] and by Zukin and Zukin,[2] PCP inhibits the NMDA receptor, has cholinergic and, at times, anticholinergic effects, inhibits reuptake of dopamine and norepinephrine, alters serotonin systems, and appears to be active at the GABA receptor. These multiple effects explain the unusual complex of clinical symptoms and the relatively unique sequencing of these effects from case to case. In addition, they explain why PCP tends not to be a preferred daily drug of abuse over decades. Like long-acting amphetamines, it has such disruptive effects on mental functions that the chronic user cannot have any kind of life. Even the most perfervid members of the drug culture usually find this unacceptable and consequently moderate their use of PCP. In the few patients I have seen in whom there has been sustained daily use over a period of years (with levels of intake at the gram-per-day level), there appeared to be serious and possibly irreversible neuropsychological impairment. The impairment precluded any kind of work or relating in social settings.

PCP, in humans, does not have an acute withdrawal syndrome, but when high doses have been taken, it may take days to weeks before neuropsychological function is normal. Luisada observed that high-dose users reported craving.[3] On clinical grounds, there appears to be no question that tolerance to PCP occurs, as some daily users need 10 times the dose of a naive user to achieve equivalent effects.

CLINICAL DISORDERS CAUSED BY PCP (OR ITS CONGENERS)[6-8]

DIAGNOSIS AND MANAGEMENT OF PCP INTOXICATION

PCP causes a unique form of intoxication. The DSM-4 criteria for this diagnosis are as follows:

DSM-4 Criteria for the Diagnosis of Phencyclidine Intoxication (292.89)

A. Recent use of phencyclidine (or a related substance)

B. Clinically significant maladaptive behavioral changes (e.g., belligerence, assaultiveness, impulsiveness, unpredictability, psychomotor agitation, impaired judgment, or impaired social or occupational functioning) that developed during, or shortly after, phencyclidine use

C. Within an hour (less when smoked, snorted, or used intravenously), two (or more) of the following signs:
   1) vertical or horizontal nystagmus
   2) hypertension or tachycardia
   3) numbness or diminished responsiveness to pain
   4) ataxia
   5) dysarthria
   6) muscle rigidity
   7) seizure or coma
   8) hyperacusis

D. The symptoms are not due to a general medical condition and are not better accounted for by another mental disorder.

   Specify if:
   With perceptual disturbances

   Specifier
   The following specifier may be applied to a diagnosis of Phencyclidine Intoxication:
   With perceptual disturbances. This specifier may be noted when hallucinations with intact reality testing or auditory, visual, or tactile illusions occur in the absence of a delirium. Intact reality testing means that the person knows that the hallucinations are induced by the substance and do not represent external reality. When hallucinations occur in the absence of intact reality testing, a diagnosis of Substance Induced Psychotic Disorder, with Hallucinations, should be considered.

The reasons for the variability of this syndrome have been discussed above. In clinical practice, this diagnosis establishes a need for at least a few hours of observation to ensure that the course is not progressing from intoxication to delirium or psychosis. The talking-down procedure described in chapter 1 may have to be abandoned if the patient cannot participate in verbal exchange, is nonresponsive, or shows signs of increased agitation in relation to attempts to engage the patient interactively. Most cases resolve with time without any kind of intervention.

MANAGEMENT OF PCP INTOXICATION PROGRESSING TO DELIRIUM OR PSYCHOSIS[3, 8, 9]

If agitation develops in the PCP-intoxicated patient, benzodiazepines should be given in sufficient dose to lessen or abolish the agitation (e.g., lorazepam IM in doses of 0.5 to 2.0 mg, depending on the degree of agitation). In persisting psychoses associated with PCP, some clinicians attempt to rid the body of PCP by acidification of the urine. Acidification of the urine is accomplished by (a) administration of ammonium chloride orally, (b) oral vitamin C and cranberry juice, and finally (c) use of a diuretic such as lasix. If the urine is not at pH 5 or below, the diuresis does not result in significant excretion of PCP. Acidification of the urine should not be attempted if there is renal or hepatic disease or if barbiturates or salicylates are also present, because acidification of urine inhibits excretion of these drugs.

Ion trapping, a technique in which the stomach is lavaged continuously, in combination with acidification of urine, has been described.[3, 9] These procedures are in a gray area between addiction medicine and emergency and intensive care medicine. As reviewed by Zukin and Zukin,[2] they may affect only a small portion of the PCP in the body and carry the risk of inducing a metabolic acidosis and renal necrosis secondary to rhabdomyolysis. Ideally, there should be full medical consultation before they are attempted, with medical treatment immediately available if problems develop. In the current environment, the addiction medicine specialist without full credentials in internal or emergency medicine needs to know the principles involved but should carry out these procedures only under the direction of a fully certified medical consultant.

In DSM-4, the coding of a drug induced psychosis is determined by the presenting symptom. In the instance of PCP psychosis, it could be 292.11, Phencyclidine Induced Psychotic Disorder with Hallucinations, or 292.12, Phencyclidine Induced Psychotic Disorder with Delusions. A PCP psychosis would not be diagnosed if it occurred solely during the course of a delirium.

In PCP delirium, patients may become comatose with their eyes open ("blank stare" or "eyes open coma"), and pupils may be constricted yet react to light. Nystagmus in all directions may be observed, only to disappear and then to return. Deep tendon reflexes (DTRs) may be hyperactive. Patients may perspire profusely. Blood pressure and pulse may be elevated, and the clinician must be mindful of the possibility of death from seizures, hyperthermia, or hypertensive crisis. Ataxia and muscle rigidity may be present. Dystonic reactions during acute PCP poisoning are also frequent. Head injuries may be mimicked in PCP-toxic patients. Urine or blood tests for PCP may not be positive in acutely toxic patients because PCP can be sequestered in the body fat. Blood levels of PCP do not correlate with the severity of clinical symptoms.

Some PCP-toxic patients may appear completely unresponsive but respond with violence or hyperactivity to any stimulation. Some clinicians advocate leaving such patients alone until they metabolize some of the drug and become more manageable. This technique is in sharp contrast to the simple reduction and/or regularization of stimuli in managing the "bad trip." If the PCP-toxic patient manifests no ability to control the effects of stimulation, stimuli should be reduced to an absolute minimum, by having the patient lie down in a quiet room covered by a blanket. Increasing clinical experience, however, indicates that most PCP-toxic patients can manage low-level regular stimuli and can therefore be managed by using the principles described in chapter 1 for the "bad trip." Early studies of PCP suggested strongly that the disorganizing effects on mental function caused by arylcyclohexylamines are dependent on sensory stimulation.

Most authors recommend butyrophenones or diazepam for control of the agitated and/or violent PCP-toxic patient, but Done believes diazepam delays excretion of PCP.[8] Luisada feels that chlorpromazine is the drug of choice in managing PCP-toxic patients and advocates its use once anticholinergic poisoning has been ruled out.[3] Luisada believes nonsedating antipsychotics do not provide the prompt response seen with chlorpromazine.

When I am consulted in PCP-toxic cases with severe behavioral disorders (e.g., extreme agitation and paranoid delusions with violent behavior), I advise giving benzodiazepine and butyrophenone together. A possible starting dose would be lorazepam 2 mg IM and haldol 5 mg IM. The patient should be observed for 20 minutes, and if there are reductions in agitation and improvements in behavior, another 20-minute period of observation is in order. If agitation and psychotic symptoms increase in the first observation period, the same dose of both butyrophenone and lorazepam should be repeated. Titrating the dose depending on clinical observation usually controls the problems. In extreme cases, some advocate electroconvulsive therapy.[10] None of the foregoing has been established by sound research, and different clinicians have different views of what is appropriate. As noted above, some argue against benzodiazepines on the grounds that they delay excretion of PCP. In my view, it is a quite justifiable tradeoff; to obtain control over homicidal behavior takes precedence over a slower biotransformation of the PCP.

There is a real risk of rhabdomyolysis when PCP-toxic patients are physically restrained. Chemical restraint should therefore be more aggressive in an attempt to achieve with drugs alone what one would achieve with physical restraint and drugs together. When PCP-toxic patients are not controllable by any means other than physical restraint, it must be ordered and the patient monitored carefully to minimize the time spent in restraint. Where possible, restraint carried out by two to four people is preferable to leather or plastic, but this is not feasible in many settings.

PCP toxicity has been observed in children who have ingested family caches of PCP or have been exposed to PCP smoke, perhaps purposefully by the parents blow-ing PCP smoke in the infant's face in an effort to quiet its crying. PCP-toxic neonates have also been observed.

MANAGEMENT OF PHENCYCLIDINE ABUSE

If patients in psychiatric wards or in therapeutic communities suffer prolonged effects from PCP, they may not be able to think accurately, or they may think so slowly or rapidly that they cannot organize their experiences. If this is the case, they should be given simple treatment regimens that do not put them under stress. Intense confrontations, or requiring them to attend group meetings with a high degree of verbal exchange, are contraindicated. The patient and other patients and staff should be oriented to the toxic effects of PCP on cognition and judgment and their implications for management. Most PCP abusers, however, are able to participate in therapeutic community or psychiatric ward dynamics after drug effects have worn off.

As reviewed by Zukin and Zukin,[2] PCP causes a psychosis that mimics naturally occurring schizophrenia. Clinical experience suggests that auditory hallucinations in PCP psychoses are more frequent than is usually observed in all other drug induced psychoses, where visual hallucinations are more frequent. Clinically, PCP also appears to cause more of a thought disorder than other psychotogens, but it is difficult to generalize because hallucinations are not present in many PCP psychoses, perceptual distortions take quite varied forms, and hallucinations, when they occur, are not always auditory. Flashbacks occur in PCP users. They can be treated according to the principles discussed in chapter 1.

HALLUCINOGENS

Hallucinogens induce, among other effects, false sensory experiences of a visual, auditory, tactile, gustatory, or kinesthetic nature. Strictly defined, hallucinations are sensory experiences of complex stimuli that do not exist (e.g., a drug toxic person sees another person who is not there, or hears voices when no one is speaking, or experiences insects crawling on the skin when no insects are present). Hallucinogens, however, are more likely to produce illusions (misperceptions of real stimuli) than they are to produce hallucinations. Under the influence of LSD, a subject may see distortions of actually existing colors; or existing stimuli may seem larger (macropsia) or smaller than they are (micropsia); alternatively, perceptions of colors or other stimuli may be intensified to the point where the colors or objects appear to be familiar yet are entirely new in some hard-to-explain way. In addition, users of hallucinogens may experience synesthesia, the experience of one sensory mode in terms of a second sensory mode (e.g., "seeing" the color of a musical tone or chord, "hearing" a color).

Hallucinogens may or may not have effects on mood. Many users of LSD, mescaline, and similar drugs report euphoria or lability of mood; less frequently, they report either no change in mood or dysphoria. Persisting dysphoria may take the form of overt loss of control, paranoia, or panic—the bad trip. Sympathomimetic effects are usual with most hallucinogens. These effects are consistent with the structure of many hallucinogens, which are closely related to amphetamines.

Hallucinogens may cause serious defects in judgment.[11] One patient I saw jumped from the roof of a three-story dormitory, acting on the delusion that he could fly. In addition, hallucinogens may produce profound distortions of body image, time sense, and sense of identity. The effects of hallucinogens on perception, mood, cognition, and body image are dose related. As the dose rises, the intensity and duration of symptoms increase; if very high doses are taken, a psychosis with adrenergic crisis may result.

Patterns of abuse of hallucinogens tend not to be stable in time; that is, unlike alcohol, nicotine, and marijuana, users tend not to take the drug daily or even frequently over long time spans. The rapid development of tolerance to most hallucinogens, if they are used frequently, may partially explain this, but the fact that hallucinogen use always carries the risk of loss of control, flashbacks, bad trips, and so forth probably accounts for why frequent hallucinogen users at 16 years of age are unlikely to be frequent hallucinogen users at age 36. For most people, these drugs appear to be too exhausting to control and too unpredictable in their effects to use on a daily basis for decades.

In the 1980s, 16 percent of the high school seniors in the United States had used hallucinogens at least once. In recent years, hallucinogen use has increased, but not to the levels of the 1980s. The data from "Monitoring the Future" for 1994 indicated a level of 8 percent of high school seniors with at least one lifetime use of LSD.[12] We do not have good data on the epidemiology of abuse because most bad trips do not come to medical attention, but many emergency rooms see clinical problems associated with hallucinogens at least occasionally. When hallucinogens do cause problems that come to medical attention, the psychiatric emergencies are usually severe.

The social setting in which hallucinogens are taken can influence the clinical pictures. If taken in the company of persons with whom the taker has highly conflictual relationships, the likelihood of problems is greatly increased, probably because any intoxicant taken under such circumstances is going to lessen controls and make fear and/or aggression more likely. As noted elsewhere in this text, some users can experience hallucinations and even mild delusions but are able to appreciate that the hallucinations or cognitive defects are drug effects. Judgment, in these instances, is intact, and there is no psychosis. DSM-4 provides a notation of this fact.

In the 1960s, when hallucinogen use, most notably LSD, was spreading, it was frequently alleged that hallucinogens caused an expansion and/or clarification of the mind, hence the term *psychedelic*. But few current observers of clinical populations with heavy hallucinogen exposure would subscribe to the notion that use of hallucinogens has advanced the maturation, motivation, or insight of users. McGlothlin and Arnold studied LSD users and found that many of them attributed positive personality changes to LSD; but a control group not experiencing LSD tended to report similar changes.[13] McGlothlin and Arnold concluded that there was little evidence that LSD use produced any so-called psychedelic changes in the groups studied.

Tolerance to hallucinogens develops rapidly and escalates sharply with repeated daily use, but the tolerance is lost as rapidly as it develops. Physical dependence of the alcohol/barbiturate type is not seen. Frequent users of high doses may experience depression, restlessness, insomnia, irritability, appetite disorders, and inability to concentrate. These effects are probably related to the stimulant properties of hallucinogens. Diazepam and routine psychological measures should provide effective clinical control of these symptoms.

HALLUCINOGEN INTOXICATION

DSM-4 Criteria for the Diagnosis of Hallucinogen Intoxication (292.89)

A. Recent use of a hallucinogen

B. Clinically significant maladaptive behavioral or psychological changes (e.g., marked anxiety or depression, ideas of reference, fear of losing one's mind, paranoid ideation, impaired judgment, or impaired social or occupational functioning) that developed during, or shortly after, hallucinogen use

C. Perceptual changes occurring in a state of full wakefulness and alertness (e.g., subjective intensification of perceptions, depersonalization, derealization, illusions, hallucinations, synesthesias) that developed during, or shortly after, hallucinogen use

D. Two (or more) of the following signs, developing during, or shortly after, hallucinogen use:
    1) pupillary dilation
    2) tachycardia
    3) sweating
    4) palpitations
    5) blurring of vision
    6) tremors
    7) incoordination

E. The symptoms are not due to a general medical condition and are not better accounted for by another mental disorder.

MANAGEMENT

In parallel with PCP, the diagnosis of hallucinogen intoxication should mandate a period of observation to determine the course. A brief period of observation will not indicate whether the intoxication episode will resolve without complications or develop into a drug induced delirium or psychosis. The management principles described in chapter 1 apply to hallucinogen abusers, as they are not unique psychopathologically. The clinician should also be aware that it is rare to encounter a patient who abuses hallucinogens and no other drugs. During some phases in a drug use career, hallucinogens may be the predominant or perhaps sole drugs of abuse, but commonly multiple substances, usually including marijuana, nicotine, and alcohol or other depressants, are involved. In my experience, patients with severe and persisting reactions to hallucinogens have had severe psychopathology antedating hallucinogen use. Psychiatric consultation is usually indicated. Ungerleider and DeAngelis advocate use of chlorpromazine if diazepam does not control symptoms.[14]

Seizures, hyperthermia, arrhythmias, and hypertension are possible expressions of toxicity from hallucinogens. These pharmacologic effects may be greatly aggravated by the reactions of the person to the hallucinatory experiences; terror or panic, for example, may be severe and persistent. Propanolol may be useful in management.

FLASHBACKS

Hallucinogen users may suffer from repeated, usually brief, experiences or fragments of experiences of a given toxic episode many days or months following the episode. Management is discussed in chapter 1.

COMMON HALLUCINOGENS

LSD.[15] LSD continues to be used by adolescents. Each generation explores this drug, then its members tend to stop using LSD as they mature. Use of the drug in the 1990s appears not to be related to the claims of transcendental experiences romanticized by Huxley, Burroughs, and Leary. Anyone working in an emergency room may see an occasional panic or psychosis from use of LSD, and it should be remembered that ordinary urine screens do not detect it. If LSD use is suspected, the laboratory should be called to see if a rapid diagnostic procedure is available for detection of LSD.

LSD—lysergic acid diethylamide—is derived from ergot, a fungus that grows on rye and other grains. LSD comes in a capsule, tablet, or liquid form. It may be absorbed on sugar cubes, in gelatin, or on blotter paper. The usual route of administration is oral, but it may be sniffed or injected. In nontolerant users, doses of 20 micrograms or more (1,000 micrograms equals 1 milligram) are effective. Stimulant or adrenergic effects usually occur immediately following ingestion. Perceptual changes begin to occur some 30 minutes to 2 hours following ingestion. This sequence is occasionally useful in diagnosis, as naturally occurring psychoses have no such sequence. The duration of effects is between 6 to 18 hours, depending on dose. As noted above, LSD effects are more likely to be bad when there are coexisting mental disorders or the person taking the drug is under severe stress. As reviewed by Ungerleider and Pechnick, there is a long series of studies indicating that LSD acts through the serotonergic system in the brain.[16]

Psilocybin. Psilocybin, a tryptamine derivative, is derived from the *Psilocybe mexicana* mushroom. It is usually sold as intact mushrooms or as a preparation of mushrooms. In chemically pure form, it may be sold as a capsule. The psychoactive dose is 4 to 10 mg. Effects on mood and cognition usually occur 30 minutes after oral administration. Perceptual changes, frequently profound, develop later. Many studies indicate that much of what is sold as psilocybin is PCP or LSD. The duration of action is approximately 2 to 6 hours.

DMT. DMT, dimethyltryptamine, is synthetic and resembles psilocybin. DMT has hallucinogenic and stimulant effects that last for 20 to 30 minutes. Because of its short duration of action, in street parlance it is sometimes called the "businessman's lunch." Parsley or some other herb is usually soaked in DMT and then smoked. A psychoactive dose is in the range of 20 to 40 mg.

Morning glory seeds. The predominant psychoactive chemical in morning glory seeds is lysergic acid-amide, which is chemically related to LSD but not as potent. Seeds are chewed or perhaps ground and then ingested. The effective dose, like LSD, is in the microgram range. Morning glory seeds can be sold legally. They are sometimes saturated with insecticides, and toxic effects can occur if enough seeds are eaten. Seeds eaten whole probably pass through the gastrointestinal tract and have no psychoactive effects.

Mescaline. Mescaline, a phenylethylamine, can be synthesized, or it may be used as a preparation, chopped or ground, of the peyote cactus button. The psychoactive dose is 300 to 500 mg. The duration of action is similar to that of LSD (12 to 18 hours). There are no unique features to the complex of stimulant, hallucinogenic, cognitive, and/or mood changes experienced, except that users become nauseated at higher rates than with other hallucinogens.

MDA. MDA, methylenedioxyamphetamine, is not currently in frequent use. It has psychoactive effects in doses of 10 mg or more. Effects begin about 30 minutes following oral ingestion and last for 8 to 12 hours. In high doses, adrenergic crises or exhaustion may occur. Hallucinations are not prominent with this drug. It has probably lost popularity because of its long duration of action with the attendant draining of the user's energies to maintain integration. (The presence of a methoxy group on an amphetamine is associated with a long duration of action.)

PMA. PMA, paramethoxyamphetamine, is usually taken orally and has more stimulant and hallucinogenic properties than MDA. Adrenergic crises may be severe. Like MDA, PMA is not used much at this time.

STP (DOM). STP or DOM (4-methyl-2,5, dimethoxyamphetamine) is usually taken orally. Stimulant effects are prominent and may last for 24 hours. It is another methoxylated amphetamine, and it too has lost favor with "street people."

Nutmeg and mace. The active ingredient of nutmeg and mace, myristicin, has stimulant and hallucinogenic properties. Myristicin is an amphetamine possibly related to trimethoxyamphetamine. Prisoners sometimes use nutmeg when they cannot obtain other intoxicants. Middle-class and street use of nutmeg is rare, probably because nausea and dysphoria are prominent if the dose is psychoactive.

COMMENTS

Therapeutic use of hallucinogens has been explored rather extensively, but to date therapeutic hallucinogen use has not won wide acceptance in the medical or psychiatric community. This is so probably for the same reasons that these drugs are used for relatively limited periods by abusers. The drugs appear to be too powerful, and the intensity and duration of their effects threaten and/or exhaust takers. The drugs also have the potential for disturbing side effects, such as panic or anxiety.

Hallucinogens greatly aggravate schizophrenia and appear to be absolutely contraindicated in schizophrenic patients. As noted in chapter 1, the administration of hallucinogens to persons who are unaware that they are being given such drugs can be devastating. Hallucinogen use is probably also absolutely contraindicated in persons with bipolar affective disorder. Lake and colleagues report a case of mania in association with LSD use that finally resolved with lithium therapy.[17]

The question of chromosomal damage from hallucinogens was much debated during the 1960s. The evidence is conflicting, and there is the possibility that it may take more than one generation before pathologic effects express themselves. Use of hallucinogens by females of child-bearing age is contraindicated.

STEROIDS

The origins of anabolic steroids can be traced back to World War II, when German soldiers were given these drugs in the belief that they would increase muscle strength and aggression. After the war, Soviet athletes, particularly weight lifters, began using steroids to increase muscle strength. At the 1956 Olympic Games, a team physician of the American national team learned of the use of testosterone by Russian weight lifters to enhance their athletic performance. He subsequently introduced the use of these anabolic steroids to American athletes.

Originally, anabolic steroid use in the United States was confined to world-class athletes. With time, however, this practice has spread to other levels of athletic competition, including professional, college, and high school sports programs. Anabolic steroid use has also spread to gyms and health spas, where individuals who are not necessarily competing in athletic events are attempting to enhance their physical appearance.

The use of steroids results in a host of side effects and adverse reactions. These effects can be both physical and psychological. Paranoid violent behavior can result from abuse of steroids.

The harmful physical side effects have been well documented. In males, these include male-pattern baldness, acne, decreased sperm production, atrophy of the testes, and enlargement of breast tissue. In females, they include virilizing side effects such as deepening of the voice, baldness, increased facial and body-hair growth, and hypertrophy of the clitoris.

Other less common effects that have been observed in steroid users include nausea, vomiting, diarrhea, abnormal liver function, healing problems, and a lowering of the HDL cholesterol level, which can increase the chances of developing coronary artery disease.

Psychological alterations can also occur in individuals who misuse steroids. A number of recent scientific studies suggests that steroids shift a person's psychological profile toward a more hostile, aggressive, and assertive nature. Additional psychological alterations that have been reported include euphoria, increases or decreases in libido, and, rarely, psychotic episodes. Steroids produce euphoric effects, and cases meeting DSM criteria for dependence have been reported. One case of HIV has been traced to needle sharing of steroids.

It has been estimated that illegal sale, or black-market activity, is responsible for an estimated 80 percent of the anabolic steroid use in the United States. The black market finds its sources through illegally diverted pharmaceutical products, clandestine manufacturing laboratories that produce counterfeit products, and smuggled steroids from other countries. These black-market anabolic steroids are then sold in mail-order magazines and at gyms and health clubs where weight lifters may gather.

"ICE"

"Ice," or "crystal meth," is a smokable form of methamphetamine, which in the past has been taken in pill form, injected into a vein, or inhaled. This means that ice is in some ways comparable to freebase cocaine or crack, in that it is a smokable form of a drug traditionally used in other ways. The chemical reactions to make ice, however, are different from those of freebasing. One similarity of ice to freebase is that ice is a more dangerous, more addicting form of a known drug. In a smokable form, the drug is delivered to the brain and other organs faster and in higher concentrations. This accentuates the toxic effects of the drug and accelerates the addiction process.

The usual pharmacological effects of the central nervous system stimulant methamphetamine include increased heart rate, headache, increased and irregular breathing, dry mouth, blurred vision, appetite suppression, and diarrhea. The central nervous system effects include overstimulation, restlessness, insomnia, euphoria, mild confusion, tremor, and subjective effects. The toxic effects of high doses may produce anginal pain and cardiovascular collapse, excess sweating and high fever (hyperthermia), convulsions, coma, cerebral hemorrhage, and death.

Use of ice is frequently in the form of a binge or "run," during which individuals use it for days without sleeping, eating, working, or going to school until they have exhausted their supply of ice and money. Then, exhausted, they may sleep for 24 to 48 hours, only to awake and prepare to do it again. As a result, individuals using ice have great difficulty maintaining job and school schedules.

The emotional and interpersonal effects of ice addiction are pervasive and devastating to users and their families. Regular users usually experience labile and chaotic emotional states with frequent episodes of agitation, anger, or aggression, followed by or associated with severe depression. Also, there is a high incidence of anxiety and panic attacks or of individuals becoming suspicious, paranoid, and frankly psychotic with delusions and hallucinations.

This drug (as others) is extremely harmful to adolescents, who are especially vulnerable to the appeal of its mood elevation and pseudostrength effects. Teenagers, who may normally at times feel insecure and helpless (or, conversely, daring and omnipotent), find that drugs and alcohol, especially ice, can cover the bad feelings and exaggerate the good. In addition, the rebelliousness and anger that adolescents frequently experience are easily distorted and more difficult to control when normal brain functioning and development is interfered with by this powerful psychotropic drug. The ability to experience and cope with the normal moods and ups and downs of life is markedly impaired by ice.

INHALANTS

Inhalants are chemicals that are volatile at ordinary temperatures and, when inhaled, have effects on mood, thinking, and feeling.[18] Some common members of the class of inhalants are toluene (airplane glue), gasoline, kerosene, carbon tetrachloride, amyl nitrite, and anesthetics such as halothane and nitrous oxide. Users soak rags in volatile substances and inhale, or "huff," the vapors, or they may use paper or plastic bags to create a closed space with a high concentration of the inhalant. "Monitoring the Future" found the lifetime use of inhalants increasing from 17.6 to 21.2 percent for eighth graders between 1991 and 1996, and a decrease from 17.6 to 16.6 percent for high school seniors in this same period.[19] These findings underscore the widespread use among young people in the United States and should alert the clinician to suspect inhalant abuse in neurologic, psychiatric, and general medical disorders in young people. Many areas of this country are relatively free of use of inhalants, while others have serious epidemics from time to time.

Inhalant abuse starts, usually, at age 12; but few of those using inhalants at age 12 are still using them at age 22. A few experimenters, usually characterized by severe psychopathology and social problems, develop long-term patterns of inhalant abuse, but most young inhalant users turn to alcohol and cannabis after using inhalants sporadically for a few weeks or months. In recent years, females appear to be involved with inhalants more than they have been in the past.

Inhalants produce varied effects, ranging from an intoxication similar to that produced by alcohol to a state of delirium with hallucinations, illusions, and delusions similar to those induced by hallucinogens. Inhalants produce intoxication rapidly, and peak intoxication from a dose usually subsides within minutes, although some users report states of intoxication that last from 30 minutes to one hour. Doses tend to be repeated in an effort to maintain a state of euphoria. Inhalants are ubiquitous in homes and stores and offer readily available intoxicants to young people who do not have funds for or perhaps access to even such common intoxicants as alcohol.

Most inhalants are also inexpensive and can be concealed easily—a tube of airplane glue, for example. The obvious possibility of toxicity, which deters most young people from using inhalants, appears to offer an element of risk that adds to the desirability of inhalants for those who experiment. The willingness to assume serious risks, often explicitly verbalized ("I'm going to fry my brain"), may be an important psychological element binding groups of inhalant users together. Solitary use of inhalants occurs, but, in general, experimentation and repeated intoxication with inhalants tends to be a group phenomenon.

Amyl and butyl nitrite, or "poppers," cause vasodilation of coronary and cerebral arteries with the induction of some hypotension. On the psychological level, users feel a "rush" and, in some instances, a loss of time sense. Amyl and butyl nitrite are used to prolong orgasm, particularly in the homosexual community. Use of nitrites in compulsive fashion is rare. Amyl and butyl nitrite are also used to counteract the "downer" effects of combinations of alcohol, marijuana, and/or other depressants. Nitrous oxide and other volatile anesthetics such as halothane are also used as intoxicants, frequently by medical personnel.

DIAGNOSIS

The DSM-4 criteria for inhalant intoxication are as follows:

DSM-4 Diagnostic Criteria for Inhalant Intoxication (292.89)

A. Recent intentional use or short-term, high-dose exposure to volatile inhalants (excluding anesthetic gases and short-acting vasodilators)

B. Clinically significant maladaptive behavioral or psychological changes (e.g., belligerence, assaultiveness, apathy, impaired judgment, impaired social or occupational functioning) that developed during, or shortly after, use of or exposure to volatile inhalants

C. Two (or more) of the following signs, developing during, or shortly after, inhalant use or exposure:
   1) dizziness
   2) nystagmus
   3) incoordination
   4) slurred speech
   5) unsteady gait
   6) lethargy
   7) depressed reflexes
   8) psychomotor retardation
   9) tremor
   10) generalized muscle weakness
   11) blurred vision or diplopia
   12) stupor or coma
   13) euphoria

   The symptoms are not due to a general medical condition and are not better accounted for by another mental disorder.

Some young people experiment with inhalants as an expression of their need to belong to a peer group. It may be a borderline call to decide if a diagnosis of abuse is justified in such a young person, especially if subsequent experience indicates that he or she has followed the usual pattern and has stopped drug use of any kind or, perhaps, is experimenting with alcohol or other drugs but does not meet the criteria for a diagnosis. The adolescent experimenter with any drugs should be educated about drugs in an effort to prevent problems. Inhalant abusers tend to use multiple substances, which frequently include nicotine, alcohol, and marijuana.

MANAGEMENT

Inhalant abusers do not come to medical attention frequently, but when they do, they are likely to have severe social, medical, and/or psychological pathology. Careful neurological and laboratory studies should be carried out because of the biological toxicity of many inhalants and the additives with which they are combined. The general management principles described in chapter 1 apply to these disorders. Family pathology may be severe. Chronic inhalant abusers have high rates of alcoholism in their families. Use of inhalants for more than a few weeks or months is highly likely to mean there is severe psychopathology, severe family pathology, and medical and neuropsychiatric consequences, as reviewed below.

Community efforts may be required if there are substantial numbers of abusers involved. Identifying the source of the supply may be important. In one such effort, airplane glue was removed from the shelves of a store supplying young adolescents. This led to the end of an epidemic of glue sniffing. Action by the families involved may also be important. Psychiatric consultation should be considered routinely to detect treatable psychiatric conditions such as depression. Removal from peer influences may also be required. A change of school, neighborhood, or even city may have to be entertained if routine treatment efforts are not successful.

MEDICAL PROBLEMS ASSOCIATED WITH INHALANTS

The major medical consequences of inhalant abuse are: respiratory depression and cardiac conduction abnormalities as acute consequences, and longer-term toxic effects on cells of the bone marrow, liver, and kidney; peripheral nerve damage; a variety of drug induced disorders, including dementia (in 20-year-old long-term users); and an increased risk of cancer.[20]

Death. Death occurs in inhalant abusers; a recent study found one inhalant-related death for every 33 cocaine related.[21] When death occurs, it appears to be related to cardiac arrythmias and respiratory depression. Because abuse of absolutely pure chemical substances is rare, the attribution of causality to one compound in a mixture is difficult. Many inhalants sensitize the myocardium to epinephrine, which can lead to arrhythmias, and this mechanism is probably involved in most inhalant deaths. Death is much more likely if a user places his or her head in a bag and then inhales volatiles. The concentration of inhalants achieved by this method can climb rapidly and be fatal.

Toxic effects on neurons are the most frequent medical complications of chronic exposure to inhalants. Toluene, N-hexane, gasoline and the gasoline additives triorthocresyl phosphate and lead, benzenes, aerosols, paint thinners, and so forth all appear to be implicated. Clinically, one encounters such manifestations as peripheral neuropathy, muscle weakness and/or atrophy, paresthesias, areflexia, cerebellar signs, and positive Babinski signs. N-hexane and aliphatic hydrocarbons (used in many glues) appear to be particularly toxic.

Bone marrow. Benzene is frequently implicated in bone-marrow toxicity. Comstock and Comstock also cite a number of cases of leukemia associated with exposure to products containing benzene.[22]

Renal. Renal failure secondary to inhalation of carbon tetrachloride has been known for a long time. Many other inhalants are toxic for renal cells, hematuria and proteinuria being early manifestations.

Liver. Damage to the liver appears to occur after exposure to chlorinated hydrocarbons and gasoline.

Methemoglobinemia. Methemoglobinemia occurs with use of nitrites; if there are clinical symptoms such as weakness, it should be tested for.

Immunosuppressant effects of nitrites. As reviewed by Lange and Fralich, a number of recent studies indicate that nitrite inhalation adversely affects a number of cells important in immune response and may facilitate viral replication.[23]

Drug induced delirium and dementia. Those few people who use inhalants heavily over a decade, after first use at age 12, can have a severe intractable dementia by the age of 21. These users center their lives on acquiring and using inhalants, and they tend to have severe medical as well as psychiatric pathology. Any young person with an inhalant induced delirium should be the focus of vigorous prevention efforts, which should involve what is usually a grossly dysfunctional family.

COMMENTS

This chapter is intended as an introduction to clinical problems related to inhalant abuse; it is not a thorough review of the pharmacology and toxicology of these substances. For such a review, see the cited works by Zukin and Zukin,[2] Sharp and Rosenberg,[18] and Karch.[20] From a clinical point of view, chronic use appears to be associated with a substantial danger of toxicity to the brain and other organs in the body. The workup of any abuser of volatiles should be meticulous in searching for such toxic effects, particularly since they are probably reversible if properly treated, and cessation of volatile abuse can be achieved. Many inhalants do not appear on routine toxicology screens, so the laboratory must be asked if it can test for the suspected drug. If toluene use is suspected, the laboratory should be asked to test for hippuric acid, as it is a relatively stable breakdown product of toluene.

REFERENCES

1. Johnstone M, Evans V, Baigel S. Sernyl, (CL-395) in clinical anesthesia. *Br J Anesth* 31:433–439, 1958.
2. Zukin SR, Zukin RS. Phencyclidine, in Lowinson JH, Ruiz P, Millman RB, et al (eds), *Substance Abuse: A Comprehensive Textbook.* Baltimore, MD, Williams & Wilkins, 1992.
3. Luisada PV, The Phencyclidine Psychosis: Phenomenology and Treatment in PCP-Phencyclidine Abuse: An Appraisal, National Institute on Drug Abuse Research Monograph Series 21, Rockville, MD, 1978.

4. Soine WH. Phencyclidine contaminant generates cyanide (letter). *N Engl J Med* 301:438, 1979.
5. Schuckit MA. *Drug and Alcohol Abuse*, ed 4. New York, Plenum, 1995, pp 206–208.
6. Fauman MA, Fauman BJ. Chronic phencyclidine (PCP) abuse: A psychiatric perspective. *J Psychedelic Drugs* 12:307, 1980.
7. Russ C, Wong D. Diagnosis and treatment of the phencyclidine psychosis: Clinical considerations. *J Psychedelic Drugs* 11:277, 1979.
8. Done AK. The toxic emergency: Phencyclidine (PCP). *Emerg Med* 12:179, 1978.
9. Dhagestani AN, Schnoll SH. Phencyclidine, in Galanter M, Kleber HD (eds), *Textbook of Substance Abuse Treatment.* Washington, DC, American Psychiatric Association Press, 1994.
10. Grover D, Yeragani VK, Keshavan MS. Improvement in phencyclidine-associated psychosis with ECT. *J Clin Psychiatry* 47:477–488, 1986.
11. Bowers MD Jr. Acute psychosis induced by psychotomimetic drug abuse. *Arch Gen Psychiatry* 27:437, 1972.
12. Report on Monitoring the Future. The University of Michigan News and Information Services, 15 December 1995, pp 2–3.
13. McGlothlin WH, Arnold DO. LSD revisited. *Arch Gen Psychiatry* 24:35, 1971.
14. Ungerleider JT, DeAngelis GG. Hallucinogens, in Lowinson, JH, Ruiz P (eds), *Substance Abuse: Clinical Problems and Perspectives.* Baltimore, MD, Williams & Wilkins, 1982.
15. Henderson L, Glass WJ. *LSD: Still With Us After All These Years.* New York, Lexington Books, 1994.
16. Ungerleider JT, Pechnik R. Hallucinogens, in Lowinson JH, Ruiz P, Millman RB, et al (eds), *Substance Abuse: A Comprehensive Textbook.* Baltimore, MD, Williams & Wilkins, 1992.
17. Lake CR, Stirba AL, Kenneman RE, et al. Mania associated with LSD ingestion. *Am J Psychiatry* 138:1508, 1981.
18. Sharp CW, Rosenberg NL. Volatile substances, in Lowinson JH, Ruiz P, Millman RB, et al (eds), *Substance Abuse: A Comprehensive Textbook.* Baltimore, Williams & Wilkins, 1992.
19. Report on Monitoring the Future. The University of Michigan News and Information Services, 15 December 1995, table 1.
20. Karch SB. *The Pathology of Drug Abuse*, ed 2. Boca Raton, FL, CRC Press, 1996.
21. Substance Abuse and Mental Health Administration, Annual Medical Examiner Data. Data from the Drug Abuse Warning Network. Department of Health and Human Services. Rockville, MD, 1995.
22. Comstock EG, Comstock BS. Medical evaluations of inhalant abusers, in Sharp CW, Brehm ML (eds), *Review of Inhalants: Euphoria to Dysfunction.* National Institute on Drug Abuse Research Monograph Series 15. Rockville, MD, 1977.
23. Lange WR, Fralich J. Nitrite inhalants: Promising and discouraging news (editorial). *Br J Addiction* 84:121–123, 1989.

12. Toxicology

The purpose of this chapter is to introduce drug treatment staff and administration to the benefits and limits of toxicology as it is used in treatment. Toxicology is also an integral element in measuring success of treatment and in epidemiology and prevention, but these areas are not within the clinical scope of this text.

VOCABULARY

The nonmedical reader of this chapter may need definitions of many of the terms used in toxicology. Some important definitions are given below; they may be repeated in the text to assist the learning process for readers who may not work regularly with chemical terms.

Chromatography. The word has two roots: *chrom,* or color, and *graphy,* or picture or writing. Loosely defined, a color picture. The word is now used to indicate any of a large number of methods of separating mixtures of molecules such as urine and blood to identify the drug components. Sometimes the process produces different colors that identify components, but it may not use color at all; for example, fragment patterns of a molecule broken up by an electron beam may define an endpoint in a chromatographic analysis.

Enzyme. A molecule that breaks down other molecules. Enzymes usually recognize and attack only certain classes of molecules, such as fats or sugars, but not other classes of molecules.

Fluorescent. Emitting light.

Gram, nanogram. These are metric weight measures. There are 454 grams in a pound. A nanogram, ng, is 1/1,000,000,000 of a gram—a very small amount indeed, one over one followed by nine zeros. A milligram is 1/1000 of a gram; a microgram is 1/1,000,000, or one millionth, of a gram; and a picogram is 1/1,000,000,000,000, or one trillionth, of a gram.

Mass spectroscopy (MS). The technique of breaking down a molecule by hitting the molecule with an electron beam. Molecules tend to break into fragments determined by their structure, and the fragmentation pattern is similar to a fingerprint in its specificity.

Metabolite. After molecules of a given drug are introduced into the body by injection, ingestion, or smoking, they are broken down by the body, usually in the liver. The breakdown products are called metabolites. Heroin is diacetyl morphine, and morphine is one of its metabolites. A single drug molecule may have many metabolites.

Molecule. The basic unit of a drug or any other substance. It has a unique structure and is made up of elements such as carbon, hydrogen, oxygen, and sulfur. Sometimes it may carry an electric charge, which may change how it interacts with other molecules.

Radioactive. Emitting electromagnetic waves, somewhat like radio waves.

Sensitivity. The ability of a test to detect different levels of concentrations of molecules. Highly sensitive tests can detect very low levels of drug molecules. Thin-layer chromatography is not as sensitive as radioimmunoassay for most drugs.

Specific gravity of urine. A medical test to determine if there are normal amounts of certain breakdown products of body metabolism in urine. When a drug user tries to dilute a urine specimen to avoid detection, this can be apparent if the specific gravity test is outside normal limits.

Specificity. The precision of detection. A highly specific method detects only the molecules of a given drug. Mass spectroscopy, or MS, is highly specific.

ANALYTIC TOXICOLOGY

Analytic toxicology—the testing of breath, urine, and blood for molecules and/or metabolites of common intoxicants such as heroin, cocaine, alcohol, and marijuana—is an essential element of modern drug treatment.[1] The use of urine screens, for clinical purposes, dates to the middle 1960's, when Drs. Vincent Dole and Marie Nyswander established methadone maintenance as an effective treatment for heroin addiction. On a clinical level, addicts in treatment knew that program counselors would be aware of any use of heroin, and that use of heroin would lead to consequences such as having to come to the clinic more often, family awareness, more frequent counseling and urine screens, reports to parole or probation officers, and the like. On the other hand, absence of heroin metabolites in urine screens would lead to increased privileges in treatment, perhaps freedom from demands of parole or probation, family affirmation, improved self-esteem, and other positive consequences. Linking the behavior of drug use firmly with a variety of positive and negative consequences through urine screens was of unquestioned value to many addicts who wanted to escape from the compulsion to use heroin. In the beginning, urine screens were limited to opiates, but over the years the technology expanded its scope and now includes many common intoxicants.

The technology of drug detection in body fluids soon came to be used diagnostically. In admission workups, a clinician could confirm the client's history and perhaps learn about drug use of which the client had no memory (because of intoxication) or awareness (because the drug was not what the client believed it to be). Diagnostic screens are particularly valuable in the emergency room, where they can rule out or rule in a suspected cause of a drug toxic state.

Quite apart from its clinical usefulness, toxicological screening came to be central to the evaluation of the effectiveness of methadone maintenance and other treatment methods. Combined with the results of research instruments, family reports, and clinical observations, a series of negative random urine screens could provide an objective element of proof that recovery had occurred. The scientific and legal communities soon recognized the value of drug screening in treatment and in demonstrating the effectiveness of treatment programs.

Recognition of the value of urine screens in the prevention of drug abuse dates from the use of urinalysis in Vietnam by Dr. Jerome Jaffe, director of the Special Action Office for Drug Abuse Prevention in the Nixon White House. Dr. Jaffe used these screens to detect and treat U.S. soldiers in Vietnam who had become heroin dependent. He and others noted that the implementation of this diagnostic and treatment effort had a robust preventive effect. When soldiers knew that they might be tested, the numbers of positive screens fell substantially.

The significance of Dr. Jaffe's observation lay dormant until a decade later, when the Department of Defense (DOD) conducted a worldwide study of U.S. naval personnel and found that 48 percent admitted to having used marijuana within a 30-day period. After a series of studies of remedial actions, DOD concluded that random urine screens with disciplinary actions for positives were the most effective deterrent. After implementing a policy based on random urine screens over a 10-year period, the Navy reduced its positive screens for all illicit drugs, including marijuana, to under 2 percent.[2]

Analytic toxicology in the workplace is a natural outgrowth of the national experiences described above. It has long been appreciated that use of intoxicants by workers is associated with absenteeism, lost productivity, increased utilization of health benefits, and industrial accidents (sometimes fatal), compared with rates observed in workers who do not use intoxicants. Despite the fact that many major industrial concerns have made substantial attempts to reduce the negative effects of drug use in the workplace, a 1991 National Household Survey, carried out by the National Institute on Drug Abuse, found that approximately 10 percent of full-time employed persons were current users of illicit drugs.[3] A number of federal agencies, including the Department of Transportation, the Nuclear Regulatory Commission, and the Department of Energy, among others, have all played a role in the federal attempt to use toxicology as a tool to reduce or prevent drug related problems in a number of domains.

The use of toxicology in the legal arena is outside the scope of this chapter. When toxicology is used for legal purposes, there must be a chain of custody which assures that a given sample has a paper trail. For clinical purposes, a rigid chain of custody is not required.

TECHNIQUES USED TO DETECT DRUGS IN BODY FLUIDS

THIN LAYER CHROMATOGRAPHY

Thin-layer chromatography (TLC) is based on the observation, in the early models of this procedure, that different molecules traveled different distances when solutions of them were placed on wet absorbent paper. It was also observed that the distance traveled tended to be constant for a given molecule; thus molecules of morphine tended to migrate to the same spot on the absorbent paper. If a solution of a known substance such as morphine is placed on a strip of wet absorbent paper and a solution of a molecule to be tested for is placed on a parallel strip of wet absorbent paper, the migration pattern of the two drugs can be compared. If the molecule to be tested migrates the same distance as the morphine, there is some evidence that the drug being tested for may be morphine. The equivalence of the two substances can be further tested by applying various dyes and examining the similarities or differences in the colors produced. The foregoing is a simplified model to illustrate the basic principle involved. In practice, the technology of chromatography usually involves substances different from the paper used in the model described above and a variety of solvents, including electric currents and gases, to produce different migration patterns for different drugs. The basic principle remains the same: the behavior of the drug to be tested for is compared with the behavior of a known drug.

TLC is cheap and quick and detects a range of drugs such as morphine, cocaine, barbiturates, and amphetamines, but it tends to detect only high-dose use of these drugs and is not highly specific. For example, it may mistake dextromethorphan for morphine. Dextromethorphan is found in many cough syrups; it has a structure like morphine, but it does not have the same effects as morphine. TLC, as it is usually done in support of treatment services, is relatively insensitive to drugs such as marijuana and phencyclidine (PCP) and may not detect common hallucinogens such as LSD at all. For all these reasons, TLC is usually used as a screening test that, if positive, requires use of one of the confirmatory tests described below.

GAS CHROMATOGRAPHY AND HIGH PERFORMANCE LIQUID CHROMATOGRAPHY

Gas chromatography (GC)—sometimes called gas liquid chromatography (GLC)—and high-performance liquid chromatography (HPLC) are drug detecting techniques, based on the behavior of molecules migrating between gas and liquid phases or between two different liquids that compare the distribution patterns with those of known drugs. These tests are much more specific than thin-layer chromatography, but they take more time and are more expensive. They are used as confirmatory tests.

IMMUNOASSAY TECHNIQUES

Immunoassay techniques rely on the fact that drugs injected into experimental animals produce antibodies, molecules formed by the interaction of the injected molecule with the immune system of the animal. The antibodies combine with the injected molecule to prevent it from having any effect, thus serving the defensive function of the immune system. Once an antibody is known, it may be synthesized in the laboratory. Because the structure of an antibody is closely related to the structure of the molecule stimulating its formation, immunoassay tends to have higher precision than ordinary TLC.

For testing purposes, a solution of the drug to be tested for is combined with a solution of antibodies. The amount of the unknown drug that combines with the antibody can be measured, and inferences can be drawn by comparing this amount with the results of doing the same procedure with known drugs such as cocaine or heroin. If the measurement depends on radioactive labeling of the antibody, the procedure is called radioimmunoassay (RIA); if the measurement depends on the labeling of the antibody with an enzyme, the procedure is called enzyme immunoassay (EIA). A common procedure today in many clinics is the enzyme multiplied immunoassay test (EMIT). Substances that give off light are said to be fluorescent; if they are used to label the drugs involved, the procedure is called fluorescent polarization immunoassay (FPIA).

Immunoassays are reasonably specific but, like TLC, require confirmatory tests because they can make mistakes in identification. Increasingly, they are being used as screening tests in place of TLC. With TLC, however, a number of drugs can be tested for simultaneously, whereas with immunoassays, the tests have to be run one drug at a time.

MASS SPECTROSCOPY

Mass spectroscopy (MS) examines the electronic "fingerprint" of a molecule by splitting the molecule apart with an electron beam. Since molecules have quite specific fragmentation patterns, this technique is highly specific and is regarded as the gold standard of testing techniques. The usual sequence in most current laboratories is to use TLC, EMIT, or RIA for screening, and then gas chromatography/mass spectroscopy in combination for confirmation.

BREATH TESTING FOR ALCOHOL

The amount of alcohol in breath is related to the amount of alcohol in blood; with higher alcohol concentrations in blood, there are correspondingly higher concentrations in breath. Testing the amount of alcohol in blood is more accurate than breath testing, but breath is good enough for clinical purposes. If a subject has taken a drink of alcohol or used a mouthwash within 15 minutes of taking a breath test, the results would not be valid, because most mouthwashes and alcoholic beverages have high concentrations of alcohol and will cause a false high reading. Breathalyzers are small and can be used in a clinic to confirm clinical suspicion that a client has been drinking. Alcohol is metabolized a little less than one drink per hour depending on a number of factors, as reviewed in the chapter on alcohol.

FACTORS INFLUENCING TOXICOLOGY TEST RESULTS

Dose of drug used. As the amount of drug used per unit of time increases, the likelihood of detection increases, because there are more molecules of the drug in the body fluid tested. The concentrations in the body are higher and remain in the body for a longer time. As noted above, TLC misses low-dose use of many of the drugs that it correctly identifies. On a clinical level, use of TLC as a screening method misses some drug use, because negative screens are not tested further. Immunoassays are more sensitive, so the physician or counselor who suspects a client is using drugs even though the client has negative TLC screens could ask for RIA or some other immunoassay test for screening purposes. Laboratories usually do not report actual levels, only whether or not they exceed the cut-off levels. Asking the lab for exact levels may confirm the clinical hunch that the patient is using.

Differences in structure of drugs. Drugs with very similar structures can have very different effects. A striking example is the drug naloxone, which is used to treat heroin overdose. Naloxone is an opiatelike drug in structure, but it does not have the sedative and intoxicating effects of heroin. A normal person taking naloxone would experience no effects, but if heroin is in the receptor sites in the brain, naloxone reverses heroin's effects and produces heroin withdrawal. There are a great many other drugs very much like one another in structure but with dramatically different effects. The relevance is that there is always some possibility with just one test and no other evidence at hand that a given positive test may have made an error, because a drug very similar in structure but with vastly different effects was present.

Age of the sample. The longer the time elapsing between use of a drug and the taking of a sample of body fluid for testing, the less likely the test will be positive. Drugs are metabolized at very different rates, but there is a general metabolism of drugs by the body as time passes. With the passage of time, drugs, in many samples, break down. This is important for legal considerations but not for clinical purposes, as testing and retesting for clinical purposes takes place in a relatively short time span.

Individual differences in metabolism. Individuals differ from one another in the rate at which their bodies break down drugs. An occasional client in a methadone program may take a dose of methadone of as much as 30 to 40 mg, observed by staff, and 24 hours later have no detectable level of methadone in blood or urine. This is not the case with most people in methadone programs, but it can and does happen. Individuals may not only differ from one another but, may differ at different times; aging, stress from family discord, severe weather changes, use of alcohol, and a host of other factors can influence how a person metabolizes a drug. Usually, stress increases the rate at which drugs are metabolized.

Drug interactions. Methadone maintained patients who are HIV-positive may be put on zidovudine. In some clients, zidovudine may speed the metabolism of the methadone, and they may need a substantial increase in dose to be comfortable. These interactions do not always occur; many patients take zidovudine and methadone with no interaction. Drugs taken for epilepsy, depression, high blood pressure, and other conditions sometimes may and sometimes may not interact with methadone.

LABORATORY CERTIFICATION AND "CUT-OFF LEVELS"

Results of drug and alcohol testing can have serious consequences in the clinical domain, as they may change treatment plans and indicate that more or less control is necessary for a given client. In the workplace and in the legal sphere, drug testing results can have similarly serious consequences. To ensure accuracy in drug and alcohol testing, the federal government charged the National Institute on Drug Abuse (NIDA) with the task of creating a national system of quality control. NIDA certifies laboratories by sending them samples of unknown drugs and examines the ability of the laboratory to detect these unknowns. When the numbers of molecules are in the low range in a test specimen, there is less accuracy. NIDA has therefore established what are called "cut-off levels." A cut-off level establishes that there is enough of a drug detected to ensure scientific accuracy. The procedures described above have different cut-off levels. Morphine, for example, has a cut-off level of 300 nanograms by GC and a cut-off level of 100 nanograms if MS is employed. Cut-off levels may change from time to time as the technology of testing becomes more sensitive and/or more specific.

NIDA Cut-off Levels and Duration of Detection for Common Intoxicants

	NIDA Cut-off Level (Nanograms)		Hours/Days After Last Use
	GC	MS	
Amphetamines	300	100	24–48 hrs.
Barbiturates	300	100	3–14 days depending on type: long/short acting
Benzodiazepines	300	100	2–9 days depending on type: long/short acting
Benzoylecognine*	300	50	2–4 days depending on dose
Opiates	300	100	1–3 days depending on dose and type
Phencyclidine (PCP)	75	10	2–8 days
Cannabinoids	20–100	10	2–42 days

* Cocaine is measured by its major metabolite Benzoylecognine

FALSE–POSITIVES, FALSE–NEGATIVES, POSITIVES FROM ACCEPTABLE SOURCES

Opiates. Poppy seeds, used in common foods such as bagels, contain enough morphine to produce urine levels of morphine well above the cut-off points cited above. In one study reported in a NIDA monograph, the ingestion of three poppy-seed bagels produced morphine levels in urine above 2500 ng/ml.[4] Such levels in urine can be achieved without being accompanied by blood levels sufficient to produce sedation, intoxication, or any behavioral effect. Urine concentrates drugs; although concentrations of drugs in urine may be high, they are often not high enough in blood to influence behavior.

If a client claims ingestion of poppy seeds as a cause of a positive urine for morphine, there is no way to disprove this. This may be a positive from an acceptable source. If there is a metabolite of heroin in the urine (6-monoacetyl morphine), this constitutes proof of heroin use, as there is no acetylated morphine in poppy seeds. Heroin is diacetyl morphine, and it does not occur naturally. Patients should be told not to consume poppy seeds so that these questions do not arise.

A client taking prescribed codeine, possibly after dental procedures, may have levels of morphine in urine above cut-off levels because one of the metabolites of codeine is morphine. If heroin use is suspected in such a case, there is no way to settle the matter on the basis of urine results unless a heroin metabolite is detected. Detection of heroin metabolites is not likely, because heroin is rapidly metabolized to morphine; one would have to take a urine sample very close to the time of heroin use to detect these metabolites.

As noted above, TLC is not very sensitive and misses low levels of street use of many common intoxicants. The staff of a treatment program must realize that a negative urine screen means there has been no high dose or very recent use of street drugs. The lack of sensitivity of TLC leads to what are called false-negatives. Immunoassays are more sensitive than TLC, but they have the problem of false-positives. GC/MS procedures are not likely to produce either false-positives or false-negatives.

Cocaine. Cocaine, like heroin, is metabolized rapidly. Urine screens are obtained usually at a time far enough removed from the time of use so that cocaine is not detected. The major metabolite of cocaine is benzoylecognine, and this metabolite may be detected one to two days after use, depending on dose. A common claim in drug treatment is that novocaine used in dentistry has produced a urine positive for benzoylecognine. If only TLC or EIA has been employed, this claim cannot be discounted, but if GC/MS confirmation has been carried out, the claim is certainly false.

Amphetamines. TLC and EIA can misidentify as amphetamine a wide range of drugs used in many over-the-counter medications. These drugs often have structures similar to amphetamine, and this is the basis of the false-positives. A common claim from clients testing positive for amphetamines is that they are taking cold or headache medications that contain amphetamine-like drugs. Here again, the confirmatory tests discriminate precisely. Clients can be counseled by medical staff about alternatives to the over-the-counter drugs they are taking.

Ambient air. Studies conducted by NIDA indicate that a person not smoking marijuana but who is near someone who is can inhale enough marijuana to have urinary levels at or near the cut-off levels. The drug culture has long recognized this as a "contact high." Under most conditions of use—such as in a large room or outdoors—it is not likely that ambient air can account for positives above current cut-off levels. The NIDA studies indicate that to reach current cut-off levels, a person must be in a small, confined space and be exposed to very high concentrations of smoke for a long period of time.[5] If these questions come up clinically, one can ask the laboratory for quantitative levels. If they are much higher than the cut-off levels, the presumption is that they must come from direct smoking of marijuana.

On a clinical level, patients should be counseled to leave situations in which marijuana is being used: "If they light up, you light out."

Phencyclidine (PCP) can also be inhaled from ambient air in sufficient dose to be detectable in urine. In fact, some infants have had near-lethal induction of coma from use by their parents. Crack cocaine can also be inhaled from the air in sufficient dose to cause problems for children. It is not possible to conduct experiments with crack cocaine, so we do not have the same kinds of data that we have for marijuana and ambient air in adults. It is conceivable that adults could get enough cocaine from ambient air to be positive. Clients in treatment should, of course, avoid any scene where crack cocaine, phencyclidine, or marijuana is being used.

MONITORING OF SAMPLE ACQUISITION

Because clients trying to avoid detection of drug use may substitute clean urine for their own, many treatment programs have direct visual confirmation that a given urine specimen is, in fact, from the client. A variant of this practice is to monitor the temperature of the urine. If the circumstances of delivery of a sample are controlled (e.g., no access to warm water), the sample should be between 90 and 98 degrees F. If it is not, another sample is taken. Some clients may drink large volumes of fluid to dilute the urine and perhaps get under the cut-off level. The specific gravity of the urine can be tested and a given sample invalidated if the specific gravity is outside normal limits. Most programs require the person to be tested to put aside all bags and excess clothing and to deliver a specimen in a bathroom without warm water and with blue dyes in toilet water to avoid its use in the dilution of samples.

It is important to communicate with the laboratory if clinical findings suggest that an exotic or a "designer drug" may be involved in a given case. Fentanyl and related compounds and drugs such as MDA or MDMA are not detected even in high concentrations. The laboratory must be alerted to these possibilities, and it can then adjust its techniques.

HAIR AS A SPECIMEN FOR DETECTING DRUGS

We do not have the space to discuss in any detail detection of drugs in anything other than routine urine samples, but the reader should be aware that hair can be used to detect drugs. Although this method is not yet accepted by the clinical/scientific community, hair analysis is accepted by the courts.[6] The human hair follicle extracts molecules of common intoxicants and incorporates them into the keratin of hair, which is a very stable specimen. The poet Shelley had miliary tuberculosis with a great deal of pain and toward the end of his life took a great deal of laudanum (a mixture of alcohol and morphine). When his body was exhumed over 180 years later, his hair was positive for morphine. It takes three days for the keratin containing the drug molecules to grow above the scalp level, so hair samples are not useful in detecting drug use in this period. Because hair grows about one-half inch a month, a three-inch segment of hair constitutes a record of the past six months of drug use.

The amount of drug incorporated into keratin is dependent on its concentration in the bloodstream. This permits judgments about when in the recent months there was more or less drug use. Hair samples are thus both qualitative and quantitative. Hair analysis could come into use in all clinics, if for no other reason than to assist managed care companies in measuring effectiveness of treatment. The scientific community is hesitant about hair, because the variability of levels of incorporation between the sexes and between racial groups has not been worked out. There is some evidence that variations in hair melanin may lead to variations in the amount of drug incorporated. In addition, there is concern that ambient contamination could lead to positive results in an innocent person, with the potential for very severe consequences. There is also concern that some hair-dressing procedures obscure drug testing results. In my opinion, these issues will be worked out and we will have another tool, and a quite valuable one, in working with drug dependent populations.

REFERENCES

1. Verebey K. Diagnostic laboratory: Screening for drug abuse, in Lowinson JH, Ruiz P, Millman RB, et al (eds), *Substance Abuse: A Comprehensive Textbook*. Baltimore, MD, Williams & Wilkins, 1992.
2. Swotinsky RB. *The Medical Review Officer's Guide to Drug Testing*. New York, Van Nostrand Reinhold, 1992, p 26.
3. National Institute on Drug Abuse. Summary of Findings from the 1991 National Household Survey on Drug Abuse. NIDA Capsule C-86-13 rev. Rockville, MD, 19 December 1991.
4. Selavka CM. Poppy seed ingestion as a contributing factor to opiate-positive urinalysis results: The Pacific perspective. *J Forensic Sci* 36:685–696, 1991.
5. Hawks RL, Chiang CN. Examples of specific drug assays in urine testing for drugs of abuse. NIDA Research Monograph 73, 1986, p 86.
6. Cone EJ. Testing human hair for drugs of abuse. I. Individual dose and time profiles of morphine and codeine in plasma, saliva, urine, and beard compared to drug induced effects on pupils and behavior. *J Anal Toxicol* 14:1–7, 1990.

Index